God Has Spoken

Volume I:

SEEING CHRIST IN THE OLD TESTAMENT

Part Two

God Has Spoken

Vol. I:

Seeing Christ in the Old Testament Part Two (Isaiah to Malachi)

STEPHEN KAUNG

CHRISTIAN FELLOWSHIP PUBLISHERS, INC.
NEW YORK

GOD HAS SPOKEN, VOLUME I:
SEEING CHRIST IN THE OLD TESTAMENT,
PART TWO (ISAIAH TO MALACHI)

ISBN 13: 978-0-935008-97-5
ISBN 10: 0-935008-97-7

Available from the Publishers at:
11515 Allecingie Parkway
Richmond, Virginia 23235
www.c-f-p.com

Printed in the United States of America

FOREWORD

"The word of God is living and operative" (Hebrews 4:12a). It is "living" and not just letter because it gives life. The Scriptures are "operative" because they contain not only theological ideas to be pondered but also spiritual realities to be experienced. For "every scripture is divinely inspired [God-breathed], and profitable for teaching, for conviction, for correction, for instruction in righteousness; that the man of God may be complete, fully fitted to every good work" (II Timothy 3:16-17).

"Ye search the scriptures," said the Lord Jesus Christ, "for ye think that in them ye have life eternal, and they it is which bear witness concerning me; and ye will not come to me that ye might have life" (John 5:39-40). It behooves us, therefore, to diligently read the Bible and meditate on it.

To encourage God's people to study God's word, brother Stephen Kaung delivered a series of messages on the sixty-six books of the Bible. Commencing in 1983, each Lord's day the survey of one book was shared from the New Testament; and a similar sharing from the Old Testament commenced in 1986. Each message is merely a panoramic view of each book of the Bible; a tasting of the sweetness of God's word. The aim is to provide the saints with some basic understanding in their search of God's word. These being spoken messages, no acknowledgement of the names of the many commentaries consulted is indicated.

This survey of the Holy Bible will be published as Volume I and Volume II under the overall title of *God Has Spoken*: with Volume I bearing the subtitle, *Seeing Christ in the Old Testament,* and consisting of two physical volumes—Part One (Genesis to Song of Songs) and Part Two (Isaiah to Malachi); and Volume II bearing the subtitle, *Seeing Christ in the New Testament*. May God use these volumes to increase our love for His word.

Contents — Volume I: Part Two

Unless otherwise indicated,
Scripture quotations are from the
New Translation by J. N. Darby

ISAIAH

PROPHET OF FAITH

Isaiah 1:1-2a—The vision of Isaiah the son of Amoz, which he saw concerning Judah and Jerusalem in the days of Uzziah, Jotham, Ahaz, Hezekiah, kings of Judah. Hear, ye heavens, and give ear, thou earth! for Jehovah hath spoken.

Isaiah 6:1-9a—In the year of the death of king Uzziah, I saw the Lord sitting upon a throne, high and lifted up; and his train filled the temple. Seraphim were standing above him: each had six wings; with twain he covered his face, and with twain he covered his feet, and with twain he flew. And one called to the other and said, Holy, holy, holy is Jehovah of hosts; the whole earth is full of his glory! And the foundations of the thresholds shook at the voice of him that cried, and the house was filled with smoke. And I said, Woe unto me! for I am undone; for I am a man of unclean lips, and I dwell in the midst of a people of unclean lips: for mine eyes have seen the King, Jehovah of hosts. And one of the seraphim flew unto me, and he had in his hand a glowing coal, which he had taken with the tongs from off the altar; and he made it touch my mouth, and said, Behold, this hath touched thy lips; and thine iniquity is taken away, and thy sin expiated. And I heard the voice of the Lord saying, Whom shall I send, and who will go for us? And I said, Here am I; send me. And he said, Go.

Isaiah 40:1-11—Comfort ye, comfort ye my people, saith your God. Speak to the heart of Jerusalem, and cry unto her, that her time of suffering is accomplished, that her iniquity is pardoned; for she hath received of Jehovah's hand double for all her sins. The voice of one crying in the wilderness: Prepare ye the way of Jehovah, make straight in the desert a highway for our God! Every

> *valley shall be raised up, and every mountain and hill shall be brought low; and the crooked shall be made straight, and the rough places a plain. And the glory of Jehovah shall be revealed, and all flesh shall see it together: for the mouth of Jehovah hath spoken. A voice saith, Cry. And he saith, What shall I cry?—All flesh is grass, and all the comeliness thereof as the flower of the field. The grass withereth, the flower fadeth, for the breath of Jehovah bloweth upon it: surely the people is grass. The grass withereth, the flower fadeth; but the word of our God abideth for ever. O Zion, that bringest glad tidings, get thee up into a high mountain; O Jerusalem, that bringest glad tidings, lift up thy voice with strength: lift it up, be not afraid; say unto the cities of Judah, Behold your God! Behold, the Lord Jehovah, will come with might, and his arm shall rule for him; behold, his reward is with him, and his recompence before him. He will feed his flock like a shepherd: he will gather the lambs with his arm, and carry them in his bosom; he will gently lead those that give suck.*

Let us pray:

> *Dear heavenly Father, our hearts do bow before Thee because Thou art our God and our Redeemer. We do praise and thank Thee for Thy precious word. We ask that Thy Holy Spirit wilt quicken Thy word to our hearts that through Thy word we may get a vision of Thyself and the greatness of Thy salvation. We ask in the name of our Lord Jesus. Amen.*

In the past we have shared very briefly on the Pentateuchal writings—the five books of Moses, the historical writings, the poetical writings, and the wisdom writings of the Old Testament. We will now begin sharing on this Testament's prophetical writings. But first, I wish to give a very brief introduction to these prophetical writings and to the meaning of the prophets.

In one sense, the entire Old Testament is prophetic. Bishop Westcott said: "The Old Testament is one whole prophecy. Prophetic utterances are linked together with historical facts and history compels us to look beyond." Prophets are forth-tellers delivering God's message to His people, telling them of His thoughts concerning them. And prophets are also fore-tellers, since the time that they live in is but a moment in the progressive unfolding of a divine plan. Prophets have both insight and foresight, and their foresight is because of their insight. They are people raised up by God in times of crisis. They are the champions of righteousness for their time. They serve many functions. They are preachers, teachers, statesmen, reformers, and heralds. They are the moral conscience of a given age. They are holy men of God who speak as they are moved by the Holy Spirit (see II Peter 1:21). They are very conscious of the fact that they are inspired by God. Therefore, we find that they often say, "Thus saith the Lord." At the same time, however, they are also very conscious that they do not fully understand what they have uttered.

Moreover, in reading the earlier parts of the Old Testament we discover that there were prophets well before the time of Samuel. For instance, the patriarchs were prophets; Moses, too, was a prophet. Usually, the prophets would deliver their messages orally, and then they committed them to writing.

In the Hebrew Bible the prophets are divided into two groups: former and latter. The former prophets include the historical writings of Joshua, Judges, I and II Samuel, and I and II Kings. The latter prophets are Isaiah, Jeremiah, Ezekiel, and the twelve minor prophets. Daniel is not classified among the prophets; this is because his writings are partly historical and partly prophetic; so he is placed with the latter prophetical writings already mentioned together with Ezra, Nehemiah, and I and II Chronicles.

Isaiah is considered as one of the greatest prophets. His name means "Jah saves"—"Jehovah saves"; or, "the salvation of Jehovah"—"Jehovah is salvation." We do not know of his past. We only know that he was the son of Amoz (not the prophet Amos), but evidently he came from a noble family since he had ready access to the kings of Judah and was quite familiar with the priests. Tradition says (and we do not know how true this is) that he was a cousin of King Uzziah. He lived in Jerusalem and his prophecies were directed towards Judah and Jerusalem; but, of course, we know he prophesied concerning the nations all around. He had at least two sons.

Isaiah is considered as the evangelical prophet. Some people think that he is the Paul of the Old Testament because the theme of his writings is salvation or even salvation by faith. Hosea and Micah were his contemporaries. His writings are considered as reaching the climax in Hebrew literary art. He is quoted much in the New Testament and his name is mentioned twenty-one times therein. Moreover, some have claimed that there are over 250 times in which Isaiah is quoted or alluded to in the New Testament. So we can readily see the value of the book of Isaiah.

In order to understand Isaiah we need to have some idea of the time in which he lived. Probably, Isaiah prophesied around 800 years before Christ. He prophesied in the days of Kings Uzziah, Jotham, Ahaz and Hezekiah; and his prophecies can be divided into three periods. The first was during the reigns of Uzziah and Jotham, and it was a long period. During the reigns of these two kings the nation of Judah was prosperous. They were good kings; and because they set their hearts towards the Lord, the nation was greatly blessed. But prosperity degenerated into luxury, and pure worship of God gradually fell into idolatry. Isaiah was raised up during that period as the voice of God calling His people to repent. However, because they did not repent, Isaiah pronounced God's judgment, condemnation and banishment upon Judah.

The second period was during the reign of King Ahaz, who was a wicked king; and during his reign three significant things happened. First, there was open idolatry. Second, there occurred the invasion of the land by Pekah and Rezin, the kings, respectively, of Israel and Syria. And third, Ahaz appealed to the king of Assyria for help, and that very action brought God's chosen nation into contact with world power. At that time Isaiah surveyed the situation with a telescopic sight.

The third period was during the reign of King Hezekiah. Hezekiah was one of the best kings of Judah. He restored the worship of Jehovah, but unfortunately, the people still behaved corruptly. So we read that Isaiah prophesied concerning the captivity into Babylon; and at the same time he was also prophesying about the return from captivity and even beyond that to the final gathering in of the twelve tribes of Israel and the ushering in of the millennial kingdom. So that is the prophecy of Isaiah.

Isaiah was not only a prophet, he was also a sign. In Isaiah 8 we read this: "Behold, I and the children that Jehovah hath given me are for signs and for wonders [or types] in Israel" (v. 18 mgn). So Isaiah was more than a prophet and spokesman of God; he was also a sign to the nation of Israel. His life and his word spoke to the nation. His person and his message were one, and in a very real sense, that is what a prophet should be. Isaiah had two particular sons. One was called *Maher-shalal-hash-baz,* which means "swift for spoil" or "hasty for prey" (see Isaiah 8:1). And that meaning actually serves to cover the contents of chapters 1—39 of Isaiah. The other son was named *Shear-jashub,* which means "a remnant shall return" (see Isaiah 7:3). That meaning fits in with the contents of chapters 40—66. And as was mentioned earlier, Isaiah means "the Lord saves"; and that serves to sum up the whole book.

The book of Isaiah can be divided into three parts. Chapters 1—35 are prophetic in nature, chapters 36—39 are historical, and chapters 40—66 are Messianic.

PROPHETIC PART

The first part—chapters 1—35—is prophetic, and it is the most difficult part in the book of Isaiah because the prophecies to be found therein are not arranged according to chronology. They are probably arranged according to subject matter.

Chapters 1—5 serve as the introduction to the entire book. Then, in chapter 6, we are told that Isaiah saw a vision. Now some people think this was the time when Isaiah was called to be a prophet, but others think it was a renewal of his call. Let us remember that Isaiah prophesied in the days of Kings Uzziah, Jotham, Ahaz and Hezekiah; but the vision he saw occurred at the time King Uzziah died. Probably, Isaiah and King Uzziah were very close; and hence, when King Uzziah died, Isaiah went to the temple to pray. And as he went into the temple he was given a vision. While in the temple, the veil was removed from his spiritual eyes and thus he beheld the Lord sitting on the throne. We would usually say that in the temple behind the veil—that is, in the Holiest of all—God sits upon the mercy seat. And here, the veil was removed from his spiritual eyes which enabled him to see the Lord God sitting on the throne and that His train filled the temple.

In this vision there were seraphim that appeared. Seraphim are an order of the angelic host, and their name means "burning ones" or those "on fire." These seraphim had six wings—two to cover their face, two to cover their feet, and two by which to fly. These burning ones were so close to the throne of God that they had to cover their whole being. That in itself reveals the intensity of the holiness of God. God is so holy, so uncommon, so unique, so unequal, so alone, so majestic, and so glorious that even the angelic seraphim have to cover their entire being before God. They dare not look at Him. And they have two wings with which to fly; hence, they are ready to do God's errands. Seraphim represent the holiness of God in judgment and the holiness of God in mercy. And we are told that one of them cried to another, "Holy, holy, holy is the Lord of hosts, and His glory fills the whole earth!" (see 6:3)

Some have wondered what was on Isaiah's mind when he entered the temple to pray. At that critical, transitional moment for the nation of Judah, he may have been wondering what would happen now that King Uzziah had died. And in the vision he was given to see that God was on the throne. King Uzziah had died, but the King of all kings lives forever. Thus He is still on the throne, and He rules over the whole earth. And hence, no matter what happens or what may appear to be, the glory of the Lord fills the whole earth. Isaiah saw that vision and heard the seraphim calling out: "Holy, holy, holy." To be a prophet one needs to see the vision of the Lord and needs to see the holiness of God. And with this particular prophet, upon seeing that vision, immediately, something extremely noteworthy happened in the life of Isaiah. For he cried out: "Woe unto me! for I am undone. I am a man of unclean lips dwelling among a people of unclean lips" (see 6:5).

No one can see a vision of the glory of the Lord without being smitten to the ground, without being reduced to dust and ashes, without having one's beauty turned into corruption. Isaiah was a prophet, and the strongest point of a prophet is his lips because he speaks for God. But when Isaiah beheld the glory of the Lord, he immediately became aware that his lips were the greatest weakness and the most flawed element in his life. He realized he was a man of unclean lips. Who is clean enough to speak for God? Isaiah also said that he dwelt among people of unclean lips. He felt as one who was completely undone—that is, destroyed, ruined, finished. Indeed, that is what makes a prophet: a prophet is not only one who sees the Lord, he is likewise one who in himself is ruined by the glory of the Lord. Immediately afterwards, a seraphim took a burning coal from the altar and touched the prophet's lips with it and he was purified. Until we realize our uncleanness and our unfitness, until we realize we in ourselves are completely finished, we will not be purified. In Isaiah's case, he was completely cleansed by the Lord and now prepared to receive the burden and word from God.

Then he heard the Lord's voice saying, "Whom shall I send, and who will go for us?" God had a need, and He made His need known at that moment. Immediately Isaiah responded with: "Here am I, send me." And God said, "Go" (vv. 8-9a). In other words, a prophet is a person who has received the burden of the Lord. And that burden from the Lord would cost him everything because, from the very beginning, God told him that his mission would be an unsuccessful one, in that Isaiah would not succeed in drawing the people back to God (see 6:9b-13). Yet, God's heart was so warm towards His people that, in spite of that, He would still send His prophet forth to try day and night to draw back His people. Nevertheless, even though, immediately and outwardly, his mission proved to be an impossible and unsuccessful one in the short term, we today know that it was ultimately a great success.

Isaiah was sent to Judah, God's chosen people. He prophesied mainly in Jerusalem, calling God's people to repent. He told them that God was not satisfied, that He could not be cheated by mere outward offerings, rituals and services while their hearts were far away from Him. So God called His people to return, to circumcise their hearts so that the blessing of the Lord might come upon them. But because of their stubbornness, they refused to repent. So Isaiah had to pronounce

God's judgment and condemnation upon Judah. Yet even with the words of condemnation, there fell from Isaiah's lips great promises concerning the Messiah and His salvation. So we discover in this first part of Isaiah such wonderful verses as these:

"Therefore will the Lord himself give you a sign: Behold, the virgin shall conceive and shall bring forth a son, and call his name Immanuel" (7:14).

"For unto us a child is born, unto us a son is given; and the government shall be upon his shoulder; and his name is called Wonderful, Counsellor, Mighty God, Father of Eternity, Prince of Peace" (9:6).

"And there shall come forth a shoot out of the stock of Jesse, and a branch out of his roots shall be fruitful; and the Spirit of Jehovah shall rest upon him" (11:1-2a).

Even though there were utterances of condemnation and of judgment, there were these great promises of salvation as well. And that is our God.

As we read these prophetic utterances, we do not consider them as prophecies pronounced over only Judah and Jerusalem. Yes, in their immediate application that was true; but we, as the chosen people of God today, also need to hear God's voice of old. As His current people, God desires that we serve Him with all our hearts, with all our minds, with all our souls, and with all our strength. We cannot deceive Him with lip service. He is looking upon our hearts, and He wants us to give ourselves wholly to Him and to serve Him purely. If we do not, and if we do not repent, He will discipline us. He is strict with those who are near to Him. But remember, though His discipline may appear severe, yet it is brought about out of His love. And along with His discipline God has not only promised us but has also given us One who is able to save us to the uttermost (see Hebrews 7:25a AV).

HISTORICAL PART

The second part of Isaiah is historical in content, and is found in chapters 36—39. The first two of these four chapters speak of the troubles and triumphs of King Hezekiah, whereas the next two chapters speak of his recovery from sickness and then of his folly in relation to Babylon. This historical record has been included in the writings of Isaiah for a very good reason. In a sense, this brief historical part serves as a bridge between the prophetic and Messianic parts of the book. In the prophetic part Israel is involved mostly with Assyria. And Assyria likewise looms large in the first two chapters of this second part of Isaiah. When Sennacherib, King of Assyria, came to attack Jerusalem, King Hezekiah prayed and God delivered His people. But the last two chapters (38—39) of this second part deal with Hezekiah's sickness and with the king of Babylon whose embassy to Jerusalem appeared on the scene after Hezekiah had recovered from his sickness and who then, in his folly, showed the Babylonian king's emissaries all his riches. Because of that foolishness, the whole nation of Judah was eventually taken captive into Babylon. And for the most part the Messianic section of Isaiah (40—66) deals with God's people and Babylon. So this brief historical part serves as the linking of the other two parts of Isaiah together. And what we can learn from this second or historical part of Isaiah is a very important lesson: that if we humble ourselves before God, He will exalt us; but that pride always precedes a fall.

MESSIANIC PART

The most important part of Isaiah is the third and final one, running from chapters 40 to 66. We all know that if we stand on a very high place, such as on a mountaintop, and look out from that vantage point, we can see a great deal laid out before us. Our horizon is thereby enlarged and broadened. As God's prophet, Isaiah stood in the presence of God. He was therefore on very high ground, and as he looked out, his horizon became almost unlimited. That was Isaiah's spiritual situation as the prophet of God. He could see the present and, simultaneously, the future. He could see the immediate and, at the same time, the remotest reaches of time. For a prophet, time is of little or no consequence. The reason prophecy is very difficult to grasp when we read it is because there is no time limit put upon a prophet's vision. He may be talking about the present in one sentence and in the next sentence he may have jumped into the future. Or he may be talking about the future and, suddenly, he is back again in the present. At one moment the prophet may be prophesying concerning a near-term future, but in the next moment he has leaped into the distant future. Why? It is because he has been given, as it were, the eyes and vision of God. Moreover, quite often, prophecy may be *partially* fulfilled in the immediate time-frame but *fully* fulfilled only in the remotest future. And such are the challenges involved in the study of prophecy.

Isaiah prophesied up until and well into the reign of King Hezekiah. Most commentators feel that he prophesied up to the fifteenth year of King Hezekiah because after that there does not seem to have been any further prophecy emanating from him. Some people think that Isaiah lived until the time of Manasseh, the son of Hezekiah, a most wicked king. If so, that line of tradition holds that he fled from Manasseh, hid himself in a tree, and that Manasseh immediately had him sawed in two. The hint of this is found in Hebrews 11 where is mentioned that some faithful people of old were sawed asunder (see v. 37a), and that was possibly the fate of Isaiah.

Whether Isaiah prophesied and lived until that age we do not know for certain; nevertheless, he did prophesy a long time—at least for forty-eight years, and probably for over sixty years. Most likely, in the time of Hezekiah he foresaw that Judah would be taken captive into Babylon and also predicted that the Jews would return from Babylon. Actually, if you want to know the historical background, you must understand that this Messianic part takes into account a prophesying, in its more immediate or near-term application, of the return of the Jewish remnant from Babylonian captivity. But as Isaiah was prophesying these more immediate events closer in time to himself, he went way beyond these events in his prophecy, now reaching well forward into another—and much, much later—dispersion; that is, the dispersion of the Jews in 70 A.D., after Christ was crucified, and, further, went even beyond *that* to the regathering of the tribes of Israel at the second coming of the Lord. And that would thus bring into view the millennium in his prophesying. Such, then, in brief, is the book of Isaiah's Messianic part. But, of course, we realize that Isaiah being an evangelical prophet, his prophecy was not limited to just the Jewish people. On the contrary, his prophecy extends within its vision to embracing the whole world and especially those who are redeemed by the Lord. So this Messianic part of Isaiah is very important to us who are God's people today.

This Messianic part can be neatly divided into three relatively equal sections of nine chapters each. Chapters 40—48 are devoted to the matter of redemption, chapters 49—57 are devoted to the Redeemer, and chapters 58—66 to the redeemed. The first eleven verses of chapter 40 serve as a prologue or introduction to the rest of the text of this Messianic part of the book of Isaiah. I will now briefly review this entire part with its prologue and three sections.

PROLOGUE

"Comfort ye, comfort ye my people, saith your God." The word comfort conveys the idea of more than just consolation. It actually means "to cause to breathe again." In Isaiah's prophetic vision the people of God had been under a lengthy period of oppression. They could hardly breathe, so God as it were says to them: "Breathe again." The time has come for a reviving, a recovering, a return from captivity. So through His prophet God speaks to the heart of His people by saying: "Her time of suffering is accomplished"; she—the nation of God—has suffered enough: "Her iniquity is pardoned; for she hath received of Jehovah's hand double for all her sins" (vv. 1-2). God looked upon His people and, in essence, declared: "You have suffered enough. Now I have pardoned your iniquity. And how? I have received the full payment for your sins from the One whom I will send as your Redeemer."

"The voice of one crying in the wilderness: Prepare ye the way of Jehovah, make straight in the desert a highway for our God!" (v. 3) We know today that this was fulfilled in the ministry of John the Baptist. He was sent as the forerunner of the Messiah. He was a voice crying in the wilderness, preparing a highway for God. And what is the highway for Christ? Repentance. Repentance is the way to salvation (see the early chapters of all four New Testament Gospels).

"Every valley shall be raised up"—meaning that the lowly and the humiliated will be encouraged. "Every mountain and hill shall be brought low"—the self-righteous and the presumptuous shall be humiliated. "The crooked shall be made straight"—the double-minded shall be made simple. "The rough places shall be made a plain"—the proud shall be brought into submission. In other words, repentance is called for. We need to repent of our selves, repent of our ways, and return to God. "And the glory of the Lord shall be revealed, and all flesh shall see it together: for the mouth of the Lord hath spoken" (vv. 4-5).

We know very well that salvation comes from God. It is because of His love for us that He can say, "It is enough." And He has provided for us a Redeemer so that our sins may be pardoned and we may see the glory of the Lord. But for this to occur we need to repent.

Verses 6-8 tell us that we are saved not because of what we are nor because we are worthy of salvation. No, we do not deserve anything good from God. We are like grass and our beauty is like the flower, in that the grass withereth and the flower fadeth because the breath of God blows upon it. In other words, we are convicted by the Holy Spirit that we are but sinners, and yet the word of God abideth forever. This we hear echoed in I Peter, for we are told there that we are born again by the abiding word of God (see 1:23).

Verses 9-11 tell us of the glad tidings. "Let the glad tidings be spread abroad. Do not be afraid. Behold your God! The King has come. He comes to deliver, and He is like a shepherd tending us as His lambs."

All this, then, serves as an appropriate introduction to the entire Messianic part to follow and which concludes the book of Isaiah.

REDEMPTION

The first section of this Messianic part deals with redemption. It is found from chapter 40:12 to the end of chapter 48. It tells us that our Redeemer is none other than our Creator. It is our Creator who redeems us. So far as we are concerned, we have failed. But God has sent His Servant—His Son is His Servant—and through His Son we are saved (see 42:1-16). Here we find King Cyrus being set forth as a type of the Messiah. Cyrus was used by God to allow the captive children of Israel in Babylon to return to Jerusalem to rebuild the temple (see chapters 41, 44—45). And thus he serves as a type of Christ, our Messiah, who in our day has delivered us out of the world that we might return to Him and rebuild His house; and that is redemption. Let us realize that redemption is not only a coming out of Babylon the world, it is also a returning to Jerusalem. Redemption is not merely a being set free from bondage but it is additionally a going back and building the house of God. Indeed, that is the purpose of redemption.

THE REDEEMER

The second section can be found in chapters 49—57 and is concerned with the coming Servant-Redeemer prophesied by Isaiah. And interestingly, Isaiah not only foretells the Redeemer's coming but also, and from the very outset of his prophecy, predicts that though God's Servant-Redeemer will labor mightily, even exhaustingly, He will nonetheless be rejected (see 49:1-4 mgn). We learn of the fulfillment of this prophecy in the New Testament's Gospel of John, wherein we are told at this Gospel's very beginning that God's Servant—that is, the Lord Jesus Christ—came to this world but the world and even His own people did not receive Him (see 1:9-11). Isaiah's prophecy tells us further that though God's Servant-Redeemer would labor hard, He would be rejected as though His work were a total failure and would come to nothing. Nevertheless, the Servant-Redeemer is recorded in the prophecy as saying: "My judgment is with Jehovah, and my work is with my God" (see again 49:3-4). In this very connection, we will recall how in Matthew's Gospel we learn that the Lord Jesus labored much in the Jewish towns of Chorazin, Bethsaida and Capernaum, but that the people there rejected Him. Yet on that very occasion He lifted up His eyes and said: "Yes, Father, I thank Thee, for thus has it been well-pleasing in Thy sight" (see 11:20-25).

In this second section, I think the most familiar portion is to be found in Isaiah 53 because there the sufferings of the Messiah and His triumphs are portrayed for us in such fullness. Let us recall the incident recorded in Acts 8 concerning the eunuch from Ethiopia who was reading Isaiah but did not understand. Philip the evangelist was sent by God to him, and he proceeded to explain Christ Jesus as God's suffering yet triumphant Servant-Redeemer to this eunuch from Isaiah, beginning at chapter 52 and verse 13: "Behold, my servant shall deal prudently; he shall be exalted and be lifted up, and be very high."

The word "behold" is used many times in the Scriptures. By this we realize that whenever that word appears, God wants us to pay close attention to what follows it. And here God's word says: "Behold, my servant"—which refers to the Lord Jesus—"shall deal prudently." In other words, God's Servant-Redeemer will work wisely, intelligently and with understanding. In the Hebrew original, "prudently" conveys the thought that He will bring everything to a successful conclusion; that is, He will accomplish His mission.

Then we read that God's Servant-Redeemer shall be exalted and lifted up and be very high. Some people believe this passage refers to the fact of His resurrection from the dead; that He ascended on high, and that He has taken His seat on the throne at the right hand of His Father, just as we are told in the New Testament (see Hebrews 12:2). Because of what God's Servant-Redeemer—the Lord Jesus—has done on earth, He is exalted and His name is above every name (see Philippians 2:5-9).

But, then, the following verse alludes to the Servant-Redeemer's suffering: "As many were astonished at thee—his visage was so marred more than any man, and his form more than the children of men—" (v. 14). In other words, God's Suffering-Servant—the Lord Jesus—was disfigured so completely that one could hardly recognize Him as a man. That describes the sufferings of the cross He endured, and yet out of that suffering came atonement.

"—so shall he astonish many nations" (v. 15). The whole world will be astonished because they will witness something they have never seen before and they will hear and understand something they have never heard before. It is the salvation of the Lord.

Then, of course, the marked-out chapter 53 itself describes for us in detail the sufferings of God's Servant-Redeemer who is Christ; and He shall see a seed out of the travail of His soul. This is followed by a call to come and buy without money. In other words, salvation is free to all who come to the Redeemer on that basis (see 55:1-3).

THE REDEEMED

The third section is from chapters 58—66, and is concerned with the redeemed. Who are the redeemed? It begins with a cry from God; and the cry, actually, is to "declare unto My people their transgression, and to the house of Jacob their sins" (58:1). So far as any of us is concerned, we all are but sinners; we do not deserve any redemption. Yet God's arm is not shortened, and it is He who has provided salvation for us. But then a division of the people comes in: those who continue in rebellion and in wickedness will be punished; but those who repent, who have a contrite and broken spirit and tremble at God's word, shall be delivered (see 66:1-24, especially vv. 2b, 5a). That is the remnant.

As was noted earlier, Isaiah, in his Messianic prophetical view, saw to the very end. He envisioned the millennial kingdom when Christ—God's Servant-Redeemer—shall return and judge the world and bring in His kingdom, even the new heavens and new earth. But in that same portion of his prophecy we learn that God will also set up watchmen. God wants His watchful people to cry unto Him that He will make of Jerusalem a thing of praise and of beauty. But God also wants His watchful people to speak with loud voice to Him day and night that He will speed up the work of full restoration of the whole earth (see 62:1-12, especially vv. 1, 3, 6-7).

So we find that the prophecies of Isaiah are almost limitless in both time and scope.

Let us pray:

> *Dear heavenly Father, we do praise and thank Thee that Thou art not only our Creator, Thou art also our Redeemer. We do praise and thank Thee that we who are no better than anybody else, we who deserve judgment, yet, in Thy mercy, Thou hast chosen us. Lord, we do pray that we may be a people who have a contrite and broken spirit before Thee, a people who tremble at Thy word, a*

people who are given over to Thee, a people who will be watchmen set upon the walls that we may speed up Thy work and bring back the King and the kingdom of God. Lord, we do pray that Thou wilt touch our hearts very deeply as we think of what a great salvation Thou hast provided for us. What a great Savior You are! a great Redeemer! We worship Thee. In the name of our Lord Jesus. Amen.

JEREMIAH

PROPHET OF LOVE

Jeremiah 1:1-19—The words of Jeremiah the son of Hilkijah, of the priests that were in Anathoth in the land of Benjamin: to whom the word of Jehovah came in the days of Josiah the son of Amon, king of Judah, in the thirteenth year of his reign; it came also in the days of Jehoiakim the son of Josiah, king of Judah, unto the end of the eleventh year of Zedekiah the son of Josiah, king of Judah, unto the carrying away of Jerusalem captive, in the fifth month.

And the word of Jehovah came unto me, saying, Before I formed thee in the belly I knew thee; and before thou camest forth out of the womb I hallowed thee, I appointed thee a prophet unto the nations. And I said, Alas, Lord Jehovah! behold, I cannot speak; for I am a child. But Jehovah said unto me, Say not, I am a child; for thou shalt go to whomsoever I shall send thee, and whatsoever I command thee thou shalt speak. Be not afraid of them; for I am with thee to deliver thee, saith Jehovah.

And Jehovah put forth his hand and touched my mouth; and Jehovah said unto me, Behold, I have put my words in thy mouth. See, I have this day set thee over the nations and over the kingdoms, to pluck up, and to break down, and to destroy, and to overthrow, to build and to plant.

And the word of Jehovah came to me, saying, Jeremiah, what seest thou? And I said, I see a rod of an almond-tree. And Jehovah said unto me, Thou hast well seen; for I am watchful over my word to perform it. And the word of Jehovah came to me the second time, saying, What seest thou? And I said, I see a seething-pot, and its face is from the north. And Jehovah said unto me, Out of the north shall evil break forth upon all the inhabitants of the land. For behold, I am calling all the families of the kingdoms of the north, saith Jehovah, and they shall come, and they shall set every one his throne at the entering of the gates of Jerusalem, and against all the walls thereof round about, and against all the cities of Judah: and I will pronounce my judgments against them for all their wickedness, in that they have forsaken me, and have burned incense unto other gods, and worshipped the works of their own hands.

Thou, therefore, gird up thy loins, and arise, and speak unto them all that I shall command thee: be not dismayed at them, lest I cause thee to be dismayed before them. And I, behold, I appoint thee this day as a strong city, and an iron pillar, and brazen walls, against the whole land; against the kings of Judah, against its princes, against its priests, and against the people of the land. And they shall fight against thee, but they shall not prevail against thee: for I am with thee, saith Jehovah, to deliver thee.

Jeremiah 31:31-34—Behold, days come, saith Jehovah, that I will make a new covenant with the house of Israel and with the house of Judah: not according to the covenant that I made with their fathers, in the day of my taking them by the hand, to lead them out of the land of Egypt; which my covenant they broke, although I was a husband unto them, saith Jehovah. For this is the covenant that I will make with the house of Israel, after those days, saith Jehovah: I will put my law in their inward parts, and will write it in their heart; and I will be their God, and they shall be my people. And they shall teach no more every man his neighbour, and every man his brother, saying, Know Jehovah; for they shall all know me, from the least of them unto the greatest of them, saith Jehovah: for I will pardon their iniquity, and their sin will I remember no more.

Let us pray:

Dear heavenly Father, how we do praise and thank Thee that through Thy beloved Son we are able to enter into Thy very presence and to behold the glory of the Lord. We do thank Thee for Thy presence with us, and we do ask Thee, Lord, that Thou wilt open Thy word to us. We pray that Thy word will truly become life and spirit to us. We pray that Thy word will really be so exalted in our midst that we may exalt Thy name. We commit this time into Thy hands and trust Thee to speak to each one of us. We ask in Thy precious name. Amen.

Jeremiah, like Isaiah, was God's prophet. Both were holy men of God who spoke as they were moved by the Holy Spirit. They were men of God raised up in their time to be the very conscience of the nations. They prophesied concerning condemnation, confiscation, and consolation; that is, they prophesied words of judgment, of God's visitation, and also of recovery.

In many ways these two prophets were alike. They prophesied for over forty years—a long period. Yet, as we consider them we find they were different in their persons as well as in their messages. Isaiah lived under good kings—except for Ahaz—and he lived in a time of prosperity. Jeremiah lived under wicked kings—except for Josiah—and he lived in a time of distress. Isaiah mostly prophesied in about the eighth century before Christ, whereas Jeremiah prophesied a hundred years later mostly during the seventh century. Isaiah came from a noble or possibly even a royal family of Judah, but Jeremiah came from a priestly family.

Their training was very different. Isaiah was like an eagle that soars high up in the heavens and fixes its gaze upon the sun. He saw the Lord high and lifted up on His throne. He foresaw much with regard to the Messiah—His birth, His ministry, His suffering, and His glory. Jeremiah, however, was like an ox that plowed a hard and barren field. His eyes were continually focused upon the earth, but occasionally he raised his head and saw the glory of the Lord. The prophecies of Isaiah are quite comprehensive, they having a very wide horizon. On the other hand, even though Jeremiah was raised up as a prophet not only to the nation of Judah but to all nations, his prophecies are mainly concerned with Jerusalem and Judah. Isaiah is a prophet of faith, Jeremiah is a prophet of love, and Ezekiel is a prophet of hope. Isaiah gives off the impression of having a regal bearing about him: he seems to stand aloof and alone. But Jeremiah exudes the impression of humanness: he lived among the people and thus appears to be one of us.

In order to understand the book of Jeremiah, we need to know something about the time in which he lived. We read in chapter 1: "The words of Jeremiah the son of Hilkijah, of the priests that were in Anathoth in the land of Benjamin: to whom the word of Jehovah came in the days of Josiah the son of Amon, king of Judah, in the thirteenth year of his reign; it came also in the days of Jehoiakim the son of Josiah, king of Judah, unto the end of the eleventh year of Zedekiah the son of Josiah, king of Judah, unto the carrying away of Jerusalem captive, in the fifth month" (vv. 1-3).

So from this lengthy opening passage we learn that Jeremiah prophesied in the days of Josiah king of Judah. In the thirteenth year of his reign the word of God came to Jeremiah to be God's prophet, and we are told in verse 6 that at that time he was a "child." But we must understand that this word is not a correct translation from the original. In Hebrew it is *na'ar*, which actually means "one who has not yet had a recognized place in the community." It thus refers to an unmarried young man, probably between the ages of sixteen and twenty. If the call came to Jeremiah during this age-frame, then he must have been born in the last days of King Manasseh. Now we know Manasseh was the worst king that Judah ever had, and because of his wickedness, the nation was going to be destroyed. So Jeremiah was probably born in the days of Manasseh.

Josiah, King Manasseh's successor after wicked King Amon (who only reigned two years), came to the throne when he was eight years of age, but the Bible says he did what was right in the eyes of God. Indeed, the Scriptures tell us that when Josiah became sixteen, which was in his eighth year of reign, he began to seek the God of David. Moreover, when he was twenty, which was in his twelfth year of reign, he began to cleanse Judah of idols. And when he was twenty-six, the work of reform reached its peak (for all this background, see II Chronicles 34:1-8). Hence, we see that the call of Jeremiah came just one year after Josiah began the reform. Unfortunately, however, and even though Josiah's heart was right before the Lord and he did what was right, his reform did not actually reach the hearts of the people. Outwardly, there was reform. Outwardly, the people followed the king; but inwardly, the hearts of the people were still estranged from God and they were still going after other gods.

Now God was looking for reality in His people, and because there was a lack of it, He raised up Jeremiah. On the one hand, God's prophet was sympathetic with Josiah's reform, but on the other hand, he showed the people that God was not satisfied with just these outward things. So God through Jeremiah called them to sincerely return and turn to Him with their whole hearts.

After Josiah died his son Jehoahaz became king but reigned for only three months; he was removed by the Pharaoh of Egypt who then put Jehoiakim, Jehoahaz's brother, upon the throne (see II Kings 23:30-34). Jehoiakim was actually a vassal to Egypt and became a wicked king. History tells us that when he was made king, he tried to build a great palace but there was no money; so he forced the people into compulsory labor and did not pay them their wages. He allowed Josiah's reforms to lapse, pagan practices began to reappear, and morality greatly deteriorated. Jehoiakim even killed the prophets. He was indeed a very wicked king; and Jeremiah prophesied during this declining period (see II Kings 23:34-24:6; II Chronicles 36:5-8; Jeremiah 22:18-19, 26:20-24, 36:30).

After Jehoiakim died, Jehoiachin his son came to the throne, but he was king for only three months and ten days. In fact, the king of Babylon brought him to Babylon and put Jehoiakim's brother, Zedekiah, on the throne of Judah in his stead (see II Chronicles 36:9-10). Now Zedekiah was a weak person who often wavered. He was so weak that he allowed himself to come under the control of his generals and his court officials. It was at the end of his reign, in its eleventh year, that the nation of Judah was finally destroyed and the people were taken into Babylonian captivity (see II Kings 24—25; II Chronicles 36; Jeremiah 52:1-11). Jeremiah likewise prophesied during this period as God's spokesman. To say the least it was a very difficult time, and yet Jeremiah was able to prophesy faithfully as God's representative to His people.

From reading Jeremiah 1:1-3 it would appear as though Jeremiah prophesied during three distinct periods. The first occurred during the reign of Josiah—in length probably twenty years—and his messages mainly took the form of appeals. He appealed to the people of God to repent and to return, and this was reinforced by warnings of God's visitation and His judgment. The second period in which he prophesied was during the reign of Jehoiakim that lasted for eleven years; and the prophetic messages which came forth—chiefly in the nature of warnings—deepened over time into irreversible judgment. And the third and final period occurred during the reign of Zedekiah until God's people were captured, and a remnant went into Egypt for approximately fourteen years. During that time his messages were mainly warnings of the impending judgment of God, but thank God, they were coupled with promises of recovery. So, all together, Jeremiah prophesied for over forty years.

JEREMIAH THE MAN

In studying the book of Jeremiah it is very, very important that we know Jeremiah the man. Of all the writings in the Old Testament we find that the book of Jeremiah has a distinct characteristic about it: not only is it a book of prophecy and of history, it also is a biography; in short, it is a prophetic autobiography. The life of Jeremiah is intimately intertwined with history and his prophecy. It is therefore very important to know Jeremiah the person.

The name *Jeremiah* means "Jehovah is exalted." Let us note that this was a time when the people of God rebelled against Him and brought disgrace to Him to such an extent that He had to allow His people to be taken captive and to have Jerusalem and His temple destroyed. It was a time when God was put under great reproach by His own people. Yet it was during such a time that Jeremiah was able—by both his name and message—to exalt the Lord. In his prophetic utterances he was able to exalt the Lord in His judgment; he was able to exalt the Lord even before the captor because even Babylon recognized that it was God's hand effecting Judah's captivity!

Jeremiah was the son of Hilkijah, who was not the high priest who discovered the book of the law in the temple during the reign of King Josiah. For it so happens that Hilkijah back then was a common name. Nevertheless, this Hilkijah *was* a priest, and most likely, he was a descendant of Abiathar the high priest during David's time. We know that Solomon deposed Abiathar and banished him to his house in Anathoth. And we know that Jeremiah came from a priestly family who lived in Anathoth located about three miles northeast of Jerusalem. Hence, Jeremiah was not brought up in Jerusalem, although, from Anathoth, he could see Jerusalem which was only about an hour's walk away.

Having been born into a priestly family, Jeremiah must have been trained from his childhood to be a priest because Levitical priests were to be numbered when they were only one month old (see Numbers 3:15). In other words, the training for the priesthood started very early. And although he was trained to become a priest when he was between sixteen and twenty years of age, God called him instead to be a prophet. Now a Jewish priest's role was to represent the people before God whereas a prophet's role was to represent God before the people. So as a prophet, Jeremiah sympathized fully with God. He pleaded lovingly with God's people to return to Him, but if they did not, he warned, then they would be punished. On the other hand, as a priest, Jeremiah was in full sympathy with the people of God, and when he beheld in his prophetic vision the coming irreversible destruction, his heart was broken. In other words, when God and His people were ending up on a collision course, with Jeremiah caught in the middle, it broke the prophet's heart.

So far as Jeremiah's temperament is concerned, he was more fitted to be a priest than a prophet. His temperament was rather timid, gentle, tenderhearted, and sympathetic. He loved the people, and he wanted to be loved. That is the temperament of a priest, but God had called him to be a prophet. There developed a tremendous conflict in Jeremiah between God's call, his appointed errand, and his temperament; and that created a great agony of soul in him, as we find in the book of Jeremiah. He had a priest's heart but a prophet's voice.

Sometimes Jeremiah even had controversies with God, and yet he loved God so much he always yielded. During that period his character was developed, and he was faithful to God and to His people to the very end. Even though he loved the people, he was hated by everybody; nevertheless, he stuck with them to the very end and did not seek anything for himself. He was a real man of God. Furthermore, his heart was so full of love towards God's people that when he saw them going downward and not returning in repentance, he wept over them. In that sense, he was very much like our Lord Jesus who wept over Jerusalem. In many ways Jeremiah is a type of Christ, full of tender love and sympathy. He did not weep for himself, he wept for the people of God.

Some of us may think: Did God make a wrong choice sending such a gentle, tenderhearted person to be His spokesman at such a time and having to pronounce for God such severe judgment? Yes, humanly speaking, we might indeed think that God chose the wrong person. And yet, let us approach the matter this way: If God had chosen a very strong, proud, arrogant person to deliver these messages of condemnation to His people, he would have misrepresented God. Even though God through His chosen prophet was pronouncing His judgment, God's heart was broken. So He needed someone, whose heart—like His—would be broken, to represent Him in issuing such severe words of condemnation. Let us acknowledge that God knows what He is doing.

Of all the Old Testament prophets, there was probably no one who suffered as much as Jeremiah. He was not only a weeping prophet, he was also a suffering prophet. He was one who was misunderstood by his own people. He was persecuted by kings, princes, priests, prophets and people. Besides his inward agony and being deeply torn, Jeremiah was one who outwardly suffered greatly. He was beaten, put in a dungeon, considered to be a traitor to the nation, and greatly misunderstood. Yet all the time, he loved the people and he loved God.

In the New Testament, we can think of another person—this one during the New Testament period—in almost the same way: the apostle Paul. In reading Paul's epistles one truly needs to know this person if one is to really understand his writings. Of all the apostles, how Paul suffered greatly for the name of the Lord! In a very real sense, if we are true to God, if we genuinely love God's people and sincerely desire to see them walking in the way of God, we will be misunderstood and we will be persecuted. But that is the way it is, and hence we need to be prepared for it.

Three times in the book of Jeremiah, God commanded His prophet to write down what he had prophesied. The first time is recounted in Jeremiah 30:1-3. He had prophesied for God orally first, but then, later on, God commanded Jeremiah to put it down in writing so that, one day, when God's people returned from their captivity, they could read it.

Another example of this practice can be found in Jeremiah 36:1-3. In the fourth year of King Jehoiakim, God told Jeremiah to record all which he had prophesied in warning the people, with the hope that they would return to God. So he had first spoken these things and then had them written down. However, the book was destroyed by King Jehoiakim (see 36:16-23). But we learn from the latter verses of chapter 36 that God told Jeremiah to write it down again and add much more to it (see vv. 27-28, 32). Basically, therefore, most of the text in the book of Jeremiah, having been first spoken by the prophet, was later written down in ink on a scroll. That is how we have this prophetic book. But, of course, we know there must have been some editing work done on the text as well.

We can readily see in this book that it is partly prophecy, partly history and partly biography. There are many dialogues between God and Jeremiah, and some of them are his soliloquies or his confessions. Other portions are his prophecies to Judah, Jerusalem, the people, the king, and also to the nations; and some chapters are really history.

When Jeremiah wrote this book, he employed the personal pronoun "I." Sometimes the "I" represents himself, but sometimes it represents the nation of Judah, especially the godly remnant. We can discern that there is a development in his prophecy. In the beginning there is condemnation, as it were. God condemns His people because they have left Him; they have violated His covenant. Following condemnation there comes forth judgment or visitation; God will visit upon them His judgment. And following that, God issues words of confidence accompanied by a promise that, one day, He will return to them and they will return to Him. This is the pattern which one can detect in the prophecies of Jeremiah.

In all his prophesying Jeremiah represents the moral government of God. Let us always remember that God loves His people. His heart towards them is full of affection and His thoughts towards them are peaceful and good; but because of their rebellion and out of His love for them, He has to chastise them. But we must never forget that when God chastises His people, it is with love, even, as it were, with tears in His eyes. Though the people seemed to be so blind and so hard, nevertheless, we find recorded nine times in the book of Jeremiah that God confided the following: "I rise up early and send My prophets to warn you, to try to bring you back" (see, e.g., 7:25-26; 25:4-7a; 26:4-5). Now on the one hand God knew that the people would not repent, yet on the other hand His heart towards them was so warm. He was ever trying, trying and trying. Here we see the long patience and the longsuffering of God towards His people. Moreover, for His own sake God—and even before the nation of Judah was taken into captivity—said there would be seventy years of captivity but that He would return to His people and His people would return to Him. He would make a new covenant with them. Unlike the old covenant of law, this one would be a new covenant of grace. He would do everything for them. He would change their hearts so that they would really love the Lord and enter into a blessed time with Him. So that is the gist of his prophecies.

There are many ways to divide this book. Probably the simplest way, so far as I am aware, was given by G. Campbell Morgan who observed: "Chapters 1—13 are the prophet's call and commission, chapters 14—51 are the prophet's ministry, and chapter 52 is the historical appendix."

JEREMIAH'S CALL AND COMMISSION

THE CALL COMES FROM GOD

We would like to concentrate on chapter 1 for a while because of the initial importance of the call and commission of Jeremiah. In that call and commission we can recognize the main principles of God's calling to ministry. We are all called to certain ministries. We may not be called to be a prophet, but we are all called to minister—to minister to the Lord and to the house of God. And I believe in this call of Jeremiah we can detect certain main principles governing the call to ministry.

"The word of Jehovah came." When we come to this matter of calling, the first thing we need to emphasize is the sovereignty of God. It does not begin with man; it begins with God. Everything in the spiritual realm—ministry included—has to be initiated by God, not by man. Man may have the desire to serve and man may be willing to serve, but the call has to come from God. That is the sovereignty of God. We say sometimes that God does not need volunteers, which is true: if He needs someone, He drafts him. So the word of the Lord came to Jeremiah.

GOD KNEW US

And God said, "Before I formed thee in the belly I knew thee; and before thou camest forth out of the womb I hallowed thee, I appointed thee a prophet unto the nations." Here we are shown three truths. One is that before Jeremiah was formed in his mother's womb—even before Jeremiah was—God already knew him. That is divine election. Even before the foundation of the world, before we came into being, before we were formed, God already knew us. And the word *knew* here in the Hebrew original has a deeper meaning than mere knowledge; it means "knowledge to the degree of commitment." God not only knew but He also had already committed himself to what He knew. Now I think that is marvelous. Even before the foundation of the world, God has chosen us in Christ Jesus; He knew us and knew us so well that He had fully committed himself to us to bring us to that place where we should be. I think there is nothing more reassuring than this matter of divine election. According to His foreknowledge God has predestined us to become conformed to the image of His beloved Son: indeed, "whom He has foreknown, He has called; whom He has called, He has justified; whom He has justified, He has glorified" (see Romans 8:29-30). God is committed to the one He knows.

God Hallowed Us

"Before thou camest forth out of the womb I hallowed thee." Jeremiah was formed in his mother's womb; but before he was ready to come forth from his mother's womb, God said: "I have already hallowed you and set you apart for Myself, for My service, for My purpose."

Do you not know that even before you were birthed from your mother's womb God had already set you apart for himself? You are not supposed to live a day for yourself. From the day you were born or even before you were born, you were already set apart, hallowed, sanctified. And this simply means that God has set you apart from everything else in order to separate you for himself. God has a purpose for you—which is, to fulfill His purpose.

God Appointed Us

"I appointed thee a prophet unto the nations." When Jeremiah was sometime between the age of sixteen to twenty, God's calling came to him: "I appointed you to be a prophet." It is a *divine* appointment: nobody chooses to be a prophet or to be a teacher or to be something else: it is all by His appointment. God has appointed each one of us to be what He wants us to be in order that we may serve His purpose. So when the divine calling comes, it is according to these three steps. First, God knew us; second, He hallowed us; and third, He appointed us.

The apostle Paul uttered the same truth in Galatians 1:15: "When God, who set me apart even from my mother's womb, and called me by His grace ..." Now that is not only true with Jeremiah and with

Paul, it is likewise true with each and every one of us. God has set us apart while in our mother's womb, and when the time comes, He calls us. He appoints us to do what He wants us to do. It may be as a prophet, it may be as a teacher, it may be as a housewife or a doctor or nurse or whatever; but whatever God has appointed us to do, we do it as to the Lord. It is our ministry to Him. It is our calling to serve the Lord in that capacity.

JEREMIAH'S RESPONSE

INSUFFICIENCY

Jeremiah responded by saying: "Alas, Lord Jehovah! behold, I cannot speak; for I am a child." If people think they are ready for God's call, most likely He has not called them. You may have a desire to serve God, you may even be prepared for it, but strangely, when God's call comes—if it *is* God's call—invariably, you will discover that you are not ready and are not prepared; that is to say, you will realize you are not sufficient, you are not adequate. That is the strangest thing. You may have been prepared for many years; yet, when God's call comes, you end up acknowledging that you are unready and insufficient.

Jeremiah said, "Behold, I cannot speak." Now Jeremiah was trained to be a priest, and a priest was not supposed to speak much but to work a great deal. He was trained to use his hands, not his mouth. So he said, "Lord, I cannot speak."

There was another person—Moses—who was eloquent and mighty after forty years of training in Pharaoh's palace in Egypt. He was an orator, even a warrior (the Jewish historian Josephus says he commanded an Egyptian army in South Egypt); and when he thought he could speak, he could not even convince one of his fellow citizens (see Exodus 2:11-15). After another forty years, when God's call came to him, do you recall what he said? "Lord, I cannot speak. Who am I? I cannot speak." It is true that in one sense he could not speak, because after forty years in the wilderness with no audience but a few sheep, there would have been no reason to make a speech to those dumb sheep. That lengthy experience had deprived him of all his eloquence. And it was only when his eloquence was gone that God said to Moses: "Now you can speak for Me. I will put My word in your mouth and teach you what to say" (see Exodus 2:15-22; 3:1-5, 11-12a; 4:10-12).

In serving the Lord, if we think we are sufficient or if we think we are eloquent, most likely God cannot speak through us because it is we who speak. But when we stop speaking, then God is able to use us to speak.

Jeremiah had said to God, "I cannot speak." So God said, "Fine, that is the kind of person I want to use." Whereupon God touched his mouth and put words in his mouth. How important that is! A prophet is not supposed to speak his own words; he is to speak the word of God. But if he knows how to speak and talks a lot, how will anyone know who is talking—God or that person? So Jeremiah, with God's help, discovered his insufficiency.

In II Corinthians 2 and 3 the apostle Paul wrote very much concerning the actual source of our sufficiency in ministering God's word. Indeed, Paul asked: "Who is sufficient for such a thing?" (see 2:16) Our sufficiency, our adequacy, he made clear, is in God. It is He who makes us adequate, not we ourselves. How can we serve God? We cannot. How can we be ministers of the new covenant? We cannot. It is too serious a work, because its very nature is life and death to souls. In and of ourselves we cannot do that, but our sufficiency and our adequacy is to be found only in God (see especially 2:14—3:6).

Too Young

The second excuse Jeremiah put forth to God was: "I am a child." He was between sixteen and twenty years old at this moment, not fully grown yet. Now I wonder whether Jeremiah was chosen because God could not find a more mature person or was it that God purposely chose an immature person? We read in I Corinthians 1 that God chooses the foolish to confound the wise—that He chooses the mean and lowly person, the ignoble person, the weak person and the nobody so that no one can boast (see vv. 25-29). And here, God chose a youth not fully grown. Such is the sovereignty of God.

JEREMIAH'S MINISTRY

God made Jeremiah a prophet, and as God's prophet, he had two works to do. Negatively, he was to pluck up, break down, destroy and overthrow. Positively, he was to build and plant. It would seem as though the negative work is double the positive. Actually, God's purpose is always positive. He wants to build; He wants to plant. In the New Testament we find the same idea being expressed. In I Corinthians 3 Paul writes on how to build and to plant (see vv. 1-15). We are God's plant; we are God's building. So far as life is concerned, we are like a plant that God is going to plant. So far as growth is concerned, we are like a building, like a house. So God's purpose is to plant and to build; but before He can do this, He has to pluck up, break down, destroy and overthrow because there are so many things which are not of himself. We as the church are like the nation of Israel; back then, there was so much in that nation which had to be eliminated before God could do the work of building. There was so much which had to be broken down and plucked up before God could plant and build. God has to do this negative work.

Even today, God is confronted with the same issue. In the church of God there is so much which needs to be dealt with and eliminated before God is able to really plant and build. Unfortunately, it seems that He has to spend a great deal of time doing the negative work before He can actually do the work He wants to do. Such is the work and ministry of a prophet.

In the days of Jeremiah there were false prophets telling the people: "Peace, peace. Everything is all right; go on. Nothing is wrong. We have the temple here in Jerusalem and God dwells in the temple. He will never leave us. Nobody can really overthrow us. Peace, peace." But there is no peace for the wicked. These were false prophets trying to please the people (see Jeremiah 7:1-4; 8:11; 14:13-15; 23:16-17). But a true prophet is one who is able to deliver the message to the effect that anything which is not of God has to be cleared away so that He is able to plant and build what is His.

And God said: "I make you a prophet. You go to whomsoever I send you. You say whatever I have told you to say. You will be against kings, priests, the people, nations; but I will make you as a strong city, as an iron pillar, and as a brazen wall against the whole land." In the end Jeremiah seemed to be against everybody but it was because everybody was against God.

Let me ask, Do you want to be popular? If the world is against God, if even the religious world is against Him, you have to be *Antipas*—that is, against all (see Revelation 2:13). But of course, that broke the heart of Jeremiah; and if you, too, are faithful to God, it will break your heart as well.

JEREMIAH'S VISIONS

An Almond Tree

Then, still in Jeremiah chapter 1, we see that God, in order to strengthen His commission to Jeremiah, gave him two visions. The first vision: "The word of Jehovah came to me, saying, Jeremiah, what seest thou? And I said, I see a rod of an almond-tree. And Jehovah said unto me, Thou hast well seen; for I am watchful over my word to perform it" (vv. 11-12).

God showed Jeremiah a rod of an almond tree. And Jeremiah, who had been trained to be a priest, knew exactly what He meant by doing so. For Jeremiah was quite familiar with the incident related in the book of Numbers chapter 17. We will recall that certain of the children of Israel had made the claim that everybody was holy and could thus serve God, so why was it that only Aaron could serve as priest? In response, God told each tribe to take a dead rod and leave it overnight before the ark of God. The next day, only Aaron's rod had budded, and it bore almond flowers. Because of that, Aaron was indisputably chosen to minister to God.

How can we serve God? We cannot serve Him with a dead rod. In other words, we are all as dead rods, and as such we cannot serve God with our natural energy; for that would be dead worship and dead service. We can only serve God with what is resurrected. The almond tree is the first tree which buds after winter. Therefore, in Scripture it always speaks of resurrection. God in essence was saying to Jeremiah: "You are going to serve Me in the power of My resurrection life." That is the only way to serve God. And Jeremiah understood.

Seething Pot

The second vision God gave to His prophet was of a seething pot with its face from the north. God was showing Jeremiah that this was to be the thrust of his prophecy. Judgment would come from the north and the people of God would be punished; yet it was going to come because of God's love towards them. So this was Jeremiah's call and his commission.

The Need for Jeremiahs Today

What does God want us to learn from this book of Jeremiah? Jeremiah lived towards the end of the nation of Judah. This people was a covenant people with God. He had covenanted with them at Mt. Sinai; but from that time forward and even up to the time when they were not faithful to God; instead, that nation was destroyed, this covenanted people had consistently and persistently violated God's covenant: they worshiped the works of their own hands; they brought disgrace to God and to His name. Yet here was a man who—by his very name and presence— was able to exalt God in that kind of situation. He was there representing God among this rebellious people, and he was there calling them to return to Him. In a sense, when they heard Jeremiah, they heard the voice of God pleading with them. He was not able to bring the nation back to God—the nation instead went into captivity—and yet, his ministry was not in vain because there was a remnant who heard Jeremiah. Eventually, a remnant returned from Babylonian captivity to rebuild the house of God and bring in the new covenant. Now that is the story of Jeremiah.

We today are living at the end of the church age. We, too, are a covenanted people. God has made a new covenant with us sealed by the blood of His beloved Son. It is a covenant of grace. The covenant which God has covenanted with us far surpasses the one He made with the children of Israel, which was a covenant of law: "If you do this, then I will be your God." Indeed, we are a privileged people because God has covenanted with us on the basis of a new covenant. According to this new covenant He in essence is saying: "I will do everything. All you need to do is respond to Me, respond to My grace.

Do not waste My grace, do not fall from My grace. That is all you need to do." Nevertheless, even toward the end of the first century, the church had left its first love (see Revelation chapters 2—3). All the way through, the church of God has been drifting further and further apart from the grace of God. The church worships the works of her own hands and has become a world institution. Outwardly, God is worshiped but there is no reality there. God is not happy. He is not satisfied. And hence, throughout the ages, He has continually sent His prophets to His church to point out to them what is wrong and urging them to return and turn back to God.

Now, though, we are at the very last stage. Apostasy is upon us and this is the time when we need Jeremiahs. We need people like Jeremiah who are in full sympathy with God, not people who will condemn others arrogantly, for that misrepresents God. God's heart is broken over His people who are scattered and without shepherds, harassed and deceived. God wants people like Jeremiah who can weep with Him; who are able, yes, to pronounce strong words—yet with tears; who are in full sympathy with God, desiring that there would be a return of His people to the new covenant in order to know and experience the grace of God and to be a testimony for Him in these last days.

God needs Jeremiahs today—weak perhaps, timid perhaps, and yet, they love God more than anything else. They are willing to lay down their lives and stand with Him against all opposition, even though sometimes, under trial, there is weakness. Jeremiah may have appeared weak before God but he never appeared weak before the people. He was faithful to God's command; and that is what we need to learn. May God raise up among His people many Jeremiahs who understand His heart and who will cry over His people. And though they may not see the whole church restored, God will restore a remnant who will be faithful to Him. I believe this is the challenge of the book of Jeremiah.

Let us pray:

Dear heavenly Father, we do praise and thank Thee for giving us this book of Jeremiah. We do pray that the spirit of Jeremiah may come upon us so that in these last days among Thy people we may humbly serve Thee and serve Thy people with faithfulness. Oh, how our hearts do cry out to Thee that Thy people will hear Thy voice and return to Thee and to that covenant relationship with Thee so that we may glorify Thy name. We ask in the name of our Lord Jesus. Amen.

LAMENTATIONS

GOD OF MERCY

Lamentations 1:1—How doth the city sit solitary that was full of people! She that was great among the nations is become as a widow; the princess among the provinces is become tributary!

Lamentations 3:19-33—Remember thou mine affliction and my wandering, the wormwood and the gall. My soul hath them constantly in remembrance, and is humbled in me.—This I recall to heart, therefore have I hope.

It is of Jehovah's loving-kindness we are not consumed, because his compassions fail not; they are new every morning: great is thy faithfulness. Jehovah is my portion, saith my soul; therefore will I hope in him.

Jehovah is good unto them that wait for him, to the soul that seeketh him. It is good that one should both wait, and that in silence, for the salvation of Jehovah. It is good for a man that he bear the yoke in his youth:

He sitteth solitary and keepeth silence, because he hath laid it upon him; he putteth his mouth in the dust, if so be there may be hope; he giveth his cheek to him that smiteth him; he is filled full with reproach.

For the Lord will not cast off for ever; but if he have caused grief, he will have compassion according to the multitude of his loving-kindnesses: for he doth not willingly afflict or grieve the children of men.

Lamentations 5:19-22—Thou, Jehovah, dwellest for ever; thy throne is from generation to generation.

Wherefore dost thou forget us for ever, dost thou forsake us so long time?

Turn thou us unto thee, Jehovah, and we shall be turned; renew our days as of old.

Or is it that thou hast utterly rejected us? Wouldest thou be exceeding wroth against us?

Let us pray:

Dear heavenly Father, how we do praise and thank Thee for Thy mercy, for Thy grace, for Thy love towards us. We thank Thee that through Thy beloved Son Thou hast redeemed us and drawn us unto Thyself that we may enter into the holiest of all and be in Thy presence to behold the glory of the Lord. Oh, our Father, how we are thankful for all Thou hast done for us in Christ Jesus. We do thank Thee for giving us Thy word, Thy precious word, Thy living word. We do look to Thy Holy Spirit to quicken Thy word to our hearts that Thou mayest speak to each one of us to the praise of Thy glory. We commit this time into Thy hands, trusting Thy Holy Spirit to do His work. In the name of our Lord Jesus. Amen.

This book of Lamentations in the Hebrew manuscript is usually entitled with the Hebrew word for our English word *how*; for that is the first word in this book. It is just like the Hebrew manuscripts of Proverbs and the five books of Moses; they are all called by the first word in the book. But occasionally it is entitled with the Hebrew word for lamentations. The rabbis of old therefore called it Lamentations; and in the Septuagint—which is the Greek translation of the Old Testament Hebrew manuscript done in Alexandria in Egypt—it is also called Lamentations. Even though in the original this book's author is anonymous, nevertheless, according to tradition and according to the Jewish Talmud, people believe that it was written by Jeremiah. As a matter of fact, in the Septuagint this book's text is prefaced by these words: "And it came to pass after Israel had been taken captive and Jerusalem had become desolate that Jeremiah sat and wept, lamenting with this lament over Jerusalem and said." So it is now generally believed that these five lamentations in the book's five chapters were actually written by the prophet Jeremiah.

Lamentation was a very common practice in the ancient days. People would compose and sing lamentations over a deceased friend or relative, and this is evident even in the Scriptures. David lamented the deaths of Saul and Jonathan (see II Samuel 1). He lamented the death of Abner, the captain of the host of Israel (see II Samuel 3). Jeremiah lamented the death of King Josiah (see II Chronicles 35:25). They not only lamented the death of some deceased person, it was also extended to lamenting the destruction of a city or a nation. For instance, Amos lamented over Israel (see Amos 5:1), and Jeremiah lamented over Jerusalem and Judah (see Jeremiah 7:29; 9:20). And Ezekiel lamented over the city of Tyre (see Ezekiel 27:2ff.). So in the Scriptures we find that lamentations are a very common thing. Whenever something sad or sorrowful happened, there would often be a lamentation offered up.

The five lamentations now to be considered were offered up over the destruction of Jerusalem and the captivity of the people of God. The first four are arranged in alphabetic, acrostic order. In the Hebrew alphabet there are twenty-two letters; and the first, second, and fourth lamentations each have twenty-two verses and each verse begins with a Hebrew letter in sequential alphabetic order. In the third lamentation, however, there are a total of sixty-six verses, with every three verses beginning with the same letter of the Hebrew alphabet—but again, all set in alphabetic sequence. So these are called acrostic poems. The fifth lamentation is not composed as an acrostic but is nonetheless a poem because it employs the literary device of parallelism—that is, a reiteration of the same thing in similar phrases. We may therefore legitimately say that all five lamentations are poems.

There are a few poems in the book of Psalms written in the same acrostic fashion—especially Psalm 119. In this particular psalm there are twenty-two divisions of eight verses each, and each and every one of these twenty-two divisions begins with a letter of the Hebrew alphabet in proper order; and thus it is acrostic in form. Someone has made this comment, which I think is a very good one: "It takes all the human language in its fullness to sing the praise of the law of God." That is Psalm 119. But it also takes the whole human language, but to a lesser extent, to lament the neglect and the violation of the law of God.

As has been noted, Lamentations is a book of poems. It is not history, nor is it prophecy. Yet it does contain some historical background and does possess a prophetic outlook. Being poems, these lamentations, like music, are something which you cannot really analyze. If we try to analyze a poem, we shall miss the point. A poem is that which you have to feel, and that is the reason why the best way to approach this book of Lamentations is not by analyzing it but by trying to enter into its spirit. Such is the best way to study Lamentations.

We thank God that the book of Lamentations has been included in the Bible. It, like all the other Bible books, is the word of God. It has a very definite place and a very important place in God's word. We thank God for that because Lamentations shows that our God is not unmindful of our sufferings nor unmindful of our sorrows. He listens to our cries. As a matter of fact, He stores up our tears in His bottle, in His vessel (see Psalm 56:8). Our God is not One who is hard or cold or distant. He is One who is warm and sympathetic, who feels for us and who loves us. So Lamentations, inasmuch as it is in the word of God, truly gives us great comfort and encouragement; for by its inclusion we come to know that our God is One who is very near to us and that we are very dear to Him. In our afflictions, He is there with us. When we go through water and fire, He goes through such situations with us. It is not at all the case that when we are in sufferings, God is laughing at us or that our suffering has nothing to do with Him. To the contrary, as we go through any pain or sorrow or suffering, we find that He is going through such experience together with us. He feels how we feel. This is our God.

Furthermore, we can sense in these Lamentations the Spirit of God. The Spirit of God is speaking or expressing himself through the spirit of the prophet Jeremiah. God suffers so much in the sufferings of His people. It is not unlike the experience which parents have. When the children are suffering, the parents actually suffer more than the children. God so loves His people and He so much desires to bless them; and yet, because of the iniquities of His people, He has to discipline those whom He loves dearly. Indeed, it hurts Him more than the people He disciplines. So here, through these lamentations of the prophet Jeremiah, we can discern the heart of God. Every letter is written with tears, and every word is the sound of a broken heart. God is heartbroken over His people. It is the very Spirit of God; and it can also be said, speaking in New Testament terms, that it is the Spirit of Christ.

When the Lord Jesus was on earth, He was here to declare the Father. He came to the earth from the Father to tell us how much God loves us, that God is love. Yet, He was misunderstood; He was rejected. In spite of that, the Lord Jesus, at His last entry into Jerusalem, looked over that city and wept over it (see Luke 19:41ff.). And as Jesus was being led on His way up to Calvary's hill, He even told the wailing women following Him this: "Weep not for Me but weep for yourselves and for your children" (see Luke 23:28). Here we see in Jesus the heart of God so full of love, so full of compassion. And because He loves us so much, He went to the cross and died in our stead in order that we might be redeemed.

Actually, in these lamentations the prophet Jeremiah was representing several parties. On the one hand, he was in full sympathy with God. He knew how God loved His people, but he also knew that God, being righteous, had to discipline His people. So he stood with God, declaring that He was righteous in punishing, disciplining and chastening His people. But it was a chastening out of love, not out of hate. On the other hand, the prophet Jeremiah represented the people who suffered so greatly, and because of that, Jeremiah wept. His tears ran down like a river.

Jeremiah also represented the godly remnant among God's people. When His chastening came upon the nation, many of the people's hearts were still hardened; but there was a godly remnant. They acknowledged that God was righteous in disciplining them, and they submitted themselves under His mighty hand in repentance and looked to His mercies. So Jeremiah also represented these people.

As we said before, God needs Jeremiahs today. He needs people who are in full sympathy with Him. How He is misunderstood today! When people are suffering for their iniquities, they put the blame on God as though He were a cold, hard and harsh God. They do not realize that He suffers more than they do. He needs a people who understand Him, who understand that He is a God of love. He sometimes has to discipline, especially His own people; nevertheless, it is out of love, not hatred. We also need people like Jeremiah who are sympathetic with the people themselves. When people suffer in the world, and especially in the household of God, people will at times stand aloof and say: "Well, that is what they deserve to have." But we need people like Jeremiah who will identify with the sufferings of people and suffer together with them. Furthermore, we likewise need people like Jeremiah who will represent the godly remnant. The hope is there that there will be a godly remnant who will submit to God's mighty hand and look to Him for mercy. That is the way He will show mercy, yet not only to the remnant but even to all the people.

THE FIRST LAMENTATION

The first lamentation of this book begins with "How": "How doth the city sit solitary that was full of people! She that was great among the nations is become as a widow; the princess among the provinces is become tributary!" This lament tells of the woes, the sorrows and the sufferings of God's people.

THE SECOND LAMENTATION

The second lamentation also begins with "How": "How hath the Lord in his anger covered the daughter of Zion with a cloud! He hath cast down from the heavens unto the earth the beauty of Israel, and remembered not his footstool in the day of his anger." This lament reveals the source of their woes: that they all come from none other than God. And that makes it even more difficult.

THE THIRD LAMENTATION

The third lamentation serves as the turning point. Here we learn that a godly remnant, through the discipline of the Lord, have submitted themselves under His mighty hand, acknowledging that He is righteous. Yet, they are looking to Him for mercy, knowing that He is a God of mercy. So this development is the turning point. We are all especially familiar with verses 22-24: "It is of Jehovah's loving-kindness we are not consumed." If God should deal with us according to our iniquities, where would we be? We would all be dead, for that is what we deserve. But it is the loving-kindness of the Lord that we are not consumed. Our God is full of mercy, and that is the only reason we are not consumed.

"Because his compassions fail not." He loves us; and because He loves us, therefore, He is merciful towards us. We may recall from the New Testament Gospels how the Lord would say again and again: "I have pity upon them," or how the record would note that He "was moved with compassion." When the Lord saw the multitudes, they were to Him like sheep without a shepherd. One day when He was tired, He led His disciples to a retreat to rest for a while; but upon seeing the crowds there, how His heart was touched: full of compassion, He gave himself to those people. On another occasion, when the multitudes had already been with Him for three days and no longer had anything to eat, the disciples came to the Lord Jesus and said, "Send them away that they may get food." But the Lord responded by saying: "No, I have pity upon them"; and He fed them with seven loaves and a few small fish (see Matthew 15:29ff.). Again and again, when people came to Him, the Lord had compassion. The leper came to Him and said, "If You will," and the Lord, "moved with compassion" for him, touched him and said, "I will" (see Mark 1:40-41). Our God is full of compassion and full of love.

"They are new every morning." The compassion and love of God are new every morning. New—yet not in the sense that it has to be novel, but new in the sense that it is always fresh and living: His new compassion over our old problems; His new compassion over even our new problems. Every morning His love is there waiting for us, prepared for us, provided for us. As the psalmist once said: "His anger is only for a moment, but His favor is for a lifetime. In the night there may be weeping, but in the morning there will be rejoicing" (see Psalm 30:5). Such is our God; and hence, whatever may happen in the night, in the morning, let us look up, for His compassion is there waiting for us. He is the resurrection and the life.

"Great is thy faithfulness." Our God is faithful. He is faithful to himself. We are told in II Timothy that we may be unfaithful, but He remains ever faithful because He cannot deny himself. Sometimes we are not faithful, but our God is always faithful to himself: He is faithful to His word, to His promise, and to His covenant with us. He always remains faithful. When we look back, we can see how faithful God is to us.

"Jehovah is my portion, saith my soul." This soul—the prophet Jeremiah—was in tremendous sufferings. Jerusalem was destroyed; the temple was demolished; the people were taken captive. What sufferings! Yet in sufferings, that soul of Jeremiah's could rise up and say, "The Lord is my portion; therefore will I hope in him." Everything may go; but there is One who will never go, and that is our Lord. We may lose everything, yet the Lord is still our portion. And because He is our portion and our inheritance, therefore, He is ours; therefore, we have hope. Our hope is not in our environment, our hope is not in the things which we can see; our hope is solely in the Lord. Because He is with us, we know there is hope. So let us never give up hope. We can hope against hope, just as Abraham did when he was in a hopeless situation. He was a hundred years old and his wife was ninety, beyond the age of having a child; nevertheless, Abraham and Sarah hoped against hope because they hoped in God.

So here in this third lamentation, composed at a time of deep sufferings, the soul rose up, looked at God, confessed his sins, and trusted in His mercy. And that was the turning point in the whole matter.

THE FOURTH LAMENTATION

The fourth lamentation also begins with a "How." It tells us the reason for, or cause of, their woes. Now it is true that God's people were in deep tribulations, and these sufferings were His discipline upon them. But why is it that they were so disciplined? In this fourth lament we are told that it was because of the iniquity of the people: "How is the gold become dim!" (v. 1a) In God's eyes His people are gold, they are most precious to Him. They shall indeed shine, but at this time the gold had become dim. "The most pure gold had changed!" (v. 1b) God had not changed; it was the people who had changed. God never changes. He is the same yesterday, today, and forever (see Hebrews 13:8). He has a name that is always the same. Who, then, has changed? The people of God have changed; and as a result, "the stones of the sanctuary poured out at the top of all the streets!" (v. 1c) The reason there was such destruction was because God's people had changed.

THE FIFTH LAMENTATION

Finally, we see that the fifth lamentation is actually a prayer. "Remember, O Jehovah, what is come upon us; consider, and see our reproach" (v. 1). Here we learn that the soul has turned to the Lord and has asked Him to remember and be merciful. "Thou, Jehovah, dwellest for ever; thy throne is from generation to generation" (v. 19). You, oh God, never change. You are always there, seated on the throne. Your throne is from generation to generation. You are ruling, controlling, and overruling everything. Therefore, we look to You for mercy.

"Turn thou us unto thee, Jehovah, and we shall be turned" (v. 21a). Sometimes we ourselves are unable to turn back to the Lord. He is the only One who is able to turn us. Now how will the Lord turn us to himself so that He may return to us? It is by way of chastening. Often we do not understand why God chastens us. We are like children who do not understand why their parents chasten them to discipline them; on the contrary, they feel that if their parents truly loved them, they would let them go. Yet, this is the only way we can be turned back to God. If He does not chasten us but lets us go or lets go of us, we are finished. But God will not let us go. He will discipline us because, through discipline, we may be turned back to Him, thus enabling Him to return to us. So this is actually the way God wants to show mercy towards us. If we refuse discipline, we will not turn back to God and thus we hinder God's returning to us. In summary, therefore, this entire set of lamentations can be summed up in the words of Hebrews 12:5: "My son, despise not the chastening of the Lord, nor faint when reproved by him."

Our problem is that we despise the chastening of the Lord. We do not want it. We reject it. We fight against it. Yet let us not despise it. We may at times faint under it as though it is too much for us. Even so, let us not faint under His reproof, because it is His hand and He carefully measures out His discipline (see Hebrews 12:5). Sometimes earthly parents will discipline a child out of anger, and thus it is uncontrolled, and overdiscipline is the sad result; but that is not the case with our heavenly Father. When He disciplines us, He knows how much we are able to bear (see I Corinthians 10:13). Moreover, He not only knows just how much to discipline but also knows when no more is needed. So let us not despise the chastening of the Lord nor faint under His reproof (see again Hebrews 12:5).

HOW?

I would like to draw our attention especially to this word "How" with which three of the five lamentations begin. In one sense, it is one of the primary characteristics of the book of Lamentations. Life on earth is such that there will always be problems, difficulties, tribulations, trials, sufferings, sorrows, despair, depression, death. This is what earthly life is because we live in a cursed world. We cannot expect our life to be smooth sailing, full of roses. Let us bear in mind that even after we believe in the Lord and are redeemed, we still live in an unredeemed world. Because of this, when we go through life and are confronted with many problems, difficulties, misunderstandings, and all other unexplainable things, we naturally ask, "Why?" We want an explanation. We are always asking, "Why?" But do we realize that sometimes when we ask why, our spirit has turned ugly? It reveals a spirit of defiance, of unbrokenness. In Job, the oldest book in the Bible, we saw that Job was faced with a very serious problem in life. There was so much personal devastation and suffering, and Job asked: "Why? Why should I suffer? I am such a good person." And his three friends seemed to know why, and they unhesitatingly told Job. But the more they tried to explain, the worse the problem became for Job. Yet when God finally intervened, He never did explain why to Job. God simply revealed His majestic and sovereign greatness, and when Job saw the Lord, in *that* light, he capitulated: he fell on his face in dust and ashes and repented. He no longer needed to know why and he was restored.

We, like Job, may never know why. If we want to know why to every problem and every situation, perhaps we will have to wait until we see the Lord himself and then we can ask why. Perhaps at that time, you will not ask why. Let us realize that we should not ask "Why?" but instead ask "How?" *How* is a different question. *How* is asking not with a spirit of defiance but with a spirit of humility and submission. *How* is to learn what has happened. *How* is to face the facts and not try to evade the problem. *How* is to try to go back behind the problem and discover the cause. When we know *how*, then we know how to repent, return, and look to God for mercy.

Our problem is that when we are in an unpleasant or difficult situation, we do not actually know how we got into it. Or sometimes we are so blind we do not even know where we are. Now that was the situation with the church in Laodicea. The church there was in a desperate, desolate and dead situation; yet those believers thought they were rich, lacking nothing, and were absolutely fine. But the Lord told them: "You are blind, you are poor, you are miserable, you are naked; and yet you do not even know it" (see Revelation 3:14-17). If we fail to ask "How?", we shall oftentimes not know where we are: we can be deceived; and because of that, there is no salvation out of the situation. Even with the church in Ephesus, the Lord had to say this: "Remember from whence you have fallen and repent and do the first works" (see Revelation 2:1-5). We need to know how we have fallen so we can repent and return to God. Therefore, whenever we are in a difficult situation, let us not ask "Why?" Let us ask "How?" Then the Lord may reveal to us how we got into that situation so that we may learn the lesson and return to God in humility and brokenness and look for His mercy. And His mercy endures forever.

SORROW THAT LEADS TO SALVATION

We like to read from God's word those things which are uplifting or which exhort us; we do not like to read things which are depressing. Some people say that reading Lamentations is a very depressing experience, but we have to face life in reality. Life is not all comedy; life consists of tragedy, too; hence, we need Lamentations. I thank God for this book in the Bible. It is very, very helpful, especially because it shows us that there is a kind of sorrow which can bring in salvation. We will recall those words of Jesus in the so-called Sermon on the Mount: "Blessed are they that mourn, for they shall be comforted" (Matthew 5:4). And we may also remember the Scripture which states that the sorrow which is according to God brings in repentance to salvation but that worldly sorrow works death (see II Corinthians 7:10).

There are two kinds of sorrow: The sorrow of the world works death, but sorrow according to God works repentance that leads to salvation. Lamentations shows us the way of spiritual sorrow. We need to learn how to be sorrowful according to God. We need to mourn over our sins. We need to mourn over the sins of this world. We need to be sorrowful in order that we may receive mercy. These are spiritual exercises which we need. We like to be in the house of feasting and have a happy time, laughing, joking, jesting, or whatever. But the Bible tells us to "go to the house of mourning" (Ecclesiastes 7:2a) because that will make us reflect and that will give us eternal benefit. We need to have the Spirit of Christ in us, not in any sense that we are always long-faced and exuding a kind of depressed feeling to other people. No, not at all! As Christians, we should be joyful; but being joyful is different from laughing and joking all the time. Deep down in our spirit there is a joy, but it is not a contradiction. Actually, it is complementary. On the one hand, the joy of the Lord is our strength. On the other hand, we need to have the Spirit of Christ in us to mourn.

"Blessed are they that mourn, for they shall be comforted." If we have the Spirit of Christ in us, we should be mournful of our spiritual condition because we are not what we should be: we are not what God is able to bring us to. And if we really love the Lord, we ought also to be mournful over the condition of the church today. When we see the church's current condition, how can we keep from mourning? If our Lord Jesus wept over Jerusalem, should we not weep over the church of God today? This is not being said in a condescending sense or in the sense that we are better than others in God's church but in the sense of joining our spirit with other people of God in confessing our sins and asking the Lord to be merciful in turning back His people. Moreover, if we have the Spirit of Christ within us, we ought likewise to mourn for the world. Look at the sufferings of the world today! We need to cry out to the Lord that He will shorten the days of these trials and bring in His kingdom so that righteousness may rule over the earth.

Meanwhile, we need to submit ourselves all the time under the mighty hand of God. I Peter instructs us to "submit ourselves under the mighty hand of God so that in due time He will exalt us" (see 5:6). We need to maintain a spirit of humility and of submission. We need to acknowledge that God is righteous in whatever He does, and yet we look for His mercy. If we have that kind of spirit in us, God will return to us, and He will be merciful to His people. In this regard let us consider David's situation. When his son Absalom rebelled against him and David had to flee for his life, he left Jerusalem and went over the Mount of Olives, weeping as he went. Then Shimei, a man of the tribe of Benjamin, from the other side of the hill, threw stones at him and cursed him and said, "That is what you deserve." David still had his mighty men with him and one of them said: "How can he curse you who are the anointed king? Let me go over and cut off his head!" But David said: "Let him alone, let him curse. Perhaps it is the Lord who told him to curse me; and if the Lord sees that I am being cursed, perhaps He will have mercy on me" (see II Samuel 15:30, 32; 16:1, 5-13).

Now that is the kind of attitude we should have. Instead of rebelling against the discipline of the Lord, we should prostrate ourselves on the ground in dust and ashes. And when the Lord sees that this is our attitude, He will return to us. Such is the way to recovery.

Let us pray:

> *Dear heavenly Father, we do thank Thee for this book of Lamentations. Thou dost teach us to have the Spirit of Christ in order that we, too, may so sympathize with Thee, with Thy people, and with the world so that we may be able to weep when Thou weepest and that we may be able to stand in the gap—in the breach—and look for Thy mercy and for Thy returning to Thy people. So Lord, do teach us this valuable lesson during these difficult end times. We ask in Thy precious name. Amen.*

EZEKIEL

PROPHET OF HOPE

Ezekiel 1:1-4—Now it came to pass in the thirtieth year, in the fourth month, on the fifth of the month, as I was among the captives by the river Chebar, the heavens were opened, and I saw visions of God. On the fifth of the month, (it was the fifth year of king Jehoiachin's captivity,) the word of Jehovah came expressly unto Ezekiel the priest, the son of Buzi, in the land of the Chaldeans by the river Chebar; and the hand of Jehovah was there upon him.

And I looked, and behold, a stormy wind came out of the north, a great cloud, and a fire infolding itself, and a brightness was about it, and out of the midst thereof as the look of glowing brass, out of the midst of the fire.

Ezekiel 1:26-28—And above the expanse that was over their heads was the likeness of a throne, as the appearance of a sapphire stone; and upon the likeness of the throne was a likeness as the appearance of a man above upon it. And I saw as the look of glowing brass, as the appearance of fire, within it round about; from the appearance of his loins and upward, and from the appearance of his loins and downward, I saw as it were the appearance of fire, and it had brightness round about. As the appearance of the bow that is in the cloud in the day of rain, so was the appearance of the brightness round about.

This was the appearance of the likeness of the glory of Jehovah. And when I saw, I fell on my face, and I heard a voice of one that spoke.

> *Ezekiel 48:35b—And the name of the city from that day, Jehovah is there [Jehovah-Shammah].*

Let us pray:

> *Dear heavenly Father, we do praise and thank Thee that we can be in Thy presence. We look up to Thee, and we desire to see the glory of God in the face of Jesus Christ. We do commit this time into Thy hands and ask Thee that by Thy Holy Spirit Thou wilt reveal Thyself to us, to the praise of Thy glory. In the name of our Lord Jesus. Amen.*

Ezekiel means "God strengthens" or "the strength of God." Now if the thirtieth year in the first verse refers to his age (and most likely it does), then Ezekiel must have been born in the days of King Josiah when there was a great reformation occurring. During the reign of Josiah Ezekiel must have been an infant in the arms of his mother. His father's name was Buzi, and we do not know much more about him. The only other fact concerning his family background which we know for certain is that Ezekiel came from a priestly family.

The Bible refers to him as Ezekiel the priest. We do not know which course in the priestly service he belonged to, but by reading the book of Ezekiel we learn that there seemed to have been great respect shown him by the Jewish elders in the exile community. Those familiar with this book of Ezekiel may remember that they sat before him. Also, we may recall from II Kings 24 that when Nebuchadnezzar took King Jehoiachin into captivity, he brought with him the king's mother, the king's wives, the chamberlains, the more important priests, and the mighty of the land. So, most likely Ezekiel belonged to a priestly family that was rather important and prominent among the priests. We have no record in the Scriptures as to when, age-wise, the priests would begin to serve in the temple. The only hint we have is from Numbers 4 where we learn that the *Levites* began to serve at the age of thirty. At the age of twenty-five they would enter the temple to serve as apprentices. Now if these rules applied also to the priesthood, then most likely a priest would be trained from his childhood. We may remember that the priests or Levites were numbered from one month old and upward. Because of their service, they had to be trained very early; and when they reached the age of twenty-five, they would enter the temple to serve as assistants for learning how to serve.

When Ezekiel was taken into captivity, he was twenty-five years old. This event therefore occurred just at the time for him to enter the temple to serve in a practical way as an apprentice; and that must have been a circumstance which he had looked forward to with great anticipation from his childhood. Unfortunately, however, he was not allowed to serve in the temple in Jerusalem. Instead, he was taken captive into Babylon. It must have been a great disappointment to him. Just think for a moment: if you had been trained for a certain work over a very long period and the time finally arrived for you to commence serving and that opportunity was suddenly snatched from you, it would have been a great disappointment to you as it must have been to Ezekiel.

So Ezekiel was taken into Babylonian captivity; and during the first few years there, all the exiles were still hoping that in a very short while they would be allowed to return to Jerusalem. There were even false prophets—not only in Jerusalem but also among the exile community—who were prophesying that within two years they would be able to go back to Jerusalem. That gave Ezekiel some hope that he might still be able to return and serve in the temple, which at this time had not yet been destroyed.

However, in the fourth year of Ezekiel's captivity the prophet Jeremiah wrote a letter to the exiles in Babylon telling them that the captivity would be long. He wrote that God wanted them to build houses, plant gardens, and get married because they would be there for seventy years before He would recover them and return them to Jerusalem (see Jeremiah 29). At the same time, the false prophets among the exiles, Ahab and Zedekiah, were prophesying that there would be an early return; and the result was that they were killed by Nebuchadnezzar (see Jeremiah 29 again). So the hope of this young man Ezekiel of ever serving in the temple back in Jerusalem was terminated. When Ezekiel reached the age of thirty, it was the moment for him to have become a full-fledged priest serving in the temple in Jerusalem. What a glorious experience that would have been for him! But it was impossible. And yet, while in the depths of his despair, the glory of the Lord appeared to him and called him to be a prophet. It has been observed that Jeremiah was a prophet who happened to be a priest, but Ezekiel was a priest who happened to be a prophet; and there is much truth in such a statement.

Now before we go into the book of Ezekiel it would be helpful for us to know something further about the prophets. As is commonly accepted, there are considered to be four major prophets and twelve minor prophets in the Old Testament. Whether a prophet is deemed minor or major actually depends upon the length of a given prophet's canonical writings. It is not to be inferred that the major prophets are greater prophets or the minor prophets are lesser prophets. They are simply judged in this manner as determined by the length of their writings. But for convenience sake in discussing these Old Testament prophets, we classify four of them as major prophets—Isaiah, Jeremiah, Ezekiel and Daniel. Isaiah is considered to have been a great poet; Jeremiah is considered to have been a great preacher; Ezekiel, a great artist; and Daniel, a great statesman. Two of them came from priestly families: Jeremiah and Ezekiel, whereas two of them came from nobility: Isaiah and Daniel.

Ezekiel does not have the soaring, sustained flight of language found in Isaiah; neither does he have the tenderness of Jeremiah nor the vast horizon of Daniel. His particular characteristic was directness. We clearly see a directness in his writings. Isaiah lived about a hundred years before Jeremiah, and Jeremiah was about twenty years older than Ezekiel. Daniel was probably around the same age as Ezekiel.

Of these four major prophets we know that three of them were connected with Jewish exiles in one way or another. Jeremiah at first stayed in Jerusalem with the poor Jewish people after the captivity of those taken away into Babylon had occurred; but, then, later on he went into exile with the Jewish remnant of Jerusalem and Judah down into Egypt where he continued as a prophet and where, according to one tradition, he was stoned to death by those Jews who rejected his prophecies of doom for all among this remnant (see Jeremiah 42—

44). On the other hand, Ezekiel was a prophet among the exiles in Babylon; and, of course, Daniel was also a prophet in the Babylonian captivity but was situated mostly at the royal court of Babylon.

Probably, Daniel was taken into captivity eight years ahead of Ezekiel because he was taken in the third year of King Jehoiakim which was eight years before King Jehoiachin was taken. But in one sense, Ezekiel is considered to have been the only man raised up by God to be a prophet among the exiles in Babylon because, even though Daniel was there and was also given the gift of prophecy, in the most strict sense, he was not called into prophetic office. He did not serve in the office of a prophet. Instead, he lived in the palace, and his prophecies are concerned with the *outward* matters of God's kingdom in relation to the kingdoms of this world. He was there as a testimony to the sovereignty of God and as a standard of godly righteousness; he was there to be a counsel to kings and princes. So that is the reason the Jewish people do not number the book of Daniel among the prophetic writings. Instead, they place his work in with the writings called the *Hagiographa*—that is, the sacred Jewish writings—because as we have said, strictly speaking, he did not perform in the prophetic office. He was more like a seer than a prophet. But Ezekiel is quite different in that he functioned as a prophet among the exiles in Babylon by speaking to the conscience of the people. In short, his prophecies are related to the *inward* concerns of the divine kingdom.

When Ezekiel was thirty years old and without any hope of ever returning to Jerusalem to serve in the temple as a priest, the Scriptures tell us that the glory of God appeared to him by the river Chebar (see 1:1 with 1:28). Now Chebar is commonly known as Chaboras. It is a river in upper Mesopotamia which flows into the river Euphrates. When Nebuchadnezzar took the Jewish captives out of Judah, he settled them in a place by the river Chebar at the community known as Tel-abib, which is about two hundred miles above Babylon. But it was considered as Babylon because it was under Babylonian rule. It was there that the glory of the Lord appeared to Ezekiel.

Now this book of Ezekiel, in one sense, is most difficult to understand because of the kind of person its author was. To begin with, Ezekiel was a very peculiar person who was given to indulge greatly in expressing things in highly symbolic language. Indeed, because his priestly feeling was so deep, he very much liked to employ priestly symbolism to convey what he saw or thought. In this connection, throughout his book we find numerous visions, symbols, allegories, parables, metaphors, similitudes, proverbs, and prophecies of every description. Moreover, his many symbolic actions are on unusual display there. In fact, his individuality is marked by much energetic action, Ezekiel having dramatically acted things out in great symbolic detail. Possessing a highly artistic bent, he employed every imaginable literary or artistic device to paint pictures which he hoped would leave a deep impression upon the people. One cannot but be impressed by the remarkable—even extraordinary—pictures he has presented. They are quite inspiring, mysterious, even charming in some instances, and yet so terrifying. Nevertheless, by means of these various symbolic actions and portrayals, Ezekiel was continually attempting to unveil to his audience an inward reality.

Time-wise, the book of Ezekiel and his prophecies can be divided into three periods. Chapters 1—24 contain predictions having to do with events to occur *before* the siege of Jerusalem. Chapters 25—32 consist of predictions related to events which were to take place *during* the siege of Jerusalem. And chapters 33—48 record those predictions of events which would play out *after* the siege of Jerusalem. The first group of prophecies is concerned with the denunciation of Judah and of Jerusalem and of their imminent destruction. The second group of prophecies is about God's wrathful visitation upon the surrounding nations. And the third group of prophecies has to do with the recovery of the nation of Israel.

By looking more closely into the content of this book, one can probably divide it into two parts: chapters 1—32 cover the devastation and destruction of the old; while chapters 33—48 relate the bringing in of the new.

From this book of Ezekiel I would like to emphasize two points: one is the prophet's call; the other is God's glory.

EZEKIEL'S CALL

When Ezekiel was a thirty-year-old captive living along the river Chebar, the glory of the Lord appeared to him; and from that moment onward he was called to be a prophet. He was not able to serve actively as a priest, for which he had been trained; but now God called him into another office—to be a prophet and a spokesman for God. There are a few important features we should note about his call.

AN OPEN HEAVEN

First, the heavens were opened to him. That is very important for anyone who is called to be a prophet. A prophet is a person who represents the full mind of God at any given time when that mind has been lost. Let me repeat: *A prophet is a person who represents the full mind of God when that mind has been lost.* That is the reason a prophet is God's spokesman. So the first important point in being called to be a prophet is that he must have an open heaven because he is a messenger of heaven. He is to bring heaven's message to the people. When God's people forsake Him, the heavens are closed to them. There is no revelation; there is no vision; there is no word of God. Instead, the heavens are like brass—totally shut up. There is no connection or communication from above. But when the heavens are opened to a certain person, the communication is present and the message comes forth. Hence, to be a prophet one must have an open heaven. We can discern from the Scriptures how very, very important this is. Indeed, we can see this in relation to the Lord Jesus.

When Jesus was baptized, and as He came up from the water, the heavens were opened and from which there came forth a voice. At this same time the Spirit descended upon Him as a dove and rested upon Him because the Lord Jesus was called to be a prophet. He was to fulfill His function as a prophet during His three and a half years of ministry on earth and the heavens were opened to Him. So whoever is called to be a prophet needs an open heaven.

There is no reason why the heavens are not open to us today because when the Lord Jesus was crucified, thank God, the separating veil or curtain between the temple's holy place and its most holy place housing the ark of God was rent from top to bottom (see Matthew 27:51a). In other words, through the finished work of the Lord Jesus, the heavens which were closed to mankind were now opened to us who believe. We as God's people today may live under an open heaven. We may have uninterrupted communion with God. We may have precious fellowship with heaven and receive messages from heaven. This is now our portion and our inheritance. So let us never forget that today an open heaven is our inheritance. There is no reason why there should be any lack of communication between heaven and us. However, though we do have an open heaven as our inheritance, possessing our possession is another matter. In other words, though it is our privilege to enjoy an open heaven, we need to turn our hearts to heaven to in fact have that communication. II Corinthians declares that when your heart is turned to the Lord, the veil of separation is taken away. There may be a veil upon your heart, but that veil will be removed when you turn your heart to the Lord (see 3:16). As soon as you do that, you have an open heaven. That is very basic, yet also very important. All believers need to live daily beneath an open heaven because they are a heavenly people who are supposed to receive heavenly messages from the Lord. However, that alone does not make a person a prophet since every believer should be living under an open heaven anyway.

Visions of God

The heavens were opened to Ezekiel and he then said: "I saw visions of God." Not only did he live under an open heaven but he saw what was in heaven. He beheld visions of God. Now in the case of Ezekiel, these visions basically consisted of the appearance of the glory of the Lord. He saw the Lord.

We, too, need to have vision. By vision is meant that we need to see God. We need to see His Person, His purpose, His plan, His glory. The apostle Paul testified: "I have not been disobedient to the heavenly vision" (see Acts 26:19). Paul had a vision on the road to Damascus and it is referred to here by Paul as a heavenly vision. And what he saw was an enormous man—a universal man—that filled the entire universe. Christ the Head is in heaven; whereas the Head's body—the church—is spread all over the earth. And that vision which Paul saw governed his whole life and ministry. We likewise need that kind of vision which is to govern our life as well.

Paul not only mentioned the heavenly vision but in II Corinthians 12 he also spoke of the visions and revelations of the Lord which he had received as well. In other words, there were many revelations and many visions because that governing heavenly vision continued throughout his life. In his experience on the road to Damascus Paul was given to see the frame of that vision; and therefore, as he communed with the Lord all through his life that vision's frame was being filled in and the heavenly vision was being fulfilled on earth.

So we find that Ezekiel talked at length here about the visions of God. To be a prophet of God you need to have the visions of God. You need to see Him and to understand Him; you need to know His Person and His character; to know His mind, His thought and His heart; to know His purpose and His will; and to know His counsel, plan, and working. All this is important for being a spokesman of God.

Hearing the Voice of God

Not only did Ezekiel see visions of God but also God spoke to him "expressly." That is to say, Ezekiel heard the voice of God in a direct, specific, personal, experiential, and revelational way (see 1:3). We have the word of God in our hands. We study it; we may even analyze and understand it; and if not all of it, then part of it. But for someone to have that kind of knowledge, important as it is, does not make that person a prophet. It may enable him to be a teacher but not a prophet. To be a prophet one needs the word of God coming directly, personally and expressly to him. Of course, today is not as it was in the Old Testament days when the word of God had not been completed. The faith once delivered to the saints (see Jude 3b) had not yet been completed, and that is the reason why the word of God came directly to those prophets. It was words which God had never spoken before—they were new revelations. But today all the revelations of God have been completed. The faith has once and for all been delivered to the saints, and we have them all in this book we call the

Bible. Therefore, we cannot have additional revelations which are entirely new or extra or are different from what has been revealed in this Book. That is impossible today; and if anyone should claim to have such revelations, he is a *false* prophet.

However, to be a prophet, not only do you need to understand what is written in the Bible, you also need the Spirit of God to speak once again freshly. It may be the same word, but it comes forth to you in a living, personal and expressed way. Receiving only that kind of speaking makes you a prophet. In other words, a prophet—to be a prophet—must have revelation, yet not in the sense of it being extra-Scriptural, but in the sense of it constituting a respeaking by the Spirit of God to the prophet's spirit so that there is a burden created in his heart.

Actually, on one occasion Ezekiel was instructed by God to eat a scroll on which had been inscribed words from God he had received; that is to say, the word of God had to be chewed, swallowed and thus come into him and be physically assimilated by him, and hence become part of him (see 2:8—3:5). Now in spiritual terms that is what makes a person a prophet.

The Hand of God

To be a prophet, besides having the word of the Lord coming to you livingly and freshly, you will also need to experience having the *hand* of the Lord upon you. Now that may be difficult, unpleasant and painful. We certainly want the word of God to come to us, but we do not like or want to have His hand upon us. Nevertheless, God's hand *has* to be upon us in order to transform us into His word which He has spoken to us. The message has to become the man: that is, God's word has to become flesh and blood. There must be dealings and discipline in order to have that kind of transformation. Then the prophet will experience the empowering of God with him when he delivers His message.

SON OF MAN

Ezekiel was trained to be a priest, never expecting to be a prophet. A priest is not trained to speak; he is trained to serve with his hands; even so, God called Ezekiel to be a prophet. It is most interesting that only in the book of Ezekiel was a prophet called by God as son of man. Many times in the book Ezekiel received from God the appellation of son of man. Why? Naturally, we will immediately be reminded of the fact that this same title or designation is attached to another Person—even to the Lord Jesus Christ.

When the Lord Jesus was on earth, He loved to call himself "the Son of man." What is the meaning of this designation? In the Scriptures Son of man means "a man according to God's original thought and pattern." For the Christian, the Lord Jesus is *the* Son of man. He is the Man who is the original pattern of man. He is the Man whom God had in His mind when He created man. He is the Man whom God wants. Jesus is the Son of man.

Ezekiel is called son of man by God without the use of the article "the." Obviously, Ezekiel and Jesus, as persons, are so different from each other because, even though Ezekiel is called son of man, he is not *the* Son of man. He is not that perfect Man, that ideal Man, the Man after God's perfect heart. Only the Lord Jesus is *the* Son of man. He is the Man according to God's original thought and pattern. He is the pattern for all of God's people. So, not in person but in function was Ezekiel called son of man. He functioned as son of man. When man failed—that is to say, when God's chosen people failed—God called Ezekiel to be a representative man, to be a standard to show His chosen people what His man ought to be. Ezekiel was therefore more than a prophet; he was a sign as well. God raised him up to be a sign.

A WATCHMAN

When God called Ezekiel, He also appointed him to be a watchman (see 3:16-17). What was a watchman in that long-ago day? Today we do not appreciate the fuller meaning of this word; but we need to be aware that in those olden days people did not have watches or clocks. And even if they did have them, they still had a watchman serving in the nighttime. The watchman was not simply there watching the gates, walls, doors or whatever else, but he would faithfully go on his rounds to every place every hour or so and beat a gong or whatever it might have been, thus telling the time. He was one who knew the time and told the time. That was what a watchman was back then. Spiritually speaking, therefore, God appointed Ezekiel to be a watchman who would be one who knew the time in which he was living.

Too often, many of us do not know the time we are living in; therefore, we are not watchful but sleeping. We are deceived because we do not realize the time. It is very important for us to know the time. And hence a prophet must be a watchman who is given the knowledge of the time that he is living in and who is declaring it and thus making it known to the people. A prophet discerns the time and foretells what is coming—warning and reminding people—so that they, too, may be watchful, alert and prepared. I believe we very much need watchmen today.

As we have now seen, Ezekiel was called to be a prophet, son of man, a sign, and a watchman. What a responsibility he had! God sent him to the people in exile, telling him: "This is a rebellious and stiff-necked people. Whether they hear or they forbear, speak. Let them know there is a prophet among them" (see 2:3-5; cf. 3:7). The work of Ezekiel was a very, very difficult task. He was sent by God to a people in captivity, yet their hearts were still hardened. So far as the people were concerned, there was no hope; but thank God, He knew that, even among such a group of people, there would still be some who would hear, who would repent, and who would submit themselves under His mighty hand; and eventually, they would be the people who would be brought back to Jerusalem to rebuild the temple.

Outwardly Ezekiel's mission seemed to be a failure from the very beginning. God had even told him in advance that it would be an impossible task, meaning that the people would not listen to him. In another sense, however, his mission was successful because, through his prophesying faithfully to the people, some of them heard and responded positively. Zerubbabel, Joshua, Nehemiah, Ezra—these people, and others like them, eventually returned to Jerusalem to rebuild the temple and reestablish the testimony of God. That is the reason Ezekiel is considered to be the prophet of hope.

GLORY

The second point I would like to draw our attention to and emphasize has to do with the subject of *glory*. Glory is the one word which characterizes the entire book of Ezekiel. Indeed, the glory of the Lord is the primary theme of this book. Let me say at the outset here that the glory of the Lord governs all things in the universe. In the vision of God's glory, Ezekiel saw a great cloud coming from the north with a brightness within as fire burning, and he also saw four cherubim. These cherubim served as a chariot, as it were, upon which the throne of God was being drawn. And over the expanse Ezekiel beheld a throne and the appearance of a man above sitting on the throne. He could not see Him clearly, but he did see the fire—symbolizing God's brightness and glory, and he did see the rainbow—the appearance of the likeness of the glory of the Lord.

Ezekiel must have been quite familiar with this scene since in the temple at Jerusalem there was the ark, above which were two cherubim serving or functioning as the arms of the mercy seat. Furthermore, when Solomon built the temple, he had the workmen fashion two giant cherubim, and the length of their wings spanned the entire length of the holiest of all. This meant that in the holiest of all there were four cherubim along with the mercy seat. Yet even before the time of the temple, when Moses had had the ark placed in the tabernacle's holiest of all and when also every piece of furniture had been properly placed, the glory of the Lord had immediately filled the tabernacle. In other words, not only did the glory of the Lord sit upon the mercy seat in the holiest of all, but the glory also filled the whole tabernacle. That was the scene with which Ezekiel had been most familiar—whether it related to the time of the tabernacle or the time of the temple.

At this point a little historical review can be helpful. We will recall that when the children of Israel entered the Promised Land, the tabernacle had first been set up in Shiloh. But the Israelites rebelled against God and sinned against Him. And in I Samuel we read that fighting had broken out between the Israelites and the Philistines; and the Israelites were defeated. In their superstitious minds, these Israelites had thought that since the ark had fought victoriously for them previously, they could bring it to the present battlefield and God would successfully fight for them again. However, they did not know He had already left them. So they brought the ark to the battlefield, but the Israelites were defeated and the ark was captured by the Philistines. When the news reached Shiloh and Israel's high priest Eli heard it, he fell back and died. And God's word at this point in the story reads: "Ichabod—the glory is departed." The ark represented the presence of God, and now it had been captured. So how rightly could it be said: "Ichabod: the glory has departed" (see I Samuel 4:16-22).

Now after the ark departed from Shiloh, and even though it came back from the Philistines on its own, it was never returned to Shiloh but found its way here and there in Israel for many years thereafter. But, then, the ark was later brought by David to his tent which he had set up on Mount Zion. Much later, at the time when Solomon had built the temple, the ark was brought up from the tabernacle of David and was placed in the holiest of all, and the glory of the Lord filled the whole temple. Even the temple priests had to retreat from its precincts because the glory was so great. Thank God for that! Unfortunately, however, the children of Israel once again rebelled against God, having committed all kinds of abominations.

Now we do not know when the glory of the Lord ultimately left the temple in Jerusalem. We do know, though, that at the time when Isaiah went to the temple, the glory was still there. For we will recall from Isaiah 6 that he saw the glory of the Lord—God sitting on the throne with His train filling the temple—and the seraphim crying aloud: "Holy, holy, holy." But we do not know when—after that occasion—the glory finally departed, but it was obviously an empty temple which the Babylonians ultimately destroyed. Meanwhile, the children of Israel had still worshiped in the temple, but it was worship offered up in vain because God was no longer there.

We now return to Ezekiel who, hopeless and in despair, was a Babylonian captive sitting one day by the river Chebar. Suddenly, the glory of the Lord came to him—it being the same glory, the same scene, the same vision that was there in the temple in Jerusalem back in Solomon's and Isaiah's day. God was now revealing His glory once again, this time to Ezekiel.

What is glory? It cannot be summed up in just one word. On the contrary, glory is the presence of God; glory is the approval of God; glory is the satisfaction of God; glory is the fullness of God. Wherever and whenever God is present, there is glory. Whenever God is satisfied, there is glory. Whenever the fullness of God is revealed, there is glory. His glory had departed from Jerusalem's temple, and yet His glory appeared to a lone captive resting by the river Chebar in faraway Babylon. What a privilege! The glory of the Lord appeared to a person who was devastated and in despair but whose heart was nonetheless for the Lord. God was present with him. God approved of him. God was satisfied with him. And God called him to be a prophet.

From a most remarkable portion of Ezekiel, in chapters 8—12, we learn that while Ezekiel was sitting there in Tel-abib by the river Chebar, once again the glory of the Lord appeared to him and, this time, snatched him by his hair and, in a vision, carried him back to Jerusalem. In a word, the glory of the Lord was revisiting the temple there.

We said a few moments ago that the glory of the Lord governs everything. The government of God in all things is according to His glory. In short, His glory governs the entire universe. His glory governs all the kingdoms of the earth. And His glory governs His own people: every dealing, every aspect of our life is governed by God's glory. So here in this current episode involving Ezekiel the glory of the Lord appeared again in the Jerusalem temple. And what did God's glory do there? It judged His people. Glory judges because it is light, and light exposes the reality of a situation. In this vision which had come to Ezekiel and which had carried him back to Jerusalem, the children of Israel were still there; the temple was also still there; they were not yet destroyed; and, they were still worshiping in the temple, but outwardly. Everything seemed to be going on as usual; but God's glory now revealed the reality of their condition and showed the prophet Ezekiel that in the temple in Jerusalem it was merely idol worship. From the gate to the altar, the temple was full of abominations. People were in the temple, yes; but they were worshiping idols. And no wonder, therefore, that God had to destroy that temple and punish His people. It was done for His glory's sake; it was done to vindicate His glory.

Let us all realize that the glory of the Lord is the one thing which governs everything about us. It governs your life; it governs my life. It governs the life of the church; it governs the life of this world. This is the standard God will use by which to measure everything in the universe. He will measure you and me in accordance with His glory. His glory will judge us; it will also discipline us. But thank God, His glory will redeem us and it will restore us. Hence, glory is the one thing which stands out above all else in the book of Ezekiel.

Ezekiel could now realize that though the judgment was severe, it was just. Jerusalem was destroyed; the temple was destroyed; the people were scattered, even taken into captivity; and God's glory was vindicated. But that was not the end of the vision given to the prophet. For there appeared a rainbow around the throne—an indication of God's mercy. In judgment, there is mercy.

From the last part of the book of Ezekiel, in chapters 33—48, we see that after the captivity the glory of the Lord returned; yet not because of the people themselves but because of God's name. It was not because the people in and by themselves had changed but for His name's sake God himself changed the people so that His glory might reappear among them. We can see this taking place step by step, as is described for us in this last part of the book. In fact, it is God's gospel, as it were, being displayed in this Old Testament book.

In His mercy, God recovered them (see chapters 33—39). He washed away their sins with water and also gave them a new spirit. He put His Spirit in them so that they could obey Him and be His people and He could once more be their God. God restored them as His people.

In chapters 40—43 we find that the temple was restored in its fullness and accompanied by the return of God's glory to the new temple. And from chapter 44 we learn that the priesthood was restored. Then, in chapters 45—46, we behold the kingship being restored, in that the Prince—the Messiah—has come. And in chapter 47 we read that the land was restored. And finally, chapter 48 reveals that the city was restored and was now to be named "Jehovah-Shammah, the Lord is there."

All these, of course, were visions which came to the prophet Ezekiel; and they are symbolic. Some people believe that in the millennium a literal physical temple will be built according to what Ezekiel saw and described in great detail. Now it may be so; but, personally, I do not think so because God has a living temple already—the church. What is the use anymore of a temple made of stones? It is symbolic. What is the use of offering up sacrifices again? We have been told in the New Testament that Christ has been sacrificed "once and for all" (see Hebrews 7:26-27). And therefore animal sacrifices have been done away with. Physically, it is impossible, if one carefully reads all these descriptions in Ezekiel. In other words, one day, through God's own working, and according to His glory, He is going to restore all things to His original purpose: a people will be restored; a living temple will be restored to His fullness; a priesthood—a spiritual priesthood—will be restored to His glory; and the King will come. There will be princes ruling with Him and a city established whose name henceforth shall be: Jehovah-Shammah—"the Lord is there." If one reads Ezekiel 40—48 with Revelation 21—22, he will see the similarities there. In a word, the picture being painted for us by God through Ezekiel is that one day the glory of the Lord will fill the whole universe—which is the theme of glory that is central to the entire book of Ezekiel.

Hence, as we have been given to see here something of the glory of the Lord, let that glory examine us. As Paul said, "Do all things to the glory of God" (see I Corinthians 10:31). Anything which does not answer to His glory is not of God and has to be judged. It cannot be carried into eternity. But whatever is of glory, whatever is of Christ, shall indeed be carried into eternity to the glory of God.

Let us pray:

Dear heavenly Father, Moses prayed that he might see Your glory, but he could only see Your back and not Your face. Oh, how we praise and thank Thee that we can see the glory of the Lord in the face of Jesus Christ. Lord God, may it be our constant cry: "Let me see Your glory." May Your glory govern our life both individually and together. Lord, take away everything that is not of glory, that is of shame, so that when we shall see Thy face, we will not be ashamed. Oh, our cry is, "Let glory rule over the earth as water fills the sea." We ask in Thy precious name. Amen.

DANIEL

GOD IS MY JUDGE

Daniel 1:1-9—In the third year of the reign of Jehoiakim king of Judah came Nebuchadnezzar king of Babylon unto Jerusalem, and besieged it. And the Lord gave Jehoiakim king of Judah into his hand, and a part of the vessels of the house of God; and he carried them into the land of Shinar, to the house of his god; and he brought the vessels into the treasure-house of his god.

And the king spoke unto Ashpenaz the chief of his eunuchs, that he should bring of the children of Israel, both of the royal seed and of the nobles, youths in whom was no blemish, and of goodly countenance, and skilful in all wisdom, and acquainted with knowledge, and understanding science, and such as had ability in them to stand in the king's palace, and whom they might teach the learning and the language of the Chaldeans. And the king appointed unto them a daily provision of the king's delicate food, and of the wine that he drank, to nourish them three years, that at the end thereof they might stand before the king.

Now among these were of the children of Judah, Daniel, Hananiah, Mishael, and Azariah. And the prince of the eunuchs gave them names: to Daniel he gave the name Belteshazzar, and to Hananiah, Shadrach, and to Mishael, Meshach, and to Azariah, Abednego.

And Daniel purposed in his heart that he would not pollute himself with the king's delicate food, nor with the wine which he drank; and he requested of the prince of the eunuchs that he might not have to pollute himself. And God granted Daniel favour and mercy before the prince of the eunuchs.

Daniel 1:17-21—As for these four youths, God gave them knowledge and skill in all learning and wisdom; and Daniel had understanding in all visions and dreams. And at the end of the days that the king had said he should bring them in, the prince of the eunuchs brought them in before Nebuchadnezzar. And the king spoke with them; and among them all was found none like Daniel, Hananiah, Mishael, and Azariah: and they stood before the king. And in all matters of judicious wisdom, as to which the king enquired of them, he found them ten times better than all the scribes and magicians that were in all his realm.

And Daniel continued unto the first year of king Cyrus.

Daniel 12:4-13—And thou, Daniel, close the words, and seal the book, till the time of the end. Many shall run to and fro, and knowledge shall be increased.

And I Daniel looked, and behold, there stood other two, the one on this side, on the bank of the river, and the other on that side, on the bank of the river. And he said to the man clothed in linen, who was above the waters of the river, How long is it to the end of these wonders? And I heard the man clothed in linen, who was above the waters of the river; and he held up his right hand and his left hand unto the heavens, and swore by him that liveth for ever that it is for a time, times, and a half; and when the scattering of the power of the holy people shall be accomplished, all these things shall be finished.

And I heard, but I understood not. And I said, My lord, what shall be the end of these things? And he said, Go thy way, Daniel; for these words are closed and sealed till the time of the end. Many shall be purified, and be made white, and be refined; but the wicked shall do wickedly: and none of the wicked shall understand; but the wise shall understand. And from the time that the continual sacrifice is taken away, and the abomination that maketh desolate set up, there shall be a thousand, two hundred, and ninety days. Blessed is he that waiteth, and cometh to the thousand three hundred and thirty-five days! But do thou go thy way until the end; and thou shalt rest, and stand in thy lot at the end of the days.

Let us pray:

Dear heavenly Father, as we continue in Thy presence, we just look to Thy Spirit to open Thy word to our hearts that we may be drawn closer to Thee and to Thy will. We do offer ourselves to Thee for whatever Thy will shall be for this earth, and may Thy name be glorified throughout all the earth. We ask in the name of our Lord Jesus. Amen.

Daniel means "God is my Judge" or "God is Judge." He was born during the reign of King Josiah who was a good king; but Josiah died in battle with Necho, king of Egypt. After he died, his son Jehoahaz assumed the throne for three months but was deposed by King Necho, who made another son of Josiah, Jehoiakim, king of Judah instead. So in reality Jehoiakim was a vassal to the king of Egypt; but in the third year of Jehoiakim's reign, Nebuchadnezzar, the king of Babylon, defeated Necho and besieged Jerusalem. King Jehoiakim surrendered to him, and even though Nebuchadnezzar allowed Jehoiakim to continue as king over Judah, he took hostages from among Judah's royal families and nobility and carried them off to Babylon to ensure that Jehoiakim would not rebel against him. And among these hostages was a young man named Daniel.

Daniel evidently came from either a royal or a noble family. When he was taken to Babylon, he was around twenty years of age. This meant that as a teenager he had lived for a few years under that wicked King Jehoiakim; but thank God, Daniel had remained faithful to the God of his fathers.

If not already aware, we must be made aware of one significant development in world history: when Daniel was taken hostage to Babylon, the whole world situation was beginning to undergo a great change. We know that, in the past, God had called Abraham and, through him, raised up the nation of Israel, over which He was King. And to that nation as it were He gave over the government of the world. But by the third year of Jehoiakim's reign over Judah and

Jerusalem, when Jewish people began to be taken as captives, this marked the beginning of a tremendous change in the economy of God on earth because Judah, Jerusalem, and God's temple would all very soon be destroyed. And from then on, throughout the period of the Babylonian captivity, God would not be addressed as the God of the heavens and of the earth since He no longer had any testimony on the earth. The nation to whom He had given His name and the temple where His name had been set were totally destroyed, leaving God with no testimony upon the earth. Hence, during the period of Jewish captivity He was referred to as only the God of the heavens; He was not addressed any longer as the God of the heavens and of the earth. The government on the earth had now passed from the hands of the chosen people of God into the hands of the Gentiles. As a matter of fact, the "times of the Gentiles" (Luke 21:24 AV) actually began with Nebuchadnezzar and Babylon. In a word, momentous change had commenced upon the earth.

Even though God was no longer addressed as the God of the heavens and of the earth—indeed, the world seemed not to recognize Him as the God over all—nevertheless, God had not left himself without witnesses. So Daniel was raised up during this critical time to be a witness to the world. Though it did not appear that God had any visible testimony upon the earth to the fact that He was the God of the earth as well as the God of the heavens, He nonetheless had not given up His rights. He was still the God of both, despite the appearance outwardly that the government of the earth had passed into the hands of the Gentiles who neither knew Him nor recognized Him. God was still ruling over the affairs of man, and that was the testimony which was now to be entrusted to Daniel (see, e.g., Daniel 4:25).

Daniel was therefore living in the time of this tremendous pivotal change in world history. We know that his contemporaries were Jeremiah, Ezekiel, Habakkuk and Obadiah. As we learned earlier, Jeremiah had remained with the people in Judah but later on had gone down to Egypt. His burden was concerned with God's chosen people, and he was with them faithfully to the very end.

Like Daniel, Ezekiel, too, was taken into Babylonian captivity, but this had occurred some ten years later in the time of Jehoiachin, and he was living directly among the people in captivity. His burden was concerned with the temple of God because he had been brought up and trained as a priest. In Daniel's case, however, when he was taken into Babylon as a hostage, he did not live with the other Jewish captives. Instead, he lived in the royal palace and served in the governments of the world. Therefore, he was concerned with the city or kingdom of God.

It is interesting to note that in our English Bible and also in the Septuagint or Greek Bible, Daniel is listed with the so-called major prophets—Isaiah, Jeremiah, Ezekiel and Daniel—whereas in the Hebrew Bible, Daniel is not listed among any of the prophets. The Hebrew Bible is divided into three sections—the law, the prophets, and the writings—and Daniel is placed among the writings called the Hagiographa. These so-called sacred writings were composed by people like priests, seers, and others. The most likely reason why Daniel is not listed among the prophets but rather among these writings is that, though Daniel was given prophetic utterances he did not really fulfill a prophet's office like the other prophets because he did not live with the people nor prophesy to them. He lived in the palace and thus his prophecies were concerned with the nations of the world as well as with God's chosen people. Accordingly, Daniel did not fulfill the function of a prophet in the strictest sense. He was more a seer than a prophet. For this reason, he is listed in the hagiographic writings instead of among the writings of the prophets.

Daniel lived about 600 years before Christ. We find that in the Old Testament his name is mentioned by Ezekiel. In Ezekiel 14 verses 14 and 20 the prophet mentioned three very righteous men: Noah, Daniel and Job. Again, in Ezekiel 28:3, he once more mentioned Daniel's name: "... wiser than Daniel!"—thus indicating the exceptional wisdom of Daniel. And in the New Testament, we learn from Matthew 24:15 that Jesus himself mentioned his name: "... the prophet Daniel." Though the Lord Jesus did call Daniel a prophet, and he *was* a prophet, he did not fulfill the prophet's office. Hence, we can be certain that Daniel was indeed a very real person, having been attested to as such in both the Old and New Testaments.

The book of Daniel was written in two different languages: chapters 2:4—7:28 were written in Aramaic, that is, in the Chaldean language; and the rest of the book was written in Hebrew. But though these two portions were written in two different languages, it is one book, one unit; a fact that is most clear. And Daniel himself was the author of this book. Although he did not use the personal pronoun "I" until in the second part of the book, it is evident that he was the one who wrote and gave us this book.

Daniel can be roughly divided into two parts: chapters 1—6 are historical in content; chapters 7—12 are prophetic. As we look into these chapters we learn that chapters 1—4 are concerned with things which happened in the reign of Nebuchadnezzar; chapter 5, with things which happened in the reign of Belshazzar; chapter 6, in the reign of Darius; chapters 7—8, in the reign of Belshazzar; chapter 9, in that of Darius; and chapters 10—12, in that of Cyrus. So, time-wise, we can see a very clear chronological order in the book of Daniel.

As noted already, the first part of Daniel is historical and the second part is prophetic; and it has been rightly observed that this prophetic part of Daniel is apocalyptic in nature because it presents a series of supernatural visions which needed to be interpreted. The Greek word *apokalupsis*, from which is derived our English words apocalyptic and apocalypse (the latter the Greek title for the last book of our English Bible, The Revelation) means "the unveiling" or "the revealing" of truth. In this regard, the prophetic part of Daniel can therefore be likened to the book of Revelation or to part of the book of Zechariah.

The book of Daniel is very, very important because it is the key to the interpretation of the Olivet discourse of the Lord Jesus—recorded in Matthew 24—25—and the Bible's concluding book of Revelation. So in order to understand Jesus' discourse on the Mount of Olives and the book of Revelation, as well as to discern the comprehensive view of prophecy, Daniel is the key. But I fear that whenever we mention Daniel, we are more interested in his prophecies than in his person. His prophetic utterances are fascinating, and that is the thing which really attracts us; but too often, we forget about Daniel the person.

Yet half of the book of Daniel is concerned with him as a person; it is his personal history. And, of course, the other half of the book is his work of prophecy. Now in God's sight the person is always more important than his work. Yet we look at the matter differently: we view the work as much more important than the person; as long as the work gets done, it does not matter what kind of person the worker is. But that is not the way with God: He is deeply interested in the person and desires after the man more than the work; and in Daniel, I think God's view of the matter is made very evident. So we need to pay more attention to Daniel as a man of God than to the prophecies which God used Daniel to give to the world and to His chosen people.

MAN OF GOD

Now in this book God is called the God of Daniel (6:26). In the Scriptures there are a few places where God is called the God of such and such a person—for example, the God of Abraham, the God of Isaac, the God of Jacob, the God of Daniel. This must indicate that something very special is meant. Of course, in a general sense, God is our God, too: God is your God; God is my God. But for Him to be called the God of Daniel or the God of so and so must be meant to convey a very special meaning. When He is called the God of a specific person, it indicates that in and through that person God has given to the world a special revelation of himself. By means of that person, we are given new knowledge of God. Thus we can see how important that vessel must be.

God is called the God of Daniel because, in Daniel, He has made himself known to the world in a very special way which cannot be known in any other way. Even the Gentile kings, one after another, had to recognize and even voluntarily acknowledge that the God of Daniel is the God of all gods. He is the living God. He is the One who rules over all the earth, the One who sets kings up and puts them down (see 2:21), the One who is the Ruler of all the earth. In spite of the fact that the government on earth was now in the hands of the unbelieving Gentiles, God was still ruling and reigning over all. He is sovereign and therefore the Ruler not only of the heavens but also of the earth. Now this was the testimony which God had given to the world through this man Daniel.

Let me inquire, Does the world see in us that our God is the God of Daniel? Does the world see in us that God truly is sovereign, that He truly rules not only in heaven but also upon this earth? I believe this is a great testimony which the church in our day has to present to the world in the same way by which Daniel had testified for God in his day.

Daniel was a man greatly beloved by God. Again and again, the Scriptures say he was a man greatly beloved (9:23, 10:11, 10:19). In a general sense, we naturally are all beloved of God: we are beloved in the beloved Son, but that is too general a statement when it comes to certain of His followers. Among all the beloved of God there must be some who are *greatly* beloved, like Daniel. Yet let us be clear that God is not partial in any way; He loves all. So why is it that, with Daniel, God can say he is greatly beloved? There must be something in his life which answered to God's heart in a very special way.

Purity

When Daniel was taken as a hostage, he was about twenty years old, or perhaps slightly younger. On the one hand, being taken hostage must have been a very traumatic experience for him. Here he was, having been born and raised in a noble family, perhaps even among the royalty, and, as a young man, he probably had ambition to serve his nation for God. Suddenly, he was taken away captive from his home and country into a distant foreign land. That would have been a very tragic experience for a young person. He probably thought he would now be placed in a terrible situation. But soon afterwards Daniel may have thought that providence had played a trick on him because he found himself among a group of young people whom Nebuchadnezzar had chosen and brought to his palace from everywhere. They were handsome, skillful, teachable, showed promise, and could stand before the king: in fact, they were the best of the young people from all over the Empire and elsewhere. Nebuchadnezzar would have them set apart, have them trained for three years, would even give them his own dainty food and drink.

They were to be trained to eventually stand before him in the royal court. Good fortune therefore seemed to have come to Daniel. As a hostage, he was a prisoner; but, suddenly, there was a very bright future ahead for him because he was given all these opportunities.

Now suppose you were that young man (or young woman), and if such good fortune suddenly happened to you, would you lose your head? Would you forget your nation? Would you forget your people? Would you forget your personal situation? Would you seize upon the opportunity for yourself? Most young people would probably do that; but not Daniel. His parents must have been among the godly people during the reign of King Josiah. And from his youth, therefore, something of substance was built up within him; for though he was in such a foreign situation in Babylon, the Bible nonetheless could declare that "Daniel purposed in his heart …" This young man determined in his heart that he would not be polluted by anything because he wanted to keep himself pure for God. Here was a young man whose life was devoted to God and yet he found himself in the worst situation one can imagine because in the royal palace of Babylon all kinds of evil things were going on—excessive luxuries, wicked acts, jealousies and rivalries, and treacheries. Daniel had been placed involuntarily right in the midst of that kind of sordid environment; nevertheless, he purposed in his heart not to be polluted by anything; he wanted to keep himself pure for God. What a difficult purpose of heart that must have been to uphold and to maintain!

It was indeed a very difficult situation. Humanly speaking, on the one hand, Daniel had no choice. He was given the extraordinary opportunity to be where he now was, and he could not reject it. Perhaps you or I might say: "I want to keep myself pure. I will therefore reject the opportunity and not even learn. I will refuse to learn the Chaldean language; for I am a Jew." Could you or I take that position in such a case? As for Daniel, he could not do so because he was not free. On the other hand, you or I might have said: "Because the opportunity is open to me, I will enjoy it to the fullest extent possible." But not Daniel; he was level-headed. He took the opportunity to learn everything—yet not for himself but for God. He might not have known or realized what would happen or how he could serve God in such a situation, but he was prepared to serve God, no matter the circumstance. He made the most of everything for God, but in doing so he would not allow himself to be polluted by anything.

So, having purposed such in his heart, Daniel approached the prince of the stewards and said on his and his three friends' behalf: "Do not give us the king's food and the king's wine, just give us plain food." Why did he do that? There might have been several reasons. Probably the primary reason was that, in those days, the king's wine and food had been offered first to the idols. So for Daniel to eat this food and drink this wine which first had been offered to idols would pollute him, would defile him, as though he himself had countenanced the notion of idol-worship. Perhaps many of us here cannot understand this; but I can, because when I was young I had been faced with the same problem. It so happens that I came from a Buddhist family. It was a large family with four generations living in one house. Every Chinese New Year we would have a family reunion and there would perhaps be two hundred people gathered; all the numerous relatives would be present. And before we ate, all the food to be eaten was first offered to our ancestors; that is to say, it would be offered up in the idolatrous ritual of ancestor-worship. After I became a Christian, this practice became a real problem for me, and I had to refuse to eat these things. Fortunately, my aunt heard about it, and on such occasions she prepared some separate food for me.

In Daniel's time this constituted a very serious issue of conscience, because in partaking of these foods he would have been deemed to have participated in the practice of worshiping idols; and hence, Daniel could not do that because he wanted to keep himself pure for God. Now that might have been the chief reason, but there could have been some other reasons as well.

As Christians, if we want to live a life for God, we should not enjoy for ourselves all the things of the world which are made available to us. Sometimes we think as follows: "Well, I did not steal it; it is just my portion. These were given to me, so why should I not enjoy them to the fullest?" No; because if we do, somehow it will lead our hearts astray from God and towards the things of this world. Christians should live a simple life. We are to eat in order that we may have a healthy body with which to serve God, but not to the extent of living in luxury. A luxurious life is not conducive to Christian living. If Daniel had enjoyed all the king's delicate food and drink, he might have gotten drunk. That would have affected his life before God. So he would rather live a simple life in order that he might glorify God. How we—especially the young people—need to purpose in our hearts the same purpose as did Daniel. And because Daniel had such desire, God honored his purpose. He opened the way for him with the prince of the stewards (see 1:9), and thus he was able not to pollute himself with the king's food and drink.

God rewarded Daniel and those other young men with him. He gave them wisdom and understanding. In judicial matters, these young men proved to be ten times wiser than the scribes and magicians throughout the entire Empire (1:20). God honored Daniel and his friends; for because Daniel kept himself pure before God and lived such a transparent life before Him, he was granted the ability to interpret the most significant visions and dreams related to world history.

Humility

Daniel was also a humble man. God gave him great wisdom and he could interpret dreams which no one else could interpret. Nevertheless, at the time when he stood before King Nebuchadnezzar who inquired of him, "Are you able to do this?" Daniel replied: "No, I am not wiser than anyone else. It is God who wishes to reveal the secret to you" (see 2:26-29). Daniel never tried to seize any glory for himself. He knew that all glory belonged to God. He was simply a vessel in His hand. Such humility in Daniel was something highly commendable and most pleasing to God.

Righteousness

Daniel was righteous as well. The righteousness of Daniel is proverbial, like that of Noah (see again Ezekiel 14:12-14, 17-20). Of all the people in the world, in his day, Noah was the only one who was righteous before God—but, of course, this was by the grace of

God. We likewise think of Job, the most righteous man of his day. And Daniel was a most righteous person in his day, too. He stood before God and man without any fault. Even his enemies could not find fault in any of his works. Bear in mind that he was well-nigh the prime minister of the greatest imperial power in the world at that time, the mighty Medo-Persian Empire. He had to manage numberless, countless matters of every kind in the world of that era; yet his enemies could not find any fault in anything he did. And they had to acknowledge that if they were to find any fault with him at all, they had to find it in his relationship with God (see 6:1-5). Think of that! He was such a righteous person not only before God but before man as well. And because he was such a righteous person, he could even confront and advise Nebuchadnezzar, that mighty despot, by saying to his face: "You had better break away from your sins by doing righteousness, and from your iniquities by showing mercy to the poor so that your days may be prolonged" (see 4:27). Daniel could even tell the descendant of Nebuchadnezzar on the throne, King Belshazzar, that he—Belshazzar—knew all the things which had happened to Nebuchadnezzar but from which he did not learn the lesson of humility and instead became proud (see 5:22-23). Daniel was such a righteous person!

FAITHFULNESS

Moreover, Daniel was a faithful person. He was faithful to God and to all the things which were entrusted into his hand (see 6:4). He was so faithful to God that even though there was issued a royal decree which stated that within a month from then no one could request anything from any man or any god except from King Darius or else face death in the lions' den, he did not regard it. Daniel knew about the decree but he was faithful to God. For as usual, three times a day, with his window opened towards Jerusalem, he continued daily to kneel down before God in prayer. He was therefore faithful even to the possibility of death (see 6:10ff.). And because he was faithful to God, God was faithful to him. Because of his faithfulness to the things entrusted to him, he was able to serve not just one empire but through two mighty world empires.

PERSISTENCY

Furthermore, in Daniel, we find persistency. He continued from the time of Nebuchadnezzar to the first year of King Darius, a period of seventy years and more. He lived through the seventy-year Jewish captivity. With us, sometimes we may begin well, but do we continue? Daniel continued on for over seventy years. He had an excellent spirit; indeed, the very Spirit of God was in him. That was Daniel.

A WITNESS TO THE WORLD

Finally, as was noted earlier, Daniel lived during a momentous transitional period in world history. When the times of the Gentiles began, it was a very critical time. God was no longer being recognized as the God of the earth; and Daniel lived in such a time. He was a witness raised up by God to stand before the world for His righteousness and justice so as to prove to the world that He still reigns on earth and that He reigns over all the affairs of men.

Daniel's name, as was earlier noted, means "God is my Judge." I wonder if you would like to have *that* name if you knew what such a name entailed. You would no doubt like to say instead, "God is my Savior" or "God is my Helper" or "God is my Comforter"; but would you like to have a name which declares "God is my Judge"? Do you dare to stand before God as your Judge? If so what kind of life you must live! Daniel had to live a highly disciplined life because he stood before God with Him as his Judge. God judged him in everything he did, in every thought he thought, in every word he spoke. That is the meaning of Daniel—in both his name and his life—God is my Judge. What a disciplined life he must have lived to be justified before God and to be so greatly beloved by Him. And because God was the Judge of Daniel, therefore, God could be proclaimed as the Judge of the whole earth; for that was Daniel's testimony.

May God raise up many Daniels today. We are living in a world which does not recognize God as the Ruler of this earth. We are also living in a time when the testimony of Jesus is shattered, has been broken up; God's people—God's church—is all fragmented. We are living in a very wicked, perverse world as though God does not even exist. God therefore needs additional Daniels in our age as His witnesses to this world and to testify that He still lives, that He still reigns and rules over all the affairs of men because He first rules over *me*. God needs such witnesses today.

PROPHECIES OF DANIEL

The second part of Daniel is prophecy. Daniel's prophecies are the most comprehensive ever given because he prophesied over the whole span of the world's history from the beginning of "the times of the Gentiles" all the way through to the second coming of Christ and even beyond that to the establishment of the kingdom of God in the millennium. He prophesied concerning not only the destiny of this world but also that of God's chosen people. In fact, he prophesied to the very end of time. In a word, that is the sum and substance of Daniel's prophecy.

This prophetic part of the book of Daniel can be roughly divided into three sections. Chapters 7—8 consist of visions and interpretations given to Daniel in the first and third years of King Belshazzar (see 7:1; 8:1). In a vision given Daniel during the first year he saw a great sea with the four winds blowing upon it. In other words, there was an immense raging storm; and in the midst of all the confusion and turmoil he beheld four wild beasts coming up from the sea one after another. Now we know that the dream given to Nebuchadnezzar and the vision God gave to Daniel, and which are found in, respectively, chapters 2 and 7, are actually the same thing. They tell us of the times of the Gentiles. With respect to world history, the times of the Gentiles began with Nebuchadnezzar, and they will end with the second coming of Christ. For the Gentile king Nebuchadnezzar, world dominion can be likened to a tall, gigantic, brilliant, bright, imposing image of man. That is how men view power and dominion in this world. This world is like an immense impressive man: one full of brightness, with gold head, silver breast and arms, brass belly and thighs, iron legs, half iron and half clay feet and toes. In the sight of God, however, world dominion is like a succession of wild beasts: cruel, wicked, terrible.

The dream of chapter 2 was given to Nebuchadnezzar, and Daniel was the interpreter. The vision in chapter 7 was given to Daniel, and the angel of God was the interpreter; but both reflected the same meaning. Oftentimes our focus in chapter 2 is on the huge image described there, and our focus in chapter 7 is on the four beasts; but God's emphasis does not rest there. Even though this Gentile emperor saw the great image, the real emphasis of his dream lay upon the Stone that was not cut by man. For that Stone will fall upon the toes and break up that entire gigantic image, and the Stone not cut by man will grow into a great mountain and fill the whole earth. Now that is what should be the focus and emphasis of Nebuchadnezzar's dream. In other words, world empires will come and go, and one day, such will all be finished and the kingdom of God as symbolized by the Stone not cut by man will be established throughout the whole earth. Such is God's message to the world; namely, that the succession of world empires will not last forever. They will ultimately be terminated and the kingdom of God and of His Christ will rule over all the earth. And this is the hope for God's people in every age.

The matter of emphasis in chapter 7's vision of the storm and the wild beasts is to be the same. And once again, the focus and emphasis is not to be aimed at the wild beasts; on the contrary, they should be aimed at the throne that is set up. The Ancient of Days is sitting on the throne, and One like the Son of man will come, take, and possess the kingdom, dominion, power and glory of all these beastly empires. In a word, all of them will be destroyed, and "the saints of the most high places shall receive the kingdom, and they shall possess the kingdom for ever, even to the ages of ages" (7:18). Such again is the message of hope for God's people.

Let us understand today that the times of the Gentiles which began with Nebuchadnezzar are now nearing their end. Luke 21 tells us that the times of the Gentiles will be ended when Jerusalem shall no longer be trampled under the feet of the Gentiles (see v. 24). And we know that that event has already occurred (it took place back in 1967); and hence, if our understanding of prophecy is correct (and, obviously, in prophecy one can never be dogmatic because God is long-suffering, not willing that anyone should perish, II Peter 3:9), then we know for certain that we are nearing the end. Thank God that His kingdom is coming. So chapters 7 and 8 speak of the times of the Gentiles and of their end.

Coming to chapter 9, we find that one day during the first year's reign of King Darius, Daniel was praying. He was reading in Jeremiah 25 and 29 that the Babylonian captivity would last for seventy years (25:11; 29:10) and at this moment in Daniel's life there were but two years more before the seventy years would expire. So when Daniel read about that prophecy, he gave himself to fasting and prayer to the end that God's promise would come to pass. And as he was praying, God answered him by sending His angel to him giving him an answer which far-surpassed the content and purpose of his prayer. He was praying about the seventy years because in just two more years the seventy years of captivity would be coming to an end. So he was praying for his people and for the city of Jerusalem in relation to these seventy years; but when God answered his prayer, He gave him words of prophecy involving the astounding figure of seventy sevens. (The word weeks is a mistranslation of the Hebrew which should not be there. It should read seventy sevens—that is, seventy units or cycles of seven—and not seventy weeks.) Daniel had been concerned with seventy, whereas God's focus was now centered upon seventy sevens. Why? Because God desired to show His servant the whole history of His coming recovery work towards His chosen people. God was setting apart a period of seventy sevens within which to complete His work surrounding His chosen people. We can say that in one sense it was through the prayers of Daniel that in the first year of King Cyrus a decree was issued at the end of the seventy years of captivity for the children of Israel to return to Jerusalem to rebuild God's temple. But God gave Daniel a prophetic calculus which went beyond—indeed, went far *far* beyond—the seventy years of His servant's prayerful concern: God gave Daniel a period of seventy sevens for Daniel's and His people's consideration.

These seventy sevens, and employing the year-day theory of Ezekiel 4:6 whereby a day equals one year, were divided into three parts—the seven sevens, the sixty-two sevens, and the one seven—and they were to begin with the decree that the city of Jerusalem should be rebuilt. The seven sevens would cover the time (forty-nine years) which would be necessary for Jerusalem to be rebuilt as a city; and we know that in the twentieth year of King Artaxerxes Longimanus, that is, in 445 B.C., the order was given to Nehemiah to rebuild the wall of Jerusalem. It took forty-nine years (the seven sevens, 9:25) to complete the rebuilding of Jerusalem, which was undertaken during a time of troubles (see again 9:25). From 445 B.C. to the time of the Messiah the King was exactly sixty-nine sevens (the seven sevens plus the sixty-two sevens, 9:25)—483 years. If one wishes to be more exact, Christ was proclaimed as Messiah at the time He entered Jerusalem for the last time, and then He was "cut off." This, in fact, is what the prophecy foretold: "The Messiah will come, but He will be cut off" (9:26). "Cut off" is a violent term; signifying, in other words, that He would meet a violent death—even the cruel and painful death by crucifixion.

There then is a gap because the period of the one last seven still lies in the future. Meanwhile, in 70 A.D. Jerusalem and the temple would be utterly destroyed by "the people of the prince" (that is, by the Roman army under the command of Titus, son of Emperor Vespasian); and there would be frequent war until the very end (see again 9:26). Now the reason there is such a gap is because this is the age of the church—the dispensation of grace; but then will come this last prophetic period of seven years. The Antichrist will appear in disguise and make a peace pact or covenant with God's chosen people to supposedly provide them security; but in the middle of this peace pact period of seven years, he will break it and reveal his true face as the Antichrist (see 9:27). That will be the commencement of the great tribulation (Matthew 24:21) or Jacob's trouble (see Jeremiah 30:7); and at the end, the Desolater will be destroyed by the coming of Christ (see again 9:27). That is the context of chapter 9.

At the time of what is covered in chapters 10—12 Daniel was already over ninety years old; so let us never think that old men are of no use anymore. Daniel had lived through the seventy years of captivity. If it be accurate to say that he was taken as hostage when he was twenty, then after these seventy years more, he would have been ninety years old in the first year of King Cyrus when the decree was issued. So in the third year of Cyrus, he must have been ninety-two or ninety-three; which was when the greatest vision of all was given to him by God. He was given the vision which is concerned with "the time of the end" (12:4, 9), according to "that which is set down in the scripture of truth" (10:21).

Now the circumstances surrounding the reception by Daniel of this greatest vision from God are as follows. The Jewish remnant had already returned to Jerusalem in the first year of King Cyrus's reign. They had started to lay the foundation of the temple, but the work was stopped. So in the third year of King Cyrus, Daniel had become aware of what had happened in Jerusalem. God had previously said He would restore the temple and the city, but it had not yet been fully accomplished. The people had returned, the foundation had been laid, but the work was now stopped. Daniel therefore fasted and prayed before God for three weeks. He was diligently seeking Him. He wanted to know what would happen. He wanted to know what happened to that seventy sevens. While he was seeking God, and because he was one greatly beloved (see 10:11, 19), God showed him the time of the end—wonderful prophecies, prophecies that would be fulfilled in detail. There are no other prophecies in the Bible which are in such detail.

Chapter 10, as has just now been described, is more like an introduction. Chapter 11 verses 2 through 35 cover the time of Darius to Antiochus Epiphanes (the latter described in 11:21 as "a vile person" who did abominable things mentioned in vv. 21-35). Then, at chapter 11 verse 36 there is a sudden turn in the prophecy in which Antiochus Epiphanes is presented as a type of the Antichrist. So the prophecy turns to the Antichrist and reveals what the Antichrist will be like and what he will be doing, reveals how the world will be in turmoil, and finally, reveals how the time of the end shall come. Of course, even Daniel did not understand fully; and at this point he was told to close and seal the book till the time of the end when knowledge will increase, communication will be increased, and people will begin to understand (see 12:4, 8-9). As a matter of fact, today, the book of Daniel is no longer a sealed book; it is an open book to us. We know that the time of the end is near. Therefore, it says here, let those who are clean be refined and be kept pure and white before God (see 12:10).

These are very difficult times in which we are living today, but by the grace of God we should allow ourselves to be kept pure and white before God so that at His coming we will be able to see His face without being put to shame (see I John 2:28).

Daniel had to enter into his rest until the time when he will be raised up and receive his reward (see 12:13). We who are still living need always to be ready: waiting, praying, and preparing to meet the coming King.

Let us pray:

> *Dear heavenly Father, Thou hast given us this book of Daniel that we may be prepared. We praise and thank Thee that Thy word is true. We see that all things are coming to an end according to Thy word. We do praise and thank Thee that this world will soon be over and Thy kingdom shall come upon this earth. During this period, oh Lord, we do pray that Thou wilt raise up many Daniels who will be witnesses to Thee, who will bear testimony that Jesus is King, that His kingdom is the everlasting kingdom and His dominion is forever. Lord, we do ask Thee that this book of Daniel will not be just a matter of curiosity to us but it will really stir our hearts to give ourselves over to Thee, pure as Daniel, to be Thy witness and Thy testimony. In the name of our Lord Jesus. Amen.*

HOSEA

THE LOVE OF GOD

Hosea 1:1-5—The word of Jehovah that came unto Hosea, the son of Beeri, in the days of Uzziah, Jotham, Ahaz, Hezekiah, kings of Judah, and in the days of Jeroboam the son of Joash, king of Israel.

The beginning of the word of Jehovah through Hosea. And Jehovah said to Hosea, Go, take unto thee a wife of whoredoms, and children of whoredoms; for the land is entirely given up to whoredom, away from Jehovah. And he went and took Gomer the daughter of Diblaim; and she conceived and bore him a son. And Jehovah said unto him, Call his name Jizreel; for yet a little, and I will visit the blood of Jizreel upon the house of Jehu, and will cause the kingdom of the house of Israel to cease. And it shall come to pass in that day, that I will break the bow of Israel in the valley of Jizreel.

Hosea 14:1-9—O Israel, return unto Jehovah thy God; for thou hast fallen by thine iniquity. Take with you words, and turn to Jehovah; say unto him, Forgive all iniquity, and receive us graciously; so will we render the calves of our lips. Assyria shall not save us; we will not ride upon horses: neither will we say any more to the work of our hands, Thou art our God; because in thee the fatherless findeth mercy.

I will heal their backsliding, I will love them freely; for mine anger is turned away from him. I will be as the dew unto Israel: he shall blossom as the lily, and cast forth his roots as Lebanon. His shoots shall spread, and his beauty shall be as the olive-tree, and his smell as Lebanon. They shall return and sit under his shadow;

> *they shall revive as corn, and blossom as the vine: the renown thereof shall be as the wine of Lebanon.*
>
> *Ephraim shall say, What have I to do any more with idols? (I answer him, and I will observe him.) I am like a green fir-tree.—From me is thy fruit found. Who is wise, and he shall understand these things? intelligent, and he shall know them? For the ways of Jehovah are right, and the just shall walk in them; but the transgressors shall fall therein.*

Let us pray:

> *Dear heavenly Father, we do thank Thee for Thy beloved Son our Lord Jesus Christ who so loved us and died for us. We do praise and thank Thee for Thy precious word that Thou hast given to us that through Thy word we may know Thee. We ask that Thy Holy Spirit will once again breathe upon Thy written word and make Thy word speak to each one of us. We ask in Thy precious name. Amen.*

We have shared briefly on the four major prophets—Isaiah, Jeremiah, Ezekiel and Daniel. God willing, we shall begin to share on the twelve minor prophets. These twelve are called minor or lesser prophets not because their messages or their prophecies are less important but because of the smaller encompassing extent of their prophecies. As a matter of fact, these twelve are the presenters of very important prophecies concerning the nation of Israel, the nation of Judah, the nations around them, and prophecies concerning the coming Messiah.

The major prophets quote the minor prophets. For instance, in Isaiah, we can find the sayings of Micah and the prophecies of Joel. Jeremiah uses Obadiah, and Ezekiel expands on the prophecies of Joel. Thus, of the twelve minor prophets, some are ahead of the major prophets timewise; and we know that the prophecies in the Old Testament are actually brought to a conclusion by these twelve minor prophets.

It is very interesting to note that from the time of Samuel to Elijah, the prophets during that period did not leave any writings for us, except perhaps for a few words to be found in the book of Kings. So the writings of these minor prophets, especially the early ones, link up with the written prophetic poems of David, Solomon, Asaph, and the psalms of Korah, and they continue on to conclude the prophecies in the Old Testament.

Among Jewish as well as Christian circles, it is commonly accepted that these twelve are a unit. So we call them the twelve, like the twelve apostles in the New Testament. Chronologically speaking, Hosea to Nahum prophesied during the pre-Assyrian and Assyrian time. Then we have Habakkuk and Zephaniah who prophesied during the Chaldean time. Finally, we have Haggai, Zechariah and Malachi who were the prophets of the post-exilic period.

Timewise, Hosea is probably not the first of the twelve, but Hosea was put at the head of the list because of the greater degree of encompassment of his prophecies. It is just like the book of Romans in the New Testament. Romans was not the first epistle written but it was placed at the head of the epistles because it is the most comprehensive one.

The name Hosea in Scripture is derived from the root name "Hoshea" in Hebrew, the same root name from which is also derived the name of Joshua in the Old Testament and Jesus in the New. It means "salvation" or "deliverance." He prophesied in the eighth century before Christ during the years of Uzziah, Jotham, Ahaz and Hezekiah—who were kings of Judah— and during the years of Jeroboam II, the son of Joash, king of Israel.

As we read this book of Hosea, we may find his language and style are somewhat difficult and also rather abrupt: he changes so swiftly from one thing to another that sometimes it is difficult to comprehend. Yet his prophecies are considered to be some of the greatest in the Bible.

It is very easy to outline this book. Roughly, it can be divided into two parts: chapters 1—3 are personal in nature, chapters 4—14 are national in content.

A PERSONAL LIFE SYMBOLIZES ISRAEL

Hosea was a prophet raised up by God to the nation of Israel's northern kingdom. He was the first prophet whose personal life was employed by God to serve as a symbol to his fellow man. His personal life is a miniature portrayal of the national life of northern Israel. His unfaithful wife is a mirror image of that nation's unfaithfulness towards God, and the faithful husband, Hosea, is a picture of the faithfulness of God towards His people.

In one sense the personal history of the prophet Hosea is very tragic. A prophet is a holy man of God who speaks for God. Yet strangely, God commanded Hosea to marry a woman of whoredoms. Now what is meant by whoredom in the Scriptures? The word signifies that one is pursuing or seeking after many objects of sinful love. Consider Hosea, who was a holy man of God, yet God ordered him to marry an unholy woman. Human dignity and personal honor were thus deeply hurt and offended; yet in obedience to God Hosea married that woman because this was an extraordinary time and God wished to use extraordinary means to speak to His people. God not only reveals himself to us by visions, He not only speaks to us by His words, but sometimes He uses dramatic actions to arrest our attention. And here God used Hosea's personal life to speak to His rebellious and unfaithful people.

In obedience to God, Hosea took to himself a woman of whoredom by the name of Gomer. Gomer means "perfection," but what kind of perfection was she? She was the daughter of Diblaim which translated from Hebrew means "a double lump of figs, sweetness." In other words, Gomer represents the sweetness of the pleasure of sins. There is a certain sweetness of pleasure in sinning, but it is the parent of destruction.

The prophet Hosea not only obeyed God's command in doing something against human honor and dignity, but he also truly loved this woman. And out of that union came forth the first son, and God said his name should be Jizreel, which means "he will scatter." God will scatter His people.

Another child, a daughter, was born, and God said that her name would be Lo-ruhamah, which means "having obtained no mercy." There will be no mercy for God's people.

Yet another son was born to Hosea and Gomer, and God said his name would be Lo-ammi, which means "not my people." Hence, by these three names God was telling His people that because of their unfaithfulness, He would scatter them, they would not obtain mercy from Him, and He would deny that they were His people.

Even after Gomer was married to this holy man and had birthed several children, her evil nature and habits were still there. So we learn from chapters 2 and 3 that she left her husband and went to another man, to whom, having now degenerated herself to such an extent, she literally sold herself as a slave. How would Hosea the holy prophet deal with such an unfaithful wife? Remarkably, God said to Hosea: "Go and buy her back" (see 3:1). So Hosea paid the price of a slave and bought her back (3:2). He loved her with such a love; he covenanted with this woman and said, "Do not do anything wrong within a period of days; keep yourself pure for many days, and I will do the same until the time comes when we can be united again" (3:3). That was the story of the prophet Hosea, a most unusual story. It is against all human reasoning, beyond human affection; yet Hosea did as God commanded him, and he did it with such love.

A BACKSLIDING NATION

Now the personal history of the prophet Hosea speaks in symbolic terms directly to the nation of Israel. In the beginning God had raised up the nation of Israel and gave them a king, David. The nation of Israel, with the house of David on the throne, was meant to represent the kingdom of God on earth. After Solomon died, however, the nation split in two: the southern nation of two tribes belonged to the house of David, and the remaining ten tribes split themselves away under Jeroboam I. The northern nation was called Israel and the southern nation was called Judah. In typology, the northern nation of Israel represents a backsliding nation because they split away from the original entity that represented the kingdom of God on earth. They were no longer under the legitimate rule of the house of David.

From I Kings 12 we learn that Jeroboam became king of the northern nation of Israel. Now at that time, even though the complete nation of Israel was split in two, the people still traveled to Jerusalem to the temple there to worship God. So in looking at the situation Jeroboam realized that if the people continued to return to Jerusalem to worship God, sooner or later they would revert back to the house of David. Therefore, out of political expediency, he had to improvise a religious measure. Accordingly, he had two golden cows built; and, of course, that was nothing new because after the children of Israel had left Egypt, and while Moses was on the mountain receiving the Ten Commandments, the children of Israel came to Aaron and said, "Fashion for us a god." Then Aaron made them a golden calf and the people worshiped it (see Exodus 32:1ff.).

So here we see Jeroboam going back through their history and extracting from it a part of that history and had two golden cows made. He cleverly placed one in Dan at the far north and installed the other at Bethel in the south, and declared: "This is your Jehovah, this is your God. You no longer need to go to Jerusalem to worship God; you can worship Him in Bethel, you can worship Him in Dan. This is Jehovah, the God that led you out of Egypt" (see I Kings 12:26ff.). At the same time Jeroboam also arranged a religious system to back up that worship. He tried to imitate everything which God had ordered for Jerusalem: he had his priests. But these priests were not Levites; and anyone who wanted to become a priest could become one. Jeroboam likewise made every arrangement for worship, just like the worship in Jerusalem; and yet it was a counterfeit: outwardly the people among the ten tribes were presumably worshiping Jehovah God, but actually they were worshiping the cows. In other words, instead of worshiping the Creator, they were now worshiping the creature—the work of man's hands. It became a nature worship; the northern nation of Israel had backslidden into nature worship.

As we further trace their history, we find that one of northern Israel's subsequent kings, Ahab, married a heathen wife, Jezebel; and through this Gentile woman foreign idols—foreign gods— were introduced into the ten-tribe kingdom. In so doing, Jezebel introduced the worship of Baal to the northern kingdom of Israel. Now Baal means "master" or "lord." Baal worship was present everywhere among the surrounding Gentile nations. Instead of continuing to worship God their Father, they began to worship Baal, a cruel, hard, bloodthirsty god. However, at its core Baal worship is nothing more than nature worship. So the whole northern nation had gone away from God into worshiping idols. They became a backslidden nation.

Moreover, it is axiomatic that wherever there is false religion there will also be corrupt behavior and manner emerging. Hence, we find that in the time of Hosea, not only were they worshiping the golden cows—the Baals—but also the whole nation—from the kings to the priests to the prophets to the people—had become corrupted with lying, cheating, bloodshedding, violence, drinking, and debauchery of every kind. As God looked upon this backslidden nation, it hurt Him deeply because He loved them dearly; and He therefore sent His prophets to warn them, to judge them, to try to restore them. Yet in spite of whatever God did to them, the people refused to repent.

In reading the book of Hosea we can easily discern that the heart of God was profoundly hurt. He said to His people of the north (6:4): "Ephraim, what shall I do to you?" (Being the largest and most central of the northern Jewish tribes, Ephraim became a name for the entire northern kingdom.) He had loved them so much, He had given them everything they had, and still they turned their backs on Him and went after idols. So God had to chastise them. Indeed, He sent rottenness to them; He even acted like a lion to tear them apart; yet they would still not repent (see 5:12, 14). They approached Assyria and Egypt for help (5:13; 7:11b); but they did not return to God, the only One who could really and truly help them. So, finally, God declared: "You are not My people any longer." In a word, God gave them up. His glory departed from them and they were taken into Assyrian captivity. And from chapters 15—17 of II Kings we learn that eventually the northern nation of Israel was completely destroyed by Assyria.

THE LOVE OF GOD

Does this mean, though, that God had given them up altogether? Does it mean that He did not love them anymore? No. Just as Hosea, when commanded by God, returned to his estranged adulterous wife and redeemed her in love, so God still loved His unfaithful people. The greatest sin to come against love is that of infidelity, and the children of Israel had committed that sin against God; and yet He still loved them.

The nation was destroyed, and during this long period of their "not being My people"—of having been set aside by God (and it has been a very long period, indeed, since the Jewish people are still in that state even today)—there had been no king, no prince, no priest, no sacrifice, no altar (see 3:4). But even during this long period, God did not, and still has not, forsaken them. On the contrary, He has been purifying them, He has continued to deal with them, always trying to instill some sense of repentance in them; and one day, His love will restore them to himself. Such is the extraordinary love of God!

We see, then, that the message of Hosea is *the love of God*. God is drawing them with cords of love (11:4). The cords are long and yet they cannot be broken. He loves them with an everlasting love.

Now we know that whatever has been written in the Scriptures is for our admonition. The personal history of the prophet Hosea taught an important lesson to the northern nation of Israel. At the same time, however, both the personal history of Hosea as well as the national history of northern Israel can teach us who are in the church today some very important lessons, and this is something we need to consider before the Lord, which is what follows next.

THE BACKSLIDING CHURCH

The northern nation of Israel is a type of the backsliding church. Christ loved the church and gave himself for her. Individually, we all were sinners. God created us with a noble purpose. He also created us according to His own image. We were His masterpiece. We were created with a capacity for knowing God, for communing with Him, for even having Him dwell in us. We were created with such a noble purpose, and yet as we review all of human history, we realize how—from our forefather Adam to us today—we have rebelled against God, how we have sinned! In short, we have all had the spirit of whoredom in us. We have gone after many objects of sinful love, and yet God still loves us. He loves us to such a degree that He sent His only begotten Son to be a man, to be like one of us. The holy God desires to be united with people like us who are nonetheless so unholy. We cannot explain such love. For a holy man of God like Hosea to be asked to marry such a woman of whoredom like Gomer is something beyond our understanding. No one would choose to do that. Even if we were forced to do so, we would refuse to do it. But let us consider God and His holiness. He is holy: Holy, holy, holy, Lord God Almighty, goes the hymn which we often sing in the church assembly. For such a holy God to condescend himself to seek after sinners such as we, it is for us such an unfathomable love; we cannot comprehend or measure it. But that is who our God is. He is love; He loves us; He loves us to such a degree that He gave His only begotten Son. His Son was willing to become a man—to be one of us, yet apart from sin, in order that He might redeem us from our sins. God brought us to himself by His love. And that is what the church is as a result.

The church is to be the bride of Christ, the beloved Son of God. On the day of Pentecost which ushered in the church the Holy Spirit came upon the assembled one hundred and twenty believers in an upper room of a home, filled them, and thereafter dwelt in them. The Holy Spirit is God. God himself came in the Person of the Holy Spirit to dwell in the church. And that is the reality of divine love. When we read church history, we find that we are God's redeemed ones; indeed, we were saved from such debauchery and such other sins; and yet, we who are called to be united with Christ in whom the Spirit of God dwells do not—just as the Israelites of old—change our habits. It seems as if, very soon, very quickly, we rebel against the One who loves us. We go off pursuing after other loves, other things. To put it simply, the church has backslidden. Instead of worshiping God we worship the work of our hands. We make Christianity a religion instead of a living faith. We create an entity called "Christianity" which is a counterfeit of the true worship of God. Outwardly, it is in the name of God, but actually, it is the work of our hands. We become adulterers and adulteresses by loving other persons or things more than God. In short, we have lost our first love. Again and again throughout church history God has sent His messengers to call His church back, and there have been revivals from time to time; but unfortunately, the impact of these revivals was felt pretty much only on the surface; they did not exert deep enough impact, and thus very soon the church returned to its backslidden state.

WAYS OF GOD

To the northern nation of Israel God had sent rottenness and moth (see 5:12). Similarly, what do we find when we survey Christianity today? Symbolically speaking, we can say that everything in it is mildewed, eaten by moth, rotten. The testimony of Jesus has been eaten up, is now weak and is corrupted. Sometimes God has to act like a lion with us in order to break us up. Whenever the church is under persecution, it seems that there is in fact somewhat of a returning; but once the pressure is gone, the old habit of infidelity returns. Is there any hope for this backslidden church? Has God given up His church?

Thank God, even in the kind of state which the northern nation of Israel descended into, God still had a few individuals who were faithful to Him. In the book of Hosea we learn that there were still some faithful people like the prophet himself. They said, "Let us return, let us seek Him" (see 6:1-3). There were still a few who desired to follow after God, and in these few the testimony of God continued. But so far as the mass of the people was concerned, it seemed to be a hopeless case.

Apostasy is upon us. In II Thessalonians it is prophesied that before the return coming of the Lord, there will be a general falling away; in fact, apostasy will prepare the way for the Antichrist. And though apostasy is already upon us, the love of God is still here.

In the book of Hosea we are given to see two important things: one is the ways of God, and the other is the love of God. Of course, the ways of God are governed by His love. The way God treated the people of Israel in the olden days is the same way God is treating His people—His church—today. He is calling us back to repentance; and if we do not repent and return to our first love, He has to judge us because He is a righteous God; He has to chastise us because He is our Father; He may even have to deal with us with drastic means; yet even so, let us bear in mind that such means are governed by love. It is God who first loved us, not we who first loved God. It is God who originates the whole process. His love is active towards us, and His love suffers long.

We know from I Corinthians 13 that the first quality of love is that "love suffers long." And hence, we have the long-suffering of God who is love (I John 4:16b). Even today the world continues to exist because of the long-suffering of God; otherwise, the world would have been destroyed long ago. The reason our Lord has not come back for His church yet is because of God's long-suffering towards the church. God gives us opportunities to repent and to return, yet how much our refusal must hurt Him, even as it must have deeply hurt Hosea when his wife left him. Nevertheless, how forgiving our God is! It is as though no matter what we do against Him, He does not mind—not that He does not suffer; indeed, God suffers greatly! Yet He endures because God, being Love, "endures all things" (I Corinthians 13:7d). And His love never changes nor ends; it is everlasting.

But when it comes to the ways of God, He has to deal with us according to His righteousness as well as according to His love. Today in Christianity it is just as it came to be with the northern nation of Israel—no king, no prince, no priests, no altar, no sacrifice, no conception, no pregnancy, no birth (see 3:4 with 9:11). That is the situation of Christianity today, but even that is the way of love. God is using such a situation to bring us back to himself.

When we reach the last chapter of Hosea, which actually provides us the theme of the book, it concludes with: "Who is wise, and he shall understand these things? intelligent, and he shall know them? For the ways of Jehovah are right, and the just shall walk in them; but the transgressors shall fall therein" (Hosea 14:9).

The ways of God are right. They are right because they are motivated by love; but the question is: What will be our reaction to His ways? If we are just and righteous, we will walk in them. In other words, we will accept the ways of God, we will justify the ways of God, we will repent. We will accept His judgment, repent, and return to Him. We will be purified in order that we may be united with Him forever. But the transgressors shall fall therein. In other words, if we continue in the way of the transgressors, there will be judgment.

If the prophecy in the book of Amos speaks of the severity of God, then the prophecy in the book of Hosea tells us of the love of God.

Let us pray:

> *Dear heavenly Father, we do praise and thank Thee for Thy everlasting love, that Thou hast loved us with an everlasting love. Lord, we do confess that we have been unfaithful, but Thou art faithful for Thou canst not deny Thyself. We do praise and thank Thee that Thou hast drawn us with cords of love. Thou wilt not let us go, but Thou wilt continue to love us until Thy love overcomes us and brings us to Thyself. Lord, we do pray that we may have our eyes opened and not fight against Thy love but yield to Thy love and walk in Thy ways. We ask in the name of our Lord Jesus. Amen.*

JOEL

THE GREAT MERCY OF GOD

Joel 1:1-4—The word of Jehovah that came to Joel the son of Pethuel.

Hear this, ye old men, and give ear, all ye inhabitants of the land. Hath this been in your days, or even in the days of your fathers? Tell your children of it, and let your children tell their children, and their children another generation: that which the palmer-worm hath left hath the locust eaten; and that which the locust hath left hath the cankerworm eaten; and that which the cankerworm hath left hath the caterpillar eaten.

Joel 2:25-32—And I will restore to you the years that the locust hath eaten, the cankerworm, and the caterpillar, and the palmer-worm, my great army which I sent among you. And ye shall eat in plenty, and be satisfied, and praise the name of Jehovah your God, who hath dealt wondrously with you: and my people shall never be ashamed. And ye shall know that I am in the midst of Israel, and that I, Jehovah, am your God, and there is none else: and my people shall never be ashamed.

And it shall come to pass afterwards that I will pour out my Spirit upon all flesh; and your sons and your daughters shall prophesy, your old men shall dream dreams, your young men shall see visions. Yea, even upon the bondmen and upon the handmaids in those days will I pour out my Spirit. And I will shew wonders in the heavens and on the earth, blood, and fire, and pillars of smoke.

The sun shall be changed to darkness, and the moon to blood, before the great and terrible day of Jehovah come.

And it shall be that whosoever shall call upon the name of Jehovah shall be saved: for in mount Zion and in Jerusalem shall be deliverance, as Jehovah hath said, and for the residue whom Jehovah shall call.

Let us pray:

Dear heavenly Father, how we do praise and thank Thee that through Thy beloved Son, we are now in Thy presence; and we do desire that the light of Thy countenance may shine upon Thy word and upon our hearts. We pray that Thy word would really be like living seed that falls into good ground and which may bear fruit unto the praise of Thy name. We ask in the name of our Lord Jesus. Amen.

The word of the Lord came to Joel the son of Pethuel. Now Joel means "whose God is Jehovah," or "Jehovah is God"; and Pethuel means "openheartedness" or "the sincerity of God." We are not given the time and the place in which the prophet Joel prophesied. We are only told that the word of the Lord came to him, and when the word of the Lord comes to a person, that makes him a prophet. So Joel is one of the prophets whom God raised up to speak to His people. But by comparing him with the other minor prophets, and by looking into his prophecies, we come to the conclusion that Joel is one of the earliest and is most likely even the earliest of the twelve minor prophets. The first reason for this conclusion is that he has been quoted by the other prophets. For instance, Amos quoted him at both the beginning and the conclusion of his prophecy. In Amos 1:2 he said, "Jehovah roareth from Zion, and uttereth his voice from Jerusalem." That is a quote of Joel 3:16: "Jehovah will roar from Zion, and utter his voice from Jerusalem." And in Amos 9:13 he said: "And the mountains shall drop new wine, and all the hills shall melt." That is a quotation from Joel 3:18: "And it shall come to pass in that day, that the mountains shall drop down new wine, and the hills shall flow with milk." And interestingly, when the major prophet Isaiah prophesied about the coming judgment day—the day of the Lord—he certainly had Joel in mind. For in chapter 13:6 of his book it reads: "Howl, for the day of Jehovah is at hand; it cometh as destruction from the Almighty." That is a quotation from Joel 1:15: "Alas for the day! for the day of Jehovah is at hand, and as destruction from the Almighty shall it come."

Hence, we may say that all the above would mean that Joel prophesied prior to the time of Amos and even before the time of Isaiah.

Second, in his prophecies Joel did not mention the sins of Judah, which the prophets Hosea and Amos condemned; nor did he mention the idol worship which had prevailed in the time of Kings Jehoram, Uzziah and Athaliah. Instead, he mentioned the Jehovah-worship that was restored during the time of King Joash under the great high priest Jehoiada and which was still existing at that time. That shows that Joel must have prophesied during the time of King Joash, perhaps within the first thirty years of his forty-year reign; and, hence, that would have been in about the middle of the ninth century B.C.—well before the prophetic ministry of any of the other minor prophets.

Third, Joel did not mention the Syrian invasion of Judah and Jerusalem. We know that this happened *at the end* of the reign of King Joash (see II Chronicles 24). There we read of the invasion of Judah by Syria; and it cost not only the treasures of the temple and the palace but eventually it also cost even the life of King Joash. So this further demonstrates that the prophecy of Joel had to have been given during the first thirty years of King Joash.

Fourth, Joel mentioned what Tyre and Sidon and the districts of Philistia did to the children of Israel: how they took away their treasures—even those of the temple—and how they sold their children as slaves. Then he predicted that they would be punished because of their sins (see 3:4-8). We read in Amos 1 that Amos prophesied the judgment which came upon Tyre. So this provides further evidence that Joel had prophesied prior to Amos.

Fifth, Joel mentioned the valley of Jehoshaphat. From II Chronicles 20 we learn that here King Jehoshaphat (who reigned over Judah from probably 870 to 845 B.C.) had won a great victory over

Moab and Ammon. So this incident of what had occurred in the valley of Jehoshaphat was still fresh in the mind of Joel (whose prophetic ministry probably began in about 840 B.C. and lasted till around 830 B.C.).

Finally, people have observed that all the minor prophets (Jonah, Amos, Hosea and Micah) who flourished in the time of Kings Uzziah (in Judah) and Jeroboam II (in Israel) seemed to have taken Joel as their model, especially in this matter of the great and terrible day of Jehovah (referred to also as “the day of the Lord”), and how it was only through repentance that judgment could be avoided. They all seemed, as it were, to have taken their cue from Joel, and this therefore dates Joel before all the other minor prophets.

So we arrive at the conclusion that Joel was the earliest of the twelve minor prophets and that he prophesied in Jerusalem concerning the ultimate destiny of Judah.

There is great similarity and also contrast between the prophet Joel and the prophet Elijah. We mentioned earlier that Joel means “Jehovah is God,” and that was the work of the prophet Elijah. We read from I Kings 18 that Elijah had challenged the people of the northern nation of Israel by saying: “How long will you halt between two opinions? If Jehovah be God, follow Him.” We also recall the dramatic contest which had then occurred on Mount Carmel, with the result being that the people bowed down and said, “Jehovah, He is God.” So the mission of Elijah was to challenge the people and bring them back to Jehovah. In other words, the Lordship of Jehovah was the burden of Elijah, and that was the same burden of the prophet Joel. Elijah maintained the Lordship of Jehovah by an act, and Joel sustained the Lordship of Jehovah by prophetic words. Elijah prophesied in the northern nation of Israel, whereas Joel prophesied in the southern nation of Judah. There is thus a very interesting comparison here between these two prophets.

THE SOUTHERN KINGDOM OF JUDAH

Outward Form of Service

We know that the northern kingdom of Israel went into apostasy; that is, they turned away from Jehovah and became a nation of idol worshipers. They committed all kinds of abominations before the Lord. Under the reign of King Joash the worship of Jehovah was restored to the southern kingdom of Judah. In II Chronicles 23—24 we read how the high priest Jehoiada had hidden the little child Joash, thus protecting him from being slaughtered by Athaliah. Then when Joash was seven years old, Jehoiada began to restore the kingdom to him; and under the advice of this good high priest, Joash repaired the temple, the house of God. In other words, during that period of time the southern nation of Judah was not in apostasy. But even though the people worshiped Jehovah as their God, God was not happy with them. They served the Lord outwardly, but inwardly their heart was not with Him. They were rather careless in their worship of God. They were not single-minded or devoted; their heart was not set towards the Lord. What God desires is the heart, not outward correctness.

This failing of the people of Judah—particularly on the part of the leaders—can easily be seen by what happened when King Joash gave the order to the Levites to collect the temple tributes from the people for repairing the house of God. These Levites were very lazy: they did not hasten to collect the Mosaic tributes, with the result being that the temple remained in a state of destruction until, finally, King Joash gave the orders to collect them. The Levites placed a box in the temple and the people began to pay their tributes, and ultimately the house was repaired. Yet even during the repairing of the house of God, the hearts of the Levites were not really in it. They seemed to be occupied with other things rather than with the service to the house of God.

Another indication that their hearts were not with God was that immediately after the high priest Jehoiada died, King Joash hearkened to the voice of the princes and forsook the house of God and began to worship idols. Under King Joash the house of God had been restored;

he had given the order to have God's house repaired. How was it, then, that so quickly after the death of the good high priest Jehoiada, this king forsook the Lord's house? The reason was that his faith in God was rather traditional and had been dependent upon somebody else. Joash himself did not have a real living relationship with God, and that explains how it came about that he turned away so quickly. Hence, we can discern from this that even though outwardly God's people—and especially the leadership—were serving Jehovah, inwardly their hearts were not perfect before Him. Their hearts were away from God, and for this reason the Lord was not satisfied.

Natural Disasters from God

So God sent the prophet Joel to them. Meanwhile, a plague of locusts had come upon the nation, and the plague was very severe. He said, "That which the palmer-worm left, hath the locust eaten; and that which the locust left, the cankerworm hath eaten, and that which the cankerworm left, hath the caterpillar eaten." Now these words may signify the different stages in the growth of the locusts or they may signify the different species of locusts involved. We do not know for sure. Nevertheless, wave upon wave of locusts had come upon the land and had devoured all the greens. Even the trees were left bare; all the fruit trees were destroyed. More than that, a drought had followed; and because of the drought, the fields were devastated. There was no harvest of crops, there was no vintage of grapes. These terrible things happened to the nation of Judah, but the people had apparently considered these events to have been nothing more than natural disasters. Indeed, these were natural disasters because they were disasters in nature; yet they did not realize that these natural disasters had come upon them as a warning from God.

How true it is that God often uses natural disasters to awaken our conscience, to bring us back to himself; but evidently, these people, who had experienced such horrific natural disasters one after another, were not awakened to the fact that God was disciplining them. They apparently did not realize that *whomever God loves He chastens*. These people were those whom He loved, and because He loved them, He had disciplined them. He had allowed these disasters and plagues to come upon the nation of Judah in order to awaken their conscience so that they might repent and turn their hearts to God. Evidently, they had not done so. They instead had complained of the lack of wine, they instead had complained of the lack of food; sad to say, their hearts had not turned to God. Therefore, the prophet Joel was sent to remind them that these had not simply been natural disasters; they had been sent by God to bring them to repentance. For the prophet declared: "Gird yourselves, and lament, ye priests; howl, ministers of the altar; come, lie all night in sackcloth, ye ministers of my God: for the oblation and the drink-offering are withholden from the house of your God. Hallow a fast, proclaim a solemn assembly, gather the elders, and all the inhabitants of the land to the house of Jehovah your God, and cry unto Jehovah" (Joel 1:13-14).

When people in this world encounter disasters, whether individually or nationally or even internationally, their natural reasoning and reaction seem to be: "Well, these are natural, and because they are natural, what can we do? We can only try to live and survive the best we can." Instead, all of us need to see that every time there is a famine, a drought, a hurricane, an earthquake, a war, or a disaster which comes upon the land and the people, it is to remind us to return to God. If we can take these disasters as His warnings to us and humble ourselves before Him, then we will be greatly benefited. Otherwise, we suffer in vain.

THE DAY OF THE LORD

The prophet prophesied and said: "These are the things that have already happened, but more terrible things will come. The day of Jehovah will come and it will be a day of gloom, a day of clouds, a day of gross darkness. It will be a great and terrible day" (2:1-2a, 11b, 31). If people do not repent, then because of His love for His people, God's hand has to come heavier and heavier upon them.

In Joel 2 is Joel's prophecy about the coming great and terrible day of the Lord, which was partially fulfilled two hundred years later by the Babylonian invasion of Israel's southern kingdom. Babylon invaded Judah, destroyed the nation, and took the people captive to Babylon. But that was only a partial fulfillment. As a matter of fact, the great and terrible day of the Lord in its fullness is an event which is yet to come in the future, and it is something which has never before happened upon this earth. Nothing can be compared with what will happen when the day of the Lord comes; nevertheless, the prophet said that there is a way to escape from the day of the Lord.

GOD'S PROVISION FOR ESCAPE

In Joel 2:12 we read, "Yet even now ..." Whether the day of the Lord prophesied by Joel refers to the Babylonian invasion of Judah or refers to the coming day when at the end there will be that great and terrible day of the Lord, in either case, there is a way which God has provided by which to escape: "Yet even now ..." How patient and merciful is our God!

"Yet even now, saith Jehovah, turn to me with all your heart, and with fasting, and with weeping, and with mourning; and rend your heart, and not your garments, and turn unto Jehovah your God: for he is gracious and merciful, slow to anger, and of great loving-kindness, and repenteth him of the evil. Who knoweth? He might return and repent, and leave a blessing behind him, an oblation and a drink-offering for Jehovah your God?" (Joel 2:12-14)

In spite of the prophecy of destruction, God always opens a way of escape if only His people will listen and will rend their hearts and not just their garments, and turn to the Lord. And why? It is because the Lord is merciful and gracious; He is full of loving-kindness, is slow to anger, and quick to forgive. Unfortunately, though, the children of Israel did not repent and return; they did not rend their hearts. Accordingly, the southern kingdom was eventually destroyed and the people were taken into Babylonian captivity. The Lord had promised that if they repented and returned, He would restore to them the years which the locusts had eaten and would fill them with such plenty that they would completely forget the famine. Yet, they did not repent.

THE WONDERFUL PROMISE OF "AFTERWARDS"

In the prophecy of Joel there is a significant insertion made at a certain point. In His great mercy God, when prophesying about destruction and then about future restoration, inserted the following further prophecy in between: "And it shall come to pass afterwards that I will pour out my Spirit upon all flesh; and your sons and your daughters shall prophesy, your old men shall dream dreams, your young men shall see visions. Yea, even upon the bondmen and upon the handmaids in those days will I pour out my Spirit. And I will shew wonders in the heavens and on the earth, blood, and fire, and pillars of smoke. The sun shall be changed to darkness, and the moon to blood, before the great and terrible day of Jehovah come. And it shall be that whosoever shall call upon the name of Jehovah shall be saved" (Joel 2:28-32a).

This is a wonderful prophecy that begins: "And it shall come to pass afterwards ..." We are told that the Hebrew word translated as "afterwards" is the same Hebrew word translated as "the last days" used by the later prophets. So in the Hebrew Old Testament we find there is this term translated as "the last days." In Isaiah, for example, we read: "at the end of the days" or "the latter days." And to repeat, that is the same Hebrew word translated as "afterwards." What is the meaning behind this phrase, "the last days"? It is a specific Hebrew expression signifying the end of the period of the law. It means that the Messiah is to be introduced. And hence, "the last days" are actually the days having to do with the Messiah.

But in the Old Testament time God's people had no revelation concerning the *two* comings of the Messiah. In other words, even though the days of the Messiah were prophesied in the Old Testament, He was sometimes prophesied as One who would come suffering and at other times He was prophesied as One coming in glory. So the Old Testament people, even the Old Testament prophets, did not know how to reconcile these two opposite descriptions of the Messiah in His coming. How could the Messiah come as the suffering One and yet at the same time come as the glorious One? It was a great puzzle to the Old Testament prophets and, of course, to the chosen people of God at that time because they had no knowledge that "the last days"—the days of Messiah—would begin with a first coming and would end with a second coming. So, "before the great and terrible day of the Lord shall come" upon the whole earth, the days of

Messiah will come first, and God said that when Messiah shall come, "I will pour out My Spirit upon all flesh and upon your sons and daughters." And we know that this prophecy was certainly fulfilled initially on the day of Pentecost.

We recall about the 120 believers who were gathered in the upper room, praying and waiting for ten days. Then on the day of Pentecost, the heaven was opened and the Holy Spirit came upon them and they were baptized in the Holy Spirit (see Acts 1 and 2). That was the beginning of the days of the Messiah. That was the beginning of "the last days," and these days of the Messiah have continued on now for some twenty centuries as the period of the church. It is the age of grace; and because of God's mercy and grace towards mankind, He inserted this period in time before the great and terrible day of the Lord comes. And what a blessing it is!

So from the day of Pentecost forward and until the second coming of Christ Jesus the Lord, the Holy Spirit is continually being poured out upon His people. And during this period, whoever shall call upon the name of the Lord shall be saved. Thank God, we have called upon the name of the Lord and we are saved. Thank God, whoever calls upon the name of the Lord during this period shall be saved and shall receive the promised Holy Spirit before the great and terrible day of the Lord shall come—that is to say—before we see the signs in the heavens and on the earth of blood and fire and pillars of smoke and darkness. All of this can be found in the book of Revelation. So thank God for His mercy and His grace. But even such a wonderful day as this will pass.

THE JUDGMENT OF THE NATIONS

In Joel chapter 3 we find the prophet returning again to describe the great and terrible day of the Lord. It is the day when God will deliver His chosen people (see 3:1); but at the same time it is the day of the judgment of the nations of this world. He will gather all the nations of the earth to the valley of Jehoshaphat (meaning "Jehovah judges" or Jehovah is judge") (see 3:2, 12). Now the valley of Jehoshaphat is the same as the valley of decision (3:12, 14). There, God (in Christ) will sit and judge all the nations (3:2, 12).

One day, all the nations of the world will gather in that valley of Jehoshaphat; but let us not think that this is impossible because, even in this little incident of the Six Days War in the Middle East today, within a very short period, the armies of many nations have gathered around that place. So the Lord said that one day He will gather all the nations to the valley of Jehoshaphat. That will be the last war, the war of Armageddon, and there He will judge the nations (see Revelation 16:12-16); and He will restore His kingdom upon this earth at last.

Such a day is coming; but if you believe, if you are prepared, if you turn your heart to Him, if you are devoted to Him and are faithful to Him, you will be gone before that day shall come because we have been promised in the New Testament that He will take us to himself (see Luke 21:36). So how important it is that we be prepared!

Now this is the historical essence of Joel's prophecy.

LESSONS FOR OUR AGE

We would next like to apply all of this from Joel to ourselves. The southern kingdom of Judah, spiritually speaking, does not represent the church in apostasy. We know that the history of the children of Israel is real but it also serves as a type or representation. God used the earthly kingdom of Israel to show us the heavenly kingdom of the heavens. In other words, we who believe in the Lord Jesus today are His heavenly nation (see I Peter 2:9; Philippians 3:20). So what we find in the Biblical history of Israel is for our edification. Whatever happened to them is for our instruction; and that is the reason we do not study the Bible merely as history, however interesting it may be, but we study it for our edification.

As the northern kingdom of Israel represents the church in apostasy, so the southern kingdom of Judah represents the church that has not yet gone into apostasy. But the church has become careless. Outwardly, the church is still maintaining everything which it is supposed to be; nevertheless, there is something missing in the heart. So the southern kingdom in Joel's time represents such a church. Or to put it another way, it actually represents what we find in Revelation 2 concerning the church in Ephesus. We know that the church there had a glorious beginning. The apostle Paul spent three years in

Ephesus until all of Asia Minor had heard of the glad tidings of the Lord. The work of God was so real and genuine that after they were converted, the people who used to delve in magic, in spiritism and in all such other activities were so utterly given to the Lord that they gathered all their magic books and burned them (and as it turned out those books were worth quite a lot of money). So the church in Ephesus at its beginning represents the church of first love: how they loved God! And how they loved the Lord Jesus! And because they loved the Lord so much, God was able to open His heart to them and reveal to them the mystery of the Christ as is presented in Paul's letter to the Ephesians. What a contrast this was to the Corinthian believers; for because they did not understand, God was unable to reveal His heart and His mystery to them as He had been able to do to the Ephesians because of their great love towards Him. It is not a question of one's brain, it is a question of one's heart that matters—not our knowledge but our heart. We sometimes think that if we are clever and bright, then we shall be able to know and comprehend all the things about God; but that is not true.

Let us never forget that the will of God is revealed to the babes—the lowly ones—but is closed to the wise and the intelligent (see Luke 10:21). If you think you are clever, wise or intelligent in and of yourself, you will never be able to know the heart and mind and purpose of God. But if you have a heart, a pure heart, then Jesus' beatitude—"Blessed are the pure in heart for they shall see God"—will become a reality for you: God will reveal all that is in His heart. In the book of Ephesians we can see how the Lord was able to pour out His heart to them; He was able to reveal to them all the secrets and the depth that is in God because of their love towards the Lord.

So Ephesus represents the church of first love. After Paul had gone from the scene the apostle John, it is asserted by early church fathers, came to help these believers, and even made his home there. They truly received much help. Moreover, before the apostle John had passed away, and while he was in exile on the Greek island of Patmos, everything went on as usual in the church of Ephesus. They continued to have works, labors, knowledge, discernment, and righteous hatred of the Nicolaitans; indeed, they had every good thing; but the Lord would nonetheless say to them: "I am against you. I am not happy with you. I am angry with you because you have left your first love." Their inner spring was gone, despite the fact that all the outward forms continued onward. Commendable habits may continue, routines may go on, worthy traditions may be maintained, yet these things in and of themselves do not satisfy God. What He desires is our heart—that first love. But that first love was now gone at Ephesus.

Now because the people of Judah had lost their first love towards God, His disciplinary hand came upon them. First the locusts, then the drought; and if they did not repent, the terrible day of the Lord would come upon them. The people were reduced to poverty. They were in lack of food; they were in lack of drink; nothing satisfied; there was no joy. Not only did *they* suffer because of their spiritual poverty, even *God* suffered because there was no longer any oblation and drink offering offered to God in His house. That was their situation, yet they were not conscious of it. They thought everything was still fine because, outwardly, Jehovah-worship continued on. What a pity! Eventually, the nation was destroyed.

REPENT AND RETURN

What can we learn from this? Let us look at the church today. Part of the church has already gone into apostasy. And as for the other part of the church, God's people still assemble together, worship services still continue, all kinds of Christian activities are engaged in, believers are still reading the Bible and praying, etc., and at the prayer meetings, there may still be a few in attendance. So, outwardly, things are proceeding forward as usual. In the beginning, there was heart, there was love; and because of love, there was labor; because of faith, there was work; because of hope, there was endurance. Now, however, the hope is no longer there, the faith is absent, and the love is lacking; yet the work, labor and endurance all continue. And in the process we may be satisfied, but God is not.

Nevertheless, can it be said that we are *really* satisfied? We are under the discipline of God; and being under His discipline, how can we be satisfied? We labor much, but we obtain little result. Do we have spiritual food? We are supposed to be in abundance, but we are in poverty! Spiritually, we are poor. When we come together, there is very little we can offer to God because we have little or nothing. Are we joyful? We are *not* joyful, we are sad. There is no drink offering; the wine is gone. We have been reduced to such spiritual poverty under the discipline of God, and yet we do not realize it. We are so blinded by the outward appearance, so obsessed in our minds by it, that we do not repent in heart and return to God.

As it was true and necessary in Joel's day, so in our day it is time for us to rend our hearts. It is time to gather the elders and gather all the people. It is time to gather all the children and even those that suck at the breasts of their mothers. It is time that we should weep before the Lord and cry to Him that He who is merciful and gracious be merciful and gracious to us. Who knows but that He will restore all the years that have been eaten by the locusts and the cankerworms (see 2:12-16).

If we look into our lives as *individuals*, do we see how many years we have misspent? Let us acknowledge that all the years we have lived for ourselves have not been lived for God. We have been occupied with the things of this world and not with the things of God. Our minds have been focused on earthly things, not on the things above. Many years of our lives have been eaten by locusts and by cankerworms; and if the Lord should count our days, I do not know how many of them would be numbered or accepted by Him (see Psalm 90:12).

But let us also look at ourselves *together* as an assembly of the Lord's people: we ought to have grown, we ought to have been able to offer God an abundant oblation and drink offering; but because of our continual spiritual poverty, how little we are able to offer Him. Many years have been eaten by the locusts; nevertheless, thank God, He promises us that if we together repent and return to Him, He will restore the years that have been consumed by the locusts.

Is it possible? We often say that time comes and goes and never returns again. That is true; but on the other hand, we know that the Lord is able to make a day a thousand years. Yes, time has gone, we have wasted these years, but by the working of His Holy Spirit the

Lord is able to restore all which has been lost during those years. He is able to produce so much in such little time that everything can be restored to the place of fullness. Only God can do that, and He promises that He will do it if we allow Him. So let us not look back, for there is nothing there to see. Instead, let us look forward! The important step is to return to the Lord with all our hearts and give ourselves to Him unreservedly and He shall indeed be able to restore all the years which have been lost. Thank God for that, and I believe this is the message which God has for us today.

Let us pray:

> *Dear heavenly Father, we do want to thank Thee for sending Thy prophet Joel to Thy chosen people to call them back to Thyself because Thy desire is to bless, is to restore to fullness. Our Father, we do thank Thee for giving this book of Joel to us that we may learn the lesson. Lord, do have mercy upon us that we may not go on as usual, as if nothing matters, nothing is changed. But Lord, do open our eyes to see that we are under Thy disciplinary hand. Oh, that we may rend our hearts and turn to Thee that Thou mayest be able to leave a blessing, not only to us but unto Thyself, because Thou art the blessed God. We bless Thee, oh Lord, in the name of our Lord Jesus. Amen.*

AMOS

THE ROAR OF JEHOVAH

Amos 1:1-2—The words of Amos, who was among the herdmen of Tekoa, which he saw concerning Israel in the days of Uzziah king of Judah, and in the days of Jeroboam the son of Joash, king of Israel, two years before the earthquake. And he said, Jehovah roareth from Zion, and uttereth his voice from Jerusalem; and the pastures of the shepherds mourn, and the top of Carmel withereth.

Amos 3:1-8—Hear this word that Jehovah hath spoken against you, children of Israel, against the whole family that I brought up from the land of Egypt, saying, You only have I known of all the families of the earth; therefore will I visit upon you all your iniquities. Shall two walk together except they be agreed? Will a lion roar in the forest when he hath no prey? Will a young lion cry out of his den if he have taken nothing? Can a bird fall in a snare upon the earth when no gin is laid for him? Will the snare spring up from the earth when nothing at all hath been taken? Shall a trumpet be blown in the city, and the people not be afraid? Shall there be evil in a city, and Jehovah not have done it? But the Lord Jehovah will do nothing, but he revealeth his secret unto his servants the prophets. The lion hath roared,—who will not fear? The Lord Jehovah hath spoken,—who can but prophesy?

Amos 9:11-15—In that day will I raise up the tabernacle of David which is fallen, and close up the breaches thereof; and I will raise up its ruins, and I will build it as in the days of old: that they may possess the remnant of Edom, and all the nations upon whom my name is called, saith Jehovah who doeth this. Behold, the days come, saith Jehovah, when the ploughman shall overtake the reaper, and the treader of grapes him that soweth seed; and the mountains shall drop new wine, and all the hills shall melt. And I will turn again the captivity of my people Israel, and they shall build the waste cities, and inhabit them; and they shall plant vineyards, and drink the wine thereof; and they shall make gardens, and eat the fruit of them. And I will plant them upon their land, and they shall no more be plucked up out of their land which I have given them, saith Jehovah thy God.

Let us pray:

Dear heavenly Father, we do praise and thank Thee that through Thy beloved Son, our Lord Jesus, we are able to come into Thy presence with holy boldness. Lord, we are here in Thy presence waiting upon Thee to hear what Thou hast to say to us. We ask Thee, Lord, that Thou wilt give us an open spirit, a teachable spirit, a hearing heart and an obedient heart. We do commit this time into Thy hands and trust Thy Holy Spirit to quicken Thy word to our hearts. To Thee be the praise. In the name of our Lord Jesus. Amen.

The name Amos means "bearer" or "heavy" and, therefore, it means "burden-bearer." He bore a burden, yet not his own but the burden of the Lord, and that made him a prophet. He was among the herdsmen of Tekoa, and Tekoa was in the land of Judah, the southern kingdom. It was a town several miles southeast of Bethlehem. It was a sandy and barren land. So instead of cultivating the fields, shepherds were tending their flocks in that place; and Amos was one of the herdsmen. The word herdsman actually means sheep master; but he was not a rich sheep master. He owned his own sheep but probably not many. Because of that, he had to supplement his living by gathering the fruit of the sycamore tree. He had to cultivate the sycamore trees and then gather the sweet juicy figs from these trees. So Amos was both a shepherd and a gatherer of the sycamore fruit.

THE DIVINE CHOICE

It seems that Amos had an ample supply for his own living, and he seemed to be quite content just to continue on as a shepherd and as a gatherer of the sycamore fruit. He did not have any aspiration or ambition to become a prophet, nor was he a son of the prophets (see 7:14-15). Whenever in the Old Testament mention is made of the sons of the prophets, such refers to the students or pupils of the prophets in the prophet school studying to become prophets. He had never received such professional training to be a prophet. Rather, while he was tending his sheep, the call of God came upon him. God called Amos to leave his country, the southern kingdom of Judah, and go to the northern kingdom of Israel to deliver a message to the people who lived there. By this we know that he had been called of God to be a prophet. It was a divine choice, determined neither by succession nor by profession.

Amos became a prophet like Elisha had become. One day Elisha was ploughing his fields with twelve yoke of oxen, busily engaged in his work, and suddenly the prophet Elijah came and placed his mantle upon him. This act meant that Elisha was henceforth called by God to be a prophet. So he left everything and followed Elijah. In this respect Amos was like Elisha in that Amos was engaged in his personal business, and the Lord called him to be a prophet.

Amos prophesied at the time when King Uzziah reigned in the southern kingdom of Judah and Jeroboam II reigned in the northern kingdom of Israel. Jewish history tells us that these two kings ruled together for some twenty-seven years, one in the south and the other in the north. Amos began to prophesy during that period for the Biblical text states that it was two years before an earthquake when the words of the Lord came to him; and since we know that this particular earthquake happened during the reign of King Uzziah, we know exactly the time during which this prophet began uttering his prophecy.

PROSPERITY MISINTERPRETED

We know this it was a time of material prosperity for both the southern kingdom of Judah as well as for the northern kingdom of Israel. Uzziah had defeated the Edomites, the Philistines and the Ammonites, and his name had spread even to the border of Egypt.

Moreover, in the northern kingdom of Israel under Jeroboam II the Syrians had been defeated, and consequently the kingdom was restored all the way from the entrance of Hamath at the far north down to the Dead Sea (see II Kings 14). So, actually, it was a time of both military power and material prosperity.

Jeroboam II was a wicked king; he did much evil in the sight of the Lord. Why was it, therefore, that during his reign God permitted the northern kingdom to experience material prosperity and military success? II Kings 14:25-28 tells us that it was during this time that Jonah was prophesying. And he prophesied that God looked upon His people and saw that they were greatly afflicted at the hands of Syria and that there was no "helper for Israel" and no freedom for the people, but that God had said that He would not blot out the name of Israel from the earth. Hence, God, in His long-suffering and mercy, allowed Jeroboam to succeed militarily. It was through the mercies of God because His heart was towards His people in their affliction and distress.

God gave the northern Israelites success and prosperity with the hope and desire that they would recognize His mercy and repent. Instead of doing that, however, they believed they were successful because of their military might and the peace which resulted from their defeat of the Syrians. So instead of returning to God, they sought after riches, wealth, luxury and ease of life; and as a consequence, there arose injustices and vices among them, and the poor were being oppressed and victimized by the rich. All kinds of sins were prevailing throughout the kingdom.

Is it not true that we sometimes think prosperity is a token of God's approval or God's blessing? But that is not always the case. On the contrary, human nature is such that, when people are in prosperity, they tend to forget God and descend into moral decay; that often seems to be the case. So was it the case here with the northern nation of Israel which was prosperous outwardly but, inwardly, it was corrupted. They were fulfilling, as it were, the measure and extent of their iniquities.

God therefore sent Amos to the northern kingdom to warn the people there as to what was going to happen to them. At that time their situation was so peaceful and so prosperous that they assumed they were under God's blessing. They had absolutely no idea that punishment would come upon them. They had no idea that possible eventual captivity was on the horizon. So it was a shock and a total surprise to them to learn that God had sent Amos to declare to them that if they did not repent, God's severe disciplinary hand would come upon them and that the nation would go into captivity.

GOD SENDS PROPHETS FROM SOUTH TO NORTH

How remarkable that Amos was sent from the southern kingdom to the northern kingdom; it was a most unusual development. Yet it was not because there was no prophet in the northern kingdom. As a matter of fact, Amos was a contemporary of Hosea who was himself prophesying there. (It may have been that Amos prophesied a little earlier than Hosea; nevertheless, they began almost in the same year.) So it was not because there was no prophet in the northern kingdom which thus compelled God to send a prophet from the south to the north.

Actually this had happened once before in Jewish history, and it had occurred at the beginning of the history of the northern kingdom of Israel. From I Kings 12 and 13 we learn about the split which took place at that time in the nation of Israel. Rehoboam became the king of the southern kingdom and Jeroboam I became the king of the northern kingdom. As a result of Jeroboam's split from Judah, ten tribes followed him, while the two tribes of Judah and Benjamin remained with Rehoboam.

Now we will recall from our earlier discussion on Hosea that after Jeroboam established his kingdom in the north, he noticed with growing concern that the people from the ten tribes still continued traveling to the temple in Jerusalem to worship God. So he realized, as was noted previously, that if people continued to do that, he would probably lose his kingdom. Out of political considerations, therefore, Jeroboam ordered two golden cows be made. Now that was not something strange to have occurred because we will recall that when the children of Israel had come out of Egypt, they fashioned a golden cow shortly after entering the wilderness (see Exodus 32:1ff.). So

Jeroboam made two golden cows and located one in Bethel to the south and one in Dan to the north and told the people: "This is your God, this is Jehovah. You do not need to go to Jerusalem; you can go to Bethel or to Dan to worship God." He thought that would inhibit the people from going to the southern kingdom. By this means he tried to strengthen his kingdom; moreover, he adopted all the rituals and the ceremonies of Jehovah-worship, made priests out of common people and not out of the Levitical tribe, and established the festivals for providing the people times of rejoicing. Thus Jeroboam imitated everything related to Jehovah-worship and even called it by the name of Jehovah; but in reality it was nothing but nature-worship (see I Kings 12:26ff.).

Now at the time when Jeroboam the king was making an offering at the altar in Bethel, God sent an unnamed prophet from the south to Bethel, who prophesied over that altar by saying that one day it would be broken down and its ashes would be poured forth. This was the first instance in which God had sent a prophet from the south to the north; and Amos was the second one to be sent—this time to Jeroboam II—in order to warn the same nation of what was going to happen. So Amos, too, went there as God had commanded him.

THE SEVERITY OF GOD

Amos was a contemporary of Hosea; but in our earlier discussion of the book of Hosea we learned that the emphasis of *his* message to the people was the loving-kindness of God. Because God loved His people so much He tried to woo them and draw them back with cords of love. But the emphasis of Amos's message was the opposite. God sent him to the northern kingdom to tell them that He was going to judge them very severely. Whereas the metaphor employed in Hosea was the cords of love, here in Amos it was the roar of the lion, thus symbolizing the impending severity of God.

Now are these two contrary emphases opposed to each other? Not at all! God often uses opposites to accomplish His purpose. For instance, Romans 11:22 states that for those who fall there is severity, but for those who are faithful there is goodness. In other words, those who fall in sin and refuse to repent will await the severity of God, but those who abide in Him will experience the goodness of the Lord. So these two messages are not opposed to each other; actually, they complement each other. Whether it is severity or goodness, both issue forth from the loving heart of God.

We know that Amos prophesied later than Joel. Joel's prophetic ministry, as we saw earlier, was the first, chronologically, of the twelve minor prophets. As a matter of fact, in his prophecy Amos took up the ending of Joel as a way to commence his own prophecy, and he also ended his prophecy by using Joel's concluding words. In other words, Amos gathered up some of Joel's words and they became the content of all his prophecies. For let us notice that whereas Joel 3:16 says that "Jehovah will roar from Zion, and utter his voice from Jerusalem," Amos 1:2 declares: "Jehovah roareth from Zion, and uttereth his voice from Jerusalem." With Joel it is, "Jehovah *will* roar"; but with Amos it is, "Jehovah *roars.*" Then Amos ended his prophecy in the same way as Joel had done. For Joel 3:18 states that when the Lord shall return to them and restore them, "the mountains shall drop down new wine, and the hills shall flow with milk." Amos uttered nearly the same words in chapter 9:13: "and the mountains shall drop new wine, and all the hills shall melt." Thus there is unity between and among all of these prophecies.

If we wish to create a theme for this book of Amos, it could be this: "The roar of Jehovah," or "The lion roars." Chapter 3 inquires: "Will a lion roar in the forest when he has no prey?" (v. 4a) Again in verse 8, it says, "The lion hath roared,—who will not fear?" The lion here signifies Jehovah or God. In other words, God roars from Zion because Zion is the place where the king resides; and He roars because of the spiritual degradation of His people. God had warned them again and again, but they would not return to Him. Therefore, the Lord roars, and who shall not fear? In fact, all facets of the prophecy which Amos prophesied against the northern kingdom of Israel came to pass just sixty years later when this kingdom was destroyed by Assyria.

Now this entire prophecy of Amos can be divided into three parts: chapters 1—2 form the first part, chapters 3—6 form the second part, and chapters 7—9, the third part.

THE LORD RULES AND OVERRULES

In the first part of Amos the word "Thus saith Jehovah" is repeated eight times. The Lord speaks. He speaks to the different nations which are mentioned there. These were the nations which bordered the nation of Israel. God started from the outside and, gradually, the prophecies came closer and closer until they touched the nation of Israel itself.

God being the God of all the earth has the right to speak to the nations. We sometimes forget that God still has the government of the earth upon His shoulder. This fact we forget because, outwardly, we see that different nations have their own government. Furthermore, we may sometimes even think that Satan, the Adversary, is the ruler of this world. Yet we forget what Daniel has made clear: that God has not given up His ownership of this earth, neither has God given up His government over all the earth. He is still the Lord of all the earth; He is still the sovereign of all the nations; government is still upon His shoulder, and, therefore, He still rules and overrules in the affairs of men. So God has every right to have His say to all the nations, and especially to those nations who immediately surrounded the nation of His chosen people.

Will the God of all the earth be unjust? When God desired to destroy Sodom and Gomorrah, Abraham approached Him and said: "Would the God of all the earth do unjustly? Certainly, You would not" (see Genesis 18:22ff.). Our God is a just God; and because He is a just God, one day, He will judge the whole world according to His justice and His righteousness. Unfortunately, people forget this. Because of the long-suffering of God, because of His great love and His patience, people overlook the fact that He is a just God who rules over the whole earth.

LONG-SUFFERING OF GOD AND FULLNESS OF INIQUITY

In these two chapters a most interesting phrase is repeated over and over again: "For three transgressions and for four." In relation to every nation it is stated like that. Now this is not a formula. On the contrary, this demonstrates two things. One is the long-suffering of

God and the other is the fullness of iniquity. On the one hand, when a nation sins, sins, and sins again, there will be divine retribution. Whatever a man sows he shall reap (see Galatians 6:7b). This is true individually as well as nationally. If you sow according to the flesh, you will reap corruption according to the flesh; if you sow according to the Spirit, you will reap eternal life according to the Spirit (see Galatians 6:8); and all this is because our God is a just God. Our God is One who suffers long; love suffers long. Out of His love, He continues to suffer as though He allows these things to continue on and on. It seems that His hand is very slow in coming forth upon us. Yet this is not because God will not judge; it is not because He gives up the world, nor because He gives up government. It is because of the long-suffering and love of God.

On the other hand, there is a facet to God's dealings with man called "the measure of the fullness of transgression" or "the fullness of iniquity." God will wait until the iniquity is full, then His hand will come down most severely upon that nation. This is fully illustrated throughout the Bible.

In Genesis 15, for example, we learn that when God was making a covenant with Abraham, He said that Abraham's descendants would be sojourners in a foreign land for four hundred years before He would give them the land of promise. This was because the iniquity of the inhabitants of that land, the Amorites, was not yet full (see vv. 12-21). In other words, it seems as though people can continue to sin and nations can continue to sin, moral decay can continue on, as though there is no God, as though He does not care. Not at all! God is waiting for iniquity to be full. God is also waiting for repentance. And if there is no repentance and sin continues on until the measure of transgression is full, then suddenly the hand of God will come upon that person or that nation because He is a just God. His wheel of justice grinds slowly but surely. So here in Amos we find each nation was mentioned in his prophecy; and because of those three and four transgressions, God's judgment would eventually come upon each nation.

These first two chapters of Amos relate how God judged those mentioned nations for their sins—both their own sins and those perpetrated against others. For one sin in particular is mentioned here: these nations' sin against God's chosen people. In other words, when God judges, He will judge according to your sins and your sin against God's people. All these prophecies were eventually fulfilled by means of Assyria's invasion of these lands and the destruction of all these nations, but we know this was just a token of God's righteous judgment upon the nations of the world.

One day, when our Lord Jesus shall return to this earth, He will judge all the nations. Matthew 25 tells us that the Lord will divide them into sheep nations and goat nations, and He will judge them according to one issue: how have they dealt with His little brother?—were they good or bad towards the little brother? Who is this little brother? Some say this little brother refers to the Jews; others say it means the Christians. Perhaps it is both. So one day, the judgment of God will come upon all the nations; and after that, righteousness shall rule over all the earth.

Today is the day of grace; but too often people do not understand grace: they abuse it, thinking that because they are under grace there will be no judgment. Yet if there is no judgment, then God is not just. God may indeed suffer long; nevertheless, one day judgment will eventually come upon this earth. Judgment will come upon all the nations of the earth, but God's judgment will be exerted most heavily upon His own people for their rebellion against Him.

PREPARE TO MEET YOUR GOD

In chapters 3—6 we find the following words repeated three times: "Hear this word." Why the repetition? Because the children of Israel were supposedly God's chosen people; and thus they should have had an ear to hear Him but did not. So three times God said, "Hear this word; hear what I am going to say to you." The Lord then said, "Of all the nations of the world, you are the only people whom I have chosen. You are the only people whom I have known, and because of this, I will judge you for all your iniquities."

Unfortunately, we sometimes think because we belong to the Lord, therefore, He will let us go ahead and do anything we want because He loves us; because He has chosen us; because He has given us so much grace. But do we realize that privilege means responsibility? Of those to whom God has given more, He will require more. Of those to whom He has committed much, He will ask much.

The children of Israel were God's people, and God reminded them how He had delivered them out of Egypt, how He had enabled them to conquer the Amorites who were stronger than they were, and how He had called them to himself to be His people in the Promised Land to serve Him as Nazarites and as Levites there. They were a most privileged people, but in spite of all these privileges, they disdained responsibility and went astray from God. Outwardly, they were still worshiping Him; but actually, the Jehovah-worship had already been changed to nature-worship. They were now worshiping the golden cows. They even called the golden cows "Jehovah." They adopted all the rituals and ceremonies which Moses had commanded, but they changed them. It was man's ways and man's ideas, and not according to the pattern which God had given them through Moses; and yet they in essence responded with: "We are the chosen people. Therefore, we are all right. When judgment comes, it will come upon the nations, not upon us." So God sent Amos to them and said: "Because you are My people, therefore, I will judge you even more severely. If you do not repent, then your judgment will be more than any other nation's because you are My people. My name is committed to you, but you have put My name to shame and reproach."

The Lord God called out to them and said, "Prepare to meet your God" (4:12). We oftentimes use this statement in preaching the gospel. We tell people to prepare to meet their God. Surely, sinners should be prepared to meet their God because He is their Maker. Sooner or later, they will have to meet Him. If they do not meet Him today in mercy and grace, they will have to meet Him in judgment at the great white throne. So the only preparation needful today to meet one's God is to repent and believe in the Lord Jesus as one's personal Savior. However, if we carefully read the context here, we shall see that this word is spoken to the believers of that day—that is, to the people of Israel, God's chosen people. God said: "I have given you enough warning and yet you still do not repent. If you do not repent, then prepare to meet your God; for it will be a terrible day" (see 4:6,

8-11). And we know that because the people of northern Israel failed to repent, they were taken into Assyrian captivity and the nation was totally destroyed. But prior to that, God was still saying to them: "Seek Me, then you will have life. Do not seek evil, but seek good" (see 5:4, 6, 14). God continued up to the very last to call them back to himself. How patient is our God!

RESTORATION NOT DESTRUCTION

In the last three chapters of Amos we find a series of visions which God gave His prophet. He showed him that He was going to destroy the nation, and Amos prayed and pleaded with the Lord, saying: "God, if Your hand comes down in this way, there will be no hope. Israel is so small that it will never be recovered." And God said, "All right, I will not do it." Again and again, God responded to Amos in this manner, but because the people would not repent, God measured them with a plumbline. Finally, because the people would not repent, they became like a basket of bad fruit which had to be completely eliminated (see 7:1-9; 8:1-2).

Towards the end of his prophetic utterances, Amos declared that the tabernacle of David which had fallen into ruin would be raised up again. This portion of Scripture is quoted by the apostle James in Acts 15. Some Jews from Jerusalem had gone to Antioch and told the Gentiles there who had become Christians that they must be circumcised and thus keep the Law of Moses. In other words, they must become Jews before they could become Christians; otherwise, they would not be saved. Consequently, there was great contention because of that teaching. The church leaders at Antioch ultimately sent Paul and Barnabas to Jerusalem to talk this issue over with the apostles and the elders there. And during this Jerusalem council, they thoroughly discussed this matter of whether the Gentiles should be Judaized in order for them to become Christians. At the very end of their discussion James remarked as follows: "The tabernacle of David shall be recovered and all the nations shall call upon the Lord" (see vv. 13-19; cf. Amos 9:11-12).

Spiritually speaking, the tabernacle of David is the church today because our David is our Lord Jesus and the church is His tabernacle.

It is called a "tabernacle" or, literally in Hebrew, a "tent" because it is not finalized yet. We as the tabernacle of the Lord today are still on a pilgrimage just as the Israelites were during their own earthly pilgrimage. One day, it will become the new Jerusalem, the holy city; but today, it is the tabernacle of David. The tabernacle of David has been raised up and all believers from the nations will have ultimately been gathered together within it (see again Amos 9:11-12 with Acts 15:16-17). All who call upon the name of the Lord shall be saved whether they be Jew or Gentile. So spiritually, this is being fulfilled in the church; but, of course, this does not mean that this will not happen to the nation of Israel. It is yet to happen—during the millennial age.

Even when God is severe in His dealings, we know that His dealing with His people is not for destruction but for restoration. There is a tremendous difference here between those who know the Lord and those who do not. For those individuals who do not know the Lord, and for those nations who do not know the Lord, when God's judgment comes upon them, that is the end; but for those who know the Lord, who are the Lord's, when God's disciplinary hand comes upon them, that is not the end. Sometimes it may look like the end, but it is not so because it is for restoration and not for destruction.

From the Scriptures we know that our Father God loves us so much; and because He loves us, He chastens us. This we find in Hebrews 12. There we read that if He does not chasten us, then we are bastards and not sons. But because we are His sons and His daughters, our Father wants us to be conformed to the image of His beloved Son Jesus. Therefore, He has to child-train us; He has to discipline us; He has to chasten us. But His chastening is not for destroying us; it is for perfecting and maturing us in order to bring us into conformity with the image of His beloved Son.

Why is it that Amos is in the Bible for us to read? It is there for the purpose of instructing us. God is speaking to us through this book that we may learn a most valuable lesson. We mentioned before that as we read in Scripture the history of the nation of Israel and of the nations, we can say that, roughly, the southern kingdom of Judah spiritually signifies the church that has not fallen into apostasy. The church may not be what it should be, but it has not yet fallen into apostasy. This situation is represented by the nation of Judah. Hence, whenever we read those prophecies concerning Judah, we can regard them as a lesson for the church as such. On the other hand, with respect to the northern nation of Israel, let us realize that from the very beginning of her history down to the very end, she was an apostate nation. From the very beginning, Jeroboam I changed Jehovah-worship into nature-worship, and that became the sin of that nation throughout her history. There was not one good king in the northern kingdom. So this nation represents the church in apostasy. And, of course, the other nations like Edom and Nineveh represent the world. If we can bear all this in mind whenever we read prophecy, we will be able to apply it properly to the relevant situation in our day.

APOSTATE CHRISTIANITY

As we have said, the northern nation of Israel represents the apostate church. Where and what is the apostate church today? If we review church history, we read that at the beginning, on the day of Pentecost, the church was born with great glory. The name of the Lord was exalted; the presence of the Holy Spirit was so real; the love of the brethren was very strong; and the testimony to the world was strong. On the one hand, people were afraid of the believers; on the other hand, they were attracted to them. The church at this time was in the original state of God's desire. And because of this, the church suffered from the hands of the world. The world did not understand them because they did not follow the world. Therefore, the church would suffer persecution throughout the centuries. But also from a review of church history, we learn that by the time of the fourth century when Emperor Constantine adopted Christianity, immediately, the church began to change. Her nature began to change from Jehovah-worship to man-worship. For political reasons, world politics entered the Christian church and began to change her very nature. Gradually, she drifted away from God's original design and became what we call Christianity. Outwardly, the people were still worshiping God, they still called upon the name of the Lord; everything was done as though nothing had changed. But it *had* changed. Instead of God-worship, there was man-worship. Instead of God's way, it was now man's way. Christianity had become a big tree from a living mustard seed; but mustard is a vegetable, not a tree. It should have been each after its own kind—that is God's divine order—but that was not the case here.

The church is supposed to be a little flock in the world; and yet, through the subtlety of Satan, it is as though the later Christianity had commenced with a popular phase but had gradually developed into a political world power. Instead of remaining a little flock it had become a big tree, full of secular power and influence. Outwardly, Christianity is prosperous today, and materially rich. Witness all these incredibly gorgeous edifices—the best, the finest, the wealthiest of these churches are the so-called cathedrals. Moreover, there are indeed all these rituals and ceremonies in worshiping God, but God has said: "I hate, I despise your feasts, and I will not smell a sweet odour in your solemn assemblies. For if ye offer up unto me burnt-offerings and your oblations, I will not accept them; neither will I regard the peace-offerings of your fatted beasts. Take away from me the noise of thy songs, and I will not hear the melody of thy lutes; but let judgment roll down as waters, and righteousness as an everflowing stream" (Amos 5:21-24).

What God wants is righteousness and justice. What He wants is love and worship towards Him, and righteousness, justice and love towards the people. But He does not want these offerings. God said: "I hate these things. I do not want to hear your songs and your music. I do not want these things." This is apostate Christianity, and people do not realize it. Instead, they say: "We are God's chosen people, we are blessed by God. Material prosperity is His blessing. It means we are approved of God." Oh, how we misunderstand God's loving heart! When God, because of His long-suffering, allowed Jeroboam II to be successful and the nation to be wealthy, it was because He did not want to wipe them out completely. He wanted to give them more time to repent, but they did not understand. They went from bad to worse.

Is this not the condition of Christianity today? We are like the Laodicean church. We do not realize that the Lord is outside the door;

we have pushed Him out. Therefore, the call of God is that to whoever will open the door, He will come in and sup with him and commune with him (see Revelation 3:14-22, especially v. 20). Oftentimes, we think of the mercies of God—and thank God for His mercies. He is most merciful; but we need to balance that aspect of God with His severity. It is a fearful thing to fall into the hands of the living God (see Hebrews 10:31).

In church history there are instances of individual Christians who have at times become apostates. In the New Testament, Paul, Peter, John and Jude all talked about apostasy. In these last days of the end times in which we find ourselves today, apostasy shall be everywhere. People will even deny the Master who has bought them with His precious blood (see II Peter 2:1; Titus 1:16; Jude 4b). In reading the Bible we discover that the disciplinary hand of God comes down very heavily upon the apostate. From church history we learn, thank God, that some people who became apostates came back to the Lord towards the very end. But there were others who never returned, and the disciplinary hand of God was heavy upon them.

We today need to be warned. We should not be careless. We should not think that because we are the Lord's, therefore, we can do whatever we wish and can get by. A person may get by now, but he cannot know for how long. So as long as God gives us life and breath, as long as it is today, let us who may have apostatized our faith return to Him and let us renew a right relationship with Him. We will discover that God's eternal thought is one of restoration. One day, the mountains will drop new wine, and all the hills will melt.

Let us pray:

> *Dear heavenly Father, we do praise and thank Thee that Thou art the Judge of all the earth; and because of this, Thou canst not but be just. We do praise and thank Thee that Thou dost suffer long, waiting for people to repent. Oh Lord, make us a people who always maintain a spirit of repentance that we may taste Thy goodness, that we may be delivered from the severity of God. Oh Lord, we do pray that Thou wilt remember Thy people everywhere upon this earth. Oh Lord, our prayer is, Turn the hearts of Thy*

people lest they fall into Thy hands. We ask in the name of our Lord Jesus. Amen.

OBADIAH

THE KINGDOM SHALL BE JEHOVAH'S

Obadiah 1-21—The vision of Obadiah. Thus saith the Lord Jehovah concerning Edom: We have heard a report from Jehovah, and an ambassador is sent among the nations. Arise ye, and let us rise up against her in battle. Behold, I have made thee small among the nations; thou art greatly despised. The pride of thy heart hath deceived thee, thou that dwellest in the clefts of the rock, whose habitation is high;—he that saith in his heart, Who shall bring me down to the ground? Though thou exalt thyself as the eagle, and though thou set thy nest among the stars, thence will I bring thee down, saith Jehovah. If thieves had come to thee, if robbers by night, (how art thou cut off!) would they not have stolen till they had had enough? If grape-gatherers had come to thee, would they not have left some gleanings? How is Esau searched! his hidden things sought out!

All the men of thy confederacy have pushed thee to the border; the men that were at peace with thee have deceived thee, they have prevailed against thee; they that eat thy bread have laid a snare under thee. There is no understanding in him. Shall I not in that day, saith Jehovah, destroy the wise men out of Edom, and understanding out of the mount of Esau? And thy mighty men, O Teman, shall be dismayed, to the end that every one may be cut off from the mount of Esau by slaughter. Because of violence against thy brother Jacob, shame shall cover thee, and thou shalt be cut off for ever. In the day that thou stoodest on the other side, in the day that strangers carried away captive his substance, and foreigners entered into his gates, and cast lots upon Jerusalem, even thou wast as one of them. But thou shouldest not have looked on the day of thy brother in the day of his disaster; neither shouldest thou have rejoiced over the children of Judah in the day of their destruction; nor have opened wide thy mouth in the day of distress. Thou shouldest not have entered into the gate of my people in the day of their calamity, nor have looked, even thou, on their affliction in the day of their calamity; neither shouldest thou have laid hands on their substance in the day of their calamity; and thou shouldest not have stood on the crossway, to cut off those of his that did escape, nor have delivered up those remaining of him in the day of distress.

For the day of Jehovah is near upon all the nations: as thou hast done, it shall be done unto thee: thy recompence shall return upon thine own head. For as ye have drunk upon my holy mountain, so shall all the nations drink continually; yea, they shall drink, and shall swallow down, and they shall be as though they had not been. But upon mount Zion shall there be deliverance, and it shall be holy; and the house of Jacob shall possess their possessions. And the house of Jacob shall be a fire, and the house of Joseph a flame, and the house of Esau for stubble; and they shall kindle in them and devour them; and there shall not be any remaining of the house of Esau: for Jehovah hath spoken it. And they of the south shall possess the mount of Esau; and they of the lowland the Philistines; yea, they shall possess the field of Ephraim and the field of Samaria; and Benjamin shall possess Gilead; and the captives of this host of the children of Israel shall possess what belonged to the Canaanites, unto Zarephath; and the captives of Jerusalem, who were in Sepharad, shall possess the cities of the south. And saviours shall come up on mount Zion, to judge the mount of Esau; and the kingdom shall be Jehovah's.

Let us pray:

Dear heavenly Father, we do approach Thy throne of grace through the blood of Thy beloved Son, our Lord Jesus, and by the new and living way that He has opened for us, knowing that He is our great High Priest. Our Father, we just come with holy boldness, knowing that we are accepted in the Beloved; and our Father, we just desire that Thou wilt open Thy word to us that we may hear Thy voice. We want to please Thee, we want to follow

Thee. We commit ourselves to Thee for this day. To Thee be the glory. In the name of our Lord Jesus. Amen.

Obadiah is the shortest of all the prophetic writings in the Old Testament, it consisting of but twenty-one verses. St. Jerome, the fourth-century Latin father of the church and noted scholar of God's word, once said, "Obadiah is the most difficult book to study." Yet the twelfth-century French mystic, Hugh of St. Victor, had this to say of this short book: "Obadiah is simple in language, manifold in thought, few in words, but abundant in meaning."

According to the letter, Obadiah delivered his prophecy against Edom; but allegorically it was issued against the world, and morally it was pronounced against the flesh. Moreover, this prophet hinted of the coming of the Lord Jesus; and at His coming the world will be destroyed, the flesh will be subdued, and freedom will be restored.

There are several Obadiahs cited in the Old Testament, but we do not know who this Obadiah was. Usually, Scripture identifies a person by saying so and so is the son of so and so; therefore, in the case of this Obadiah we do not know who he was, for the Scriptures are silent about his father. Probably, there is a spiritual meaning to this silence: it may be that the biographical facts about the prophet were hidden so that his prophecy might be made more manifest. One thing we do know: Obadiah was a prophet. His name means "servant of Jehovah" or "worshiper of Jehovah." As a servant and worshiper of the Lord, he was given a vision. So this book begins with the vision of Obadiah.

In Old Testament times prophets were also called seers; that is to say, they perceived things which other people could not. With their spiritual eyes they saw the thought, the heart and the mind of God. They not only saw, they also heard: for the opening reference to the vision of Obadiah is followed immediately by "Thus saith the Lord Jehovah." In other words, this prophet not only was given a vision, he also was given the word. He not only saw, he also heard; and this is true of all prophetic ministry. If it is a prophetic ministry, then the one who delivers such ministry must be one who not only sees and perceives but also hears.

When Moses was in the desert, he saw the burning bush. That was a vision. Then he heard the voice of the One who dwelt in that burning bush (see Exodus 3:1-6). We likewise recall Isaiah, who one day was in the temple praying. He beheld the glory and the throne of the Lord, and then he heard the voice (see Isaiah 6:1-8). The same thing was true with John in exile on the island of Patmos. He was given the vision of the seven lampstands with the Son of Man in the midst of them, and he also was given the words with which to write to the seven churches in Asia (see Revelation 1). So whenever there is prophetic ministry, we know that behind it there is that which has been seen and that which has been heard.

Not only do we not know who this particular Obadiah was, we do not even know exactly when he prophesied. The only way to judge as to when he prophesied is by looking at both internal and external evidences available to us. One piece of external evidence is to compare the words of Obadiah's prophecy with those of Jeremiah. This may give us a hint because we discover that both men's books contain words of prophecy in common. Whether it was Jeremiah who quoted Obadiah or vice versa will help us to determine when Obadiah prophesied. With respect to internal evidence, what we need to verify is whether the capture of Jerusalem mentioned in Obadiah was a prophetic past or a real past. In other words, in mentioning the capture of Jerusalem, was Obadiah referring to an event which had already happened or was he prophesying an event which was going to happen? So by these two possible evidences we may be able to judge roughly the time when Obadiah prophesied.

Now if we compare the first five verses of Obadiah with Jeremiah 49:7-22, we will find that these five verses of Obadiah are scattered throughout the sixteen verses of that part of the prophecy of Jeremiah concerning Edom and which are identical or almost identical with Jeremiah. On the other hand, in the eleven other verses of Jeremiah under discussion there are phrases and expressions which are exclusively Jeremiah's. So on the basis of these findings we come to the conclusion that it was Jeremiah who quoted Obadiah and not the reverse. Hence, Obadiah's ministry must have occurred before

Jeremiah, or at least he must have been a slightly earlier contemporary of Jeremiah's.

Moreover, when we look further into the internal evidence, we find that what Obadiah mentioned was not the *destruction* of Jerusalem but its temporary seizure and the ensuing plunder of it. As we look back into Jewish history covering the period before Jerusalem was destroyed and the Israelites were taken into Babylonian captivity, we will learn that there were five instances in which Jerusalem was broken into and plundered. The first time it happened was in the fifth year of King Rehoboam when Shishak, king of Egypt, broke into Jerusalem (see II Chronicles 12). The second occasion was when the Philistines and the Arabians entered the city of Jerusalem and plundered it. That occurred in the days of King Jehoram (see II Chronicles 21). The third instance was when Joash, king of Israel, broke into Jerusalem. That happened during the reign of Amaziah (see II Chronicles 25). And then the fourth and fifth times, Jerusalem was captured by the Babylonians—once during the reign of King Jehoiakim and the other during that of King Jehoiachin (see II Chronicles 36). So on these five occasions Jerusalem was broken into and plundered.

Here I cannot go into the details on how four of these five occasions have been eliminated thus narrowing the choice down to the one particular instance to which the prophet referred as being "the day of the distress" of Jerusalem; I will simply tell you the conclusion arrived at. Which of these five occasions the prophet actually referred to must have been the second instance when the Philistines and the Arabians broke into Jerusalem. For Obadiah mentioned that strangers and foreigners came into Jerusalem; and in reading II Chronicles 21 we learn that this had occurred just after Edom had been defeated by Judah when the Edomites had revolted against Judah's rule. When the Arabians and the Philistines broke into Jerusalem, the Edomites had tried taking their revenge against the Israelites, and that is what they did to the house of Jacob. We therefore conclude that the particular occasion of the capture of Jerusalem to which Obadiah had made reference was the second of these five instances.

Hence, by putting all these evidences together, we are of the opinion that Obadiah most likely prophesied a little ahead of Jeremiah. Jeremiah was probably Obadiah's contemporary because Jeremiah prophesied a very long time. But we must acknowledge that there are other scholars who believe that chronologically Obadiah was actually the first of the twelve minor prophets. If so, that would place him very far in advance of Jeremiah.

Nevertheless, the matter of *when* the prophet prophesied is not that important. The essential point in all this is *what* he prophesied. In other words, the message is really the most important factor to grasp hold of here; the timing or even who the prophet was is not important.

These twelve so-called minor prophets, of whom Obadiah was one, were used by God to prophesy warnings to His people, some concerning Judah and some concerning the northern kingdom of Israel. Some others prophesied against Edom and Nineveh. Here we find Obadiah's prophecy was against Edom, but we must always bear in mind that he was a Jewish prophet. So even though he prophesied against Edom, it was because of Edom's relationship with the house of Jacob.

In order to better understand this prophecy we have to know something of the history of Edom. Its history is most interesting; even so, I am afraid most people are not familiar with its history, so I must pause here to recount a little of the history of Edom.

THE SOVEREIGNTY OF GOD

The historical narrative of Edom in the Bible begins at Genesis 25. We may recall that when Rebecca was pregnant and discovered that there were two babies struggling in her womb, she went to the Lord about it and the Lord said, "Two nations are in thy womb, and two peoples shall be separated from thy bowels. One people shall be stronger than the other, and the elder shall serve the younger" (see vv. 21-23). Twin sons were born. At the time of birth, the first one that came out was covered with hair and he was red. That is the reason he was called Esau—meaning, "covered with hair." Then, the second one followed him from the womb with his hand grasping hold of

Esau's heel, and thus he was called Jacob—meaning the "heel-holder" or, "supplanter."

Before these twin sons were born, the prophecy was given: "The older shall serve the younger." In Romans 9, a chapter on the sovereignty of God, we read the following passage: "For this word is of promise, According to this time I will come, and there shall be a son to Sarah. And not only that, but Rebecca having conceived by one, Isaac our father, the children indeed being not yet born, or having done anything good or worthless (that the purpose of God according to election might abide, not of works, but of him that calls), it was said to her, The greater shall serve the less: according as it is written, I have loved Jacob, and I have hated Esau" (vv. 9-13).

Before the children were born, before they had done anything good or worthless, God had already chosen Jacob and rejected Esau. So the Bible has termed this the purpose of God according to election. Here, then, is an instance of divine election. Actually, the principle of divine election can be traced all the way back to before the foundation of the world. Even before the world's foundation God has elected or chosen some. In divine election we see unfolded both the purpose of God and the sovereignty of God. It is written: "I have loved Jacob, and I have hated Esau." Nowhere do we find that statement in the Old Testament until one comes to the very last book, Malachi; there we have the words in chapter 1:2-3, "I have loved Jacob, and I have hated Esau."

In the word of God can be found the truth called the sovereignty of God. God is sovereign. Indeed, He is the Sovereign of the universe; and because of that, He has every right to do anything which pleases Him. In other words, He does everything according to His good pleasure. There is no one who has any right to question Him. If God wants to do something, He does it and nobody can question Him. Now, of course, since He is the all-wise God, He would never do anything which is wrong: He must be right; and furthermore, there must be some reason for what He has done, but He may not explain to us the reason. In the word of God this is a very fundamental truth. It is a part of our faith: we believe in God; we believe He is sovereign; we believe there is the matter of His sovereignty; we believe God has every right to do anything He wishes; and it is His prerogative as God and we cannot question Him. All we need to do is submit to His sovereignty. That is the one attitude we must learn to have.

But this does not mean that because of the sovereignty of God man is relieved of his responsibility. Not at all! Divine election is indeed God's prerogative, but responsibility is man's. We who are created by God are endowed with moral responsibility. Even in the life of Esau, we clearly recognize this fact because the Bible says he despised the birthright. In fact, the birthright was first given to Esau because he emerged from his mother's womb first; but as the elder son he despised his birthright, and because of that, he was not able to inherit the blessing. This therefore points up the complementary truth of human responsibility.

THE EDOMITES

Now Esau was a hunter and, one day, when he returned from the fields, he was hungry, thirsty and exhausted. His brother Jacob happened to be cooking a dish of lentil soup. Esau came in and said, "Give me this soup; I am dying of hunger." And Jacob said, "If you take a vow that you will give me your birthright, then you can have the soup." So Esau said: "What is the good of a birthright? I am almost dying. You can have the birthright. Give me the red lentil soup." And that is the reason Esau was called Edom in the Scriptures thereafter because the name *Edom* means "red." So in exchange for a dish of lentil soup, Esau gave away his birthright (see Genesis 25:29-34). Nevertheless, when the time for his father Isaac's blessing came, Esau was trying to obtain the blessing, even though Jacob had stolen it from him. Because of this, Esau hated his brother.

It is important that we fully understand what happened here. The birthright was Esau's, but he despised it; and yet, when the time for the blessing of the firstborn arrived, he wanted it. He had no right to it anymore, and yet, he wanted it. And because he did not get it, he got angry with his brother. He was jealous of his brother and hated him, hoping one day to take revenge; for Esau said to himself: "I am waiting for my father to die and then I will kill him" (see Genesis 27:44). Now even though after twenty years he himself forgot about this, unfortunately, his descendants would ever afterwards harbor perpetual hatred against Jacob.

Because Esau could not obtain the blessing, he wept, he shed tears; and Hebrews 12 tells us that Esau was a profane person in having despised the birthright and would not repent; and yet he tried with tears to retrieve the blessing, but he could not (vv. 16-17). Nevertheless, his father Isaac still blessed him by saying: "Behold, thy dwelling shall be of the fatness of the earth, and of the dew of heaven from above; and by thy sword shalt thou live; and thou shalt serve thy brother; and it shall come to pass when thou rovest about, that thou shalt break his yoke from off thy neck" (Genesis 27:39-40). In other words, God gave Jacob the land of Canaan, the Promised Land; but to Esau He gave the large area of Mt. Seir, which extended from the southern tip of the Dead Sea all the way to the Red Sea. Apart from the land of Canaan, all this other region was given to Esau and came to be known as Edom or Idumea (the Greek form of Edom).

The northwestern part of this land of Idumea was a very fertile land; but on its eastern side, it was barren desert, full of mountain ranges; yet it was very beautiful. People lived in caves in Mt. Seir. They even built a city in the caves by the side of the mountain. It was almost impenetrable, and that is the description given in Obadiah. It was land good for hunting and so forth, and the descendants of Esau roamed about in it. In short, the prophetic blessing that was given to them through their ancestor Esau was Mt. Seir.

Now the Edomites, the descendants of Esau, actually developed their culture much more quickly than did the children of Jacob because of the fact, as indicated in chapter 36 of Genesis, that the Edomites were a mixed race. Esau married not only two daughters of the Hittites, that is, of the Canaanites, but he also married another daughter—this one of Ishmael. It was a very mixed race, but they developed very highly. In terms of civilization, they had prime leaders and chiefs among them. While the children of Israel were slaves in the land of Egypt, the Edomites already had chiefs of their tribes and, later on, had kings over them. So they became a highly civilized society.

We should take note that though, timewise, the first book in the Bible is Job, Job was not an Israelite. Most likely he was an Edomite; and not only that, but in the same book of Job (2:11) we read of Eliphaz, the Temanite, who lived in the north-eastern area of Edom. So this great "theologian" was also an Edomite. We can therefore see that the Edomites had developed their culture very quickly, well ahead of the house of Jacob.

Now when the children of Israel finally came out of Egypt, God told them that they should not abhor the Edomites. When an Edomite became part of the third generation, he or she could enter the assembly of the people of God because they and the Edomites were brothers (see Deuteronomy 23:7-8). However, when the children of Israel came to the border of Edom and asked for permission to go through on their way to the Promised Land (see Numbers 20), the Edomites not only refused their going through their territory, which was a straight and quicker route to the Promised Land, they even gathered an army to fight against Israel. So the children of Israel had to retreat, and for thirty-eight years they just surrounded Mt. Seir, wandering around. After thirty-eight years of wandering around, the Israelites went to the eastern side of Edom and up to the Promised Land. This, then, is how the house of Jacob suffered because of the hatred of the Edomites.

We read that after the children of Israel entered the Promised Land, they fought against the Edomites often. Under David, the Edomites were subdued; but later on, they renewed their civilization. Eventually, however, all trace of them was lost, and today we do not know who the Edomites are. We do know that at the time of Christ an Edomite—King Herod—was ruler over Judah. So when the King of kings came into this world, there was an Edomite on the throne over Judah. And that is the history of the Edomites.

Returning now to the book of Obadiah, it can be divided into three parts. Verses 1-9 contain a prophecy concerning the destruction of Edom. Verses 10-14 give the reason why. And verses 15-21 contain a prophecy concerning the day of Jehovah or the day of the Lord. When that day comes, the Edomites and all the other nations will be destroyed and "the kingdom shall be the Lord's."

THE KINGDOM SHALL BE JEHOVAH'S

What is the message of Obadiah? If we read this book casually, we may think it is simply a prophecy against Edom, that Edom will be destroyed completely; but this is not the central message. Actually, the primary message can be found in the very last sentence of the book: "The kingdom shall be Jehovah's." That is the message. In other words, no matter how much Edom hated and persecuted Jacob, ultimately Edom will be destroyed and Jacob will be established. And why? It is because Jacob represents the kingdom of God. So this message can provide a comfort to the people of God. Moreover, we can broaden our understanding of the message and say that the secular world as represented by Edom, and the religious world that is also represented by Edom, are always hateful towards the people of God. The true children of God have suffered at the hands of both the secular and religious worlds throughout history. But there is a comfort available to God's people because the day of the Lord shall come and He will judge the world, even also the religious world, and will establish His kingdom among His chosen people. So that is actually the central message of Obadiah.

FURTHER SPIRITUAL APPLICATION

FLESH VERSUS SPIRIT

Now we wish to go further in pursuing the spiritual application of Obadiah. Obadiah is not only a prophecy, it also contains a spiritual principle demonstrated to us. It is commonly accepted by Bible scholars that Edom, spiritually speaking, represents the flesh. Do we know what the flesh is? It is a twin brother of the spirit; moreover, it is not the spiritual that is born first, it is the natural that comes forth first (see I Corinthians 15:46). That which is of the flesh always comes forth first and always persecutes that which is of the spirit.

When God created man, He gave him the birthright to have dominion over all things (see Genesis 1:26, 28). But man lost his birthright through sin, and by the time of Genesis 6 man had so sinned that God's word declared that "Man had become flesh" (see v. 3).

"That which is born of the flesh is flesh" (John 3:6a). When we were born, we were born of the flesh; therefore, we were flesh. It was not that we did not have a spirit, but our spirit was dead because of sins and transgressions (see Ephesians 2:5a). Our human spirit had no contact with God the Spirit. We lived as the flesh, according to the desire of our soul and the passion of our body. Now it does not mean that there was no good in us. From the human standpoint, there are many good things in the flesh as well as many bad things. But if there was any good in the flesh, it was of no good or value to God because the Bible says the natural man does not receive the things of the Spirit of God because they are folly to him and he cannot know them because they have to be discerned by the spirit (see I Corinthians 2:14). The Scripture also says, "The mind of the flesh is enmity against God" (Romans 8:7a). Therefore, so far as the flesh is concerned, whether there is something good in it or there is something bad in it, nothing of it is acceptable to God. They that are of the flesh cannot please God (see Romans 8:8). That is what His word says. The only way for the flesh is to go to the cross to be crucified; and that is what God did to the flesh.

Before we believed in the Lord Jesus, we were flesh. We used our flesh to commit many sins but we sometimes even used our flesh to do some good. We even tried to do some good works, thinking that by doing so God might accept us. But we know that our so-called righteousnesses are as filthy rags (see Isaiah 64:6). God will not accept them. Anything which comes from the flesh is rejected by Him, and yet the flesh is full of pride.

What are the symptoms of the flesh? Number one is pride. We were all proud of ourselves. Number two is jealousy. If we find someone better than ourselves, we become jealous. Number three is hatred. We hate; but we especially hate the things of God. Because we do not have those things, we are therefore jealous of people who have them and so we hate those people. That is the flesh.

When we come to the Lord Jesus and we are saved, "that which is born of the Spirit is spirit" (John 3:6b). Thank God, we now have a spiritual life in us, but that does not mean our flesh has changed. The flesh in us is still flesh. That is the reason why, in our spiritual experience, the flesh lusts against the spirit and the spirit lusts against the flesh (see Galatians 5:17). There is a war in us between these two; but unfortunately, the flesh has been around longer and is stronger; and hence, oftentimes our spirit is being persecuted and suppressed. Today, how easily we are deceived. We think that because we have believed in the Lord Jesus, therefore, our flesh has changed. Formerly, we used our flesh to commit sin; now we will use our flesh to serve God. We use our fleshly wisdom, our fleshly talents, our fleshly energy, our fleshly experience or background or whatever it may be. We turn around and use this to serve God. And so we think God will now most certainly be pleased; but God's word tells us that the flesh cannot please Him (see again Romans 8:8). And the verdict of God is that the flesh must die; and He has condemned it on the cross of Christ (see Romans 8:3).

So what is our personal story here? Because the flesh is akin to our spirit—so close, in fact, that they are twin brothers—we often find that we are living according to the flesh instead of living according to the spirit (see Romans 8:12-14; Galatians 5:25). There is a perpetual battle going on between these two (see Galatians 5:17b). So, let us never think that the flesh will ever love the spirit; on the contrary, it has a perpetual hatred against the things of the spirit (see Romans 8:6-7). Sometimes the flesh may appear quite spiritual, but it is a counterfeit. As a matter of fact, it is persecuting the spirit; it is opposing the spirit (see again Galatians 5:17). And this is a lesson we have to learn. And it takes time to learn this. Perhaps it requires some failures in order to learn it, and that is how the apostle Paul himself learned this lesson. For in Romans 7 he stated that he thought his flesh was good: he could do the will of God; he could keep the commandments; he could please God. So he tried and tried very hard. But only after repeated failure did he come to the following conclusion: "In me, that is, in my flesh, there is no good" (see v.18a). And it is not until that moment that we are delivered from our flesh—that we begin to realize that he who is of Christ has crucified the flesh with its passions and lusts (see Galatians 5:24). So this is a lesson we have to learn. It is a very important lesson to learn, and how much time and energy are wasted because we do not know the difference between the flesh and the spirit. Only the spirit represents the kingdom of God.

A SYSTEM VERSUS LIVING FAITH

All the above has been an application to us personally, but there is another application. We can spiritually apply Edom corporately. Corporately, Edom represents that which is very close to the house of God, and yet it is the enemy of His house. In the first century it was Judaism that was the enemy of the church of God. At the beginning it was God's revelation on Mount Sinai, but when did that living faith of the children of Israel become an "ism"—Judaism as a religious system? Most likely it happened during the years of the Babylonian captivity. That living faith gradually degenerated—first through apostasy, and then into the system of Judaism, which is so close to the church of God. They in fact are twin brothers: Judaism came first and then the church of God, but oh how the former persecuted the latter! Judaism hated the church because it had lost its birthright.

To what, corporately, can we apply Edom today in our present century? I believe we can say that it is Christianity as a religious system. Christianity has gradually developed through the ages into a religious system. It has become an "ism"; and whenever living faith degenerates into an "ism"—into a system of religion—it becomes the enemy of that which is of God. In reading church history we find that when Christianity eventuated into the system of Roman Catholicism, how greatly it persecuted true believers! What hatred it had because it had lost its birthright! Somebody else had obtained the birthright. There was the jealousy, the hatred, and also the pride. Then, too, after the Reformation, when the Protestant faith became an "ism," the same thing happened. If we read the history of Protestantism, we discover that it also persecuted true believers, just as had Roman Catholicism; in this regard, it was nothing better. How many did Protestantism kill? They tied rocks to the necks of the Anabaptists and drowned them. They said, "So you want to be baptized? All right, we will baptize you." Thousands drowned as a cruel result. Whenever a living faith degenerates into an "ism"—into a religious system—it always ends up hating what is of God.

Thank God, Edom will be destroyed; whether it is the secular world or the religious world, it will be destroyed. In Revelation 17 and 18 we come upon a mystery, the great Babylon—that is, the religious world. How it drinks the blood of the saints! In chapter 18 we read how the great city Babylon, the political and economic center, engages in the trade of souls. But Babylon will fall, and the new Jerusalem shall be established. "The kingdom shall be the Lord's" (Obadiah 21b). So let us take comfort because if we want to be true to the Lord, if we desire to follow the Lamb wheresoever He goes, it will be the way of the cross; but ultimately, it shall reach the kingdom: "the kingdom shall be the Lord's." And that, as we said earlier, is the central message of Obadiah. So may the Lord help us.

Let us pray:

> *Dear heavenly Father, do open our understanding that we may see what Thou art speaking to us, both individually and corporately. We pray that we may have a vision of the flesh and of Thy judgment upon the flesh that we may side with Thee and deliver it to the cross that we may live a life that is spiritual and pleasing to Thee. We pray that we may also be given a vision of what the church of God is, the pillar and the base of truth, that we may follow Thee. Lord, we pray that we may eventually see new Jerusalem shine because the kingdom is the Lord's. Use these words to encourage us, to make us faithful in these last days. We ask in the name of our Lord Jesus. Amen.*

JONAH

GOD IS MERCIFUL

Jonah 1:1-3—And the word of Jehovah came unto Jonah the son of Amittai, saying, Arise, go to Nineveh, the great city, and cry against it; for their wickedness is come up before me. But Jonah rose up to flee unto Tarshish from the presence of Jehovah; and he went down to Joppa, and found a ship going to Tarshish; so he paid the fare thereof, and went down into it, to go with them unto Tarshish, from the presence of Jehovah.

Jonah 3:1-4—And the word of Jehovah came unto Jonah the second time, saying, Arise, go to Nineveh, the great city, and preach unto it the preaching that I shall bid thee. And Jonah arose, and went unto Nineveh, according to the word of Jehovah. Now Nineveh was an exceeding great city of three days' journey. And Jonah began to enter into the city a day's journey, and he cried and said, Yet forty days, and Nineveh shall be overthrown!

Jonah 4:10-11—And Jehovah said, Thou hast pity on the gourd, for which thou hast not laboured, neither madest it grow; which came up in a night, and perished in a night: and I, should not I have pity on Nineveh, the great city, wherein are more than a hundred and twenty thousand persons that cannot discern between their right hand and their left hand; and also much cattle?

Matthew 12:38-41—Then answered him some of the scribes and Pharisees, saying, Teacher, we desire to see a sign from thee. But he, answering, said to them, A wicked and adulterous generation seeks after a sign, and a sign shall not be given to it save the sign of Jonas the prophet. For even as Jonas was in the belly of the great fish three days and three nights, thus shall the Son of man be in the heart of the earth three days and three nights. Ninevites shall [rise] up in the judgment with this generation, and shall condemn it: for they repented at the preaching of Jonas; and behold, more than Jonas is here.

Let us pray:

Dear heavenly Father, as we continue in Thy presence, we do look to Thee to shine Thy light upon Thy word and shine Thy light upon our hearts. We pray that through Thy Holy Spirit working in us we may be drawn into Thy very thought, into Thy very mind, and into Thy very heart. Lord, we do desire to be of one mind, one heart, one spirit with Thee. We commit this time into Thy hands and look for Thy blessing. To the praise of Thy glory. In the name of our Lord Jesus. Amen.

The book of Jonah is most unusual. It is listed among the twelve minor prophets, but it is really not a prophecy; it is a history—even a personal history. Indeed, as we read the book of Jonah, we find that except chapter two—which is a prayer—it is simply straight narrative, the story of one particular man. And yet, even though it is one individual's history, hidden in that personal story is the mystery of the greatest prophecy. In its content and style, this book is more in line with what we have in the Old Testament books of I and II Kings concerning the lives of Elijah and Elisha. They were prophets, just as Jonah was a prophet; and, in the same way as with the stories of those two prophets, we find in this book of Jonah that the personal story of the prophet Jonah is being told.

Jonah was a real person because in Matthew 12 and 16 and in Luke 11 the Lord Jesus is recorded as mentioning him. Just as Jonah was a sign to the Ninevites, so the Lord Jesus served, and continues to serve, as the sign to a wicked and adulterous generation. The very name Jonah means "dove." He was the son of Amittai, which means "the truth of God." He was from Gath-Hepher—a town about a mile north of Nazareth—and was of the tribe of Zebulon in Galilee.

We learn from John 7 that the scribes and Pharisees, in their opposition to Jesus, would not recognize Him as a prophet. So they challenged Him by saying: "Has any prophet come out of Galilee?"

(see v. 52) Yet Jonah came out of Galilee. But because he had been sent to a Gentile nation, these scribes and Pharisees, out of their narrow-mindedness, most conveniently forgot about him.

Now having arisen out of Galilee, Jonah was thus a prophet of the northern kingdom of Israel. According to II Kings 14:25, he prophesied during the time of Jeroboam II which thus would have been sometime during the first half of the eighth century B.C. It was Jonah who had prophesied that God would restore the northern kingdom of Israel during the reign of Jeroboam II. So he was truly a great prophet. Now even though God used Jeroboam II to restore the territory of the northern kingdom of Israel, it was not because Jeroboam was a good king; as a matter of fact, he was a wicked king. Also, it was not because the children of Israel had repented that He restored their territory; for they did not repent. No, God restored it because He looked upon that guilty nation and saw that there was absolutely no earthly help for them; and He had previously made up His mind already not to blot out the name of Israel (see II Kings 14:26-27). So out of His compassion for that nation, He had prophesied through Jonah that He would use Jeroboam to restore the glory of the northern kingdom of Israel (see II Kings 14:25-28). In fact, we learn that during this king's long reign Israel had enjoyed great prosperity.

Jonah probably prophesied after Elisha. Indeed, it was almost as though he was succeeding Elisha. At that time the latter was also a prophet to the northern kingdom of Israel. He was a prophet of grace to that guilty nation; but Jonah most likely prophesied after Elisha, and was sent to a heathen nation to prophesy of its destruction in order that they might repent and be spared. The word of God came to Jonah: "Arise, go to Nineveh, cry against it; for their wickedness has come up before Me."

This becomes even more interesting for us if we know what Nineveh was at that time. Of course, today*, we all are aware of the news about Iraq; and actually, Nineveh—and Babylon too—were at this much earlier period within what is today the territory of modern Iraq. Nineveh had been built by Nimrod, and if we go back to Genesis

* This message was delivered in 1991.

10:10-12, we learn that he was the grandson of Ham, and that he went forth. The name Nimrod means "rebel." He was a great hunter, but he was also the first empire builder in history; for he went forth and built Babylon by the river Euphrates and built Nineveh by the river Tigris. And we believe that Mesopotamia (or modern-day Iraq) was the place where civilization first began in world history. So Nimrod was the first one in history who established large cities for his kingdom.

Thirteen hundred years later, at the time of Jonah, Nineveh had become a great city, even an exceedingly great city—so great, in fact, that it required three days' journey to traverse its precincts. It is even said that this city most probably covered some sixty to ninety miles of territory. Moreover, we know that it had one hundred and twenty thousand people who did not know their right hand from their left, which thus referred to those who were under seven years of age. And hence, during the time of Jonah, Nineveh probably possessed a population of at least six hundred thousand people. It was truly a vast city for its time; but it was also a very wicked city. It was strong but wicked, and it became the capital of the Assyrian Empire. At the time of Jonah, Assyria was a rising star in the firmament of nations. It began to build and then expand its kingdom and, of course, we know that eventually it was destroyed by the Babylonian Empire. Nevertheless, in history and in prophecy the Assyrian and Babylonian Empires were oftentimes named together as one. These two empires were referred to almost interchangeably at times because they together represented the first world empire. And we know that with the rise of the Babylonian Empire under Nebuchadnezzar, "the times of the Gentiles" had begun (cf. Luke 21:24; Romans 11:25). And if we look more closely into Biblical prophecy, we shall learn that it was prophesied that in future days the Assyrians would rise up and become the enemy of God's people. So in other words, this term Assyrian was used in a very general way to refer to what the world empire is or what the world represents, and it is always characterized as being an enemy of God's people.

FLEEING FROM THE PRESENCE OF GOD

When Jonah was commissioned by God to go to Nineveh to cry against it, he immediately fled from His presence. He did not want to go. Why? Probably it was because he was a typical, very patriotic Jew, and he had been greatly used by God to prophesy concerning the prosperity of the nation of Israel. Yet Israel was not right before God; and as a prophet, Jonah probably had a kind of premonition that God would use some Gentile power to punish and discipline Israel. And in the Scriptures, Assyria is called the rod of God's anger (Isaiah 10:5). So Jonah might have had a sense of what God would do. When God sent him to Nineveh to cry against it and declare that unless her people repented it would be destroyed within forty days, I would think that he would have been most glad to do that. However, Jonah knew God too well; he knew His character. He knew that the reason God had sent him there to cry against them was not to destroy them but to give them another opportunity to escape His wrath, and Jonah did not desire to see them have that opportunity. So instead of obeying God, he fled from His presence.

Jonah went down to the seaport of Joppa, and it so happened there was a ship going to Tarshish. Now we do not know for sure where Tarshish was located. Some say it was probably a seaport in Spain. Others have conjectured that because Solomon had sent boats from the Red Sea to gather treasures, Tarshish must have been some place in Africa. We therefore do not know for certain where Tarshish was; but the one thing we do know is that Nineveh is to the east of Palestine, and Spain and/or Africa are to the west or south of Palestine. And hence, Jonah traveled in the opposite direction from Nineveh in an attempt to flee from the presence of God.

Now do any of us really believe Jonah thought he could flee from the presence of God? Jonah was a prophet and he was most familiar with the Old Testament Scriptures. If you read his prayer found in the second chapter of Jonah, you will see that it is quotation after quotation taken from the Psalms. He was using the Psalms to express his feelings before God. So I for one do not think that he actually believed he could flee from the presence of God—especially when one considers the following passage from Psalm 139: "Whither shall I go from thy Spirit? and whither flee from thy presence? If I ascend up into the heavens thou art there; or if I make my bed in Sheol, behold, thou art there; If I take the wings of the dawn and dwell in the uttermost parts of the sea, even there shall thy hand lead me, and thy right hand shall hold me. And if I say, Surely darkness shall cover me, and the light about me be night; even darkness hideth not from thee, and the night shineth as the day: the darkness is as the light. For thou hast possessed my reins; thou didst cover me in my mother's womb" (vv. 7-13).

Jonah, being quite familiar with the Psalms, certainly knew he could not flee from God's presence. So what does it mean, "fleeing from the presence of Jehovah"? Actually, nobody can flee from the Lord's presence because He is everywhere. It really means that Jonah was thinking of turning away from being God's prophet because he did not want to bring His message to the Ninevites. In other words, Jonah was fleeing from his ministry. Perhaps there was another reason for his flight. Knowing God's heart, he thought if he should go and announce that within forty days Nineveh would be destroyed but they repented and thus God would not destroy Nineveh, then what would happen to him as a prophet? People would say he was a false prophet because his prophecy did not come true, and he would therefore lose his credibility. If so, then Jonah was more concerned with his credibility than he was with the character of God. So perhaps that was another reason why he did not wish to do what God had commanded him to do. In any case, Jonah fled. Sure enough, there was a ship going to Tarshish. So he paid the fare, went down into the ship, and thought he would soon be in Tarshish.

Sometimes we use circumstances as a guide to know the Lord's will. Yes, it is true that at times the Lord does guide us by means of circumstances, but we cannot be guided by our circumstances alone. When Jonah arrived in Joppa, there was a ship ready for him. He could therefore claim that God had provided the essential circumstance for him, and thus conclude that it must be God's will. But we know that in this instance it was precisely the opposite to God's will. When circumstances do not agree with or even oppose the direct command of God, then we know we cannot rely on circumstances to guide us. We must go by the direct will of God. Circumstances can serve sometimes as a help, but they can never serve as the sole guidance as to what is the will of God. This is something which we need never to forget.

Jonah paid the fare (actually, it was a waste of money) and went down into the ship—that is to say, he went into the hold of the ship and went to sleep; but God sent a great storm that put the ship in great danger. The sailors threw overboard most of the goods the ship was carrying in order to lighten it, but this tactic did not work. The storm grew so severe that everybody on the ship cried out to their gods for help. Then the captain found that there was a man sleeping in the hold of the ship, to whom he shouted: "Sleeper, wake up!" Is it not rather strange that a person who deliberately disobeyed God and tried to flee from Him could go to sleep? Jonah's conscience must surely have greatly bothered him; indeed, at this moment, he must have had a most wicked conscience; how, then, could he have gone to sleep? But let us understand that sometimes we may try to sleep away our wicked conscience. So much so that often, when a person is in such strain and stress, he can and does go to sleep!

We may recall Elijah in this regard, how he fled and went to sleep (I Kings 19:1-5). And let us recall the three disciples whom Jesus especially took with Him into the Garden of Gethsemane. It was such an important time and the Lord said, "Watch with Me"; but they went to sleep (see, e.g., Matthew 26:36-43). Why was this with these three and with Elijah? It was because the tension was so great; and I believe that this was the reason with Jonah as well. Jonah was so tired from bearing such a wicked conscience, fighting within himself and without, that he simply fell fast asleep.

The shipmaster, having awakened him, now said, "Arise, and cry unto your god." And they all said, everyone to his fellow, "Come, let us cast lots that we may know for whose cause this evil is upon us." God actually governed that lot, and it fell upon Jonah. So they said, "Who are you? What have you done?" Now I believe by that time Jonah realized what he had been doing and he had therefore repented before God. So he said, "I am a Hebrew; I fear God who made the heavens and the earth." And he told them that he was fleeing from the presence of the Lord. So this admission of Jonah's made everybody else on board very frightened. He had been doing the wrong thing; so they said, "What shall we do?" And Jonah said, "Throw me into the sea." The prophet realized that he had been rebellious towards God and that he should be chastised. Yet he had enough faith, believing that if he were thrown into the sea, somehow God would rescue him. But, naturally, the other people on board the ship would not do such a thing. In one sense we find the good flesh even in the natural man; for they would not at this moment do that. Instead, they tried their best to row the ship to land, but they could not do so. Meanwhile, the sea became even more tempestuous; so that, in the end, these sailors prayed to God, even to Jehovah, and said, "It is Your doing; therefore, do not let the blood of this man fall upon us." And with that, they threw Jonah into the sea. As soon as he touched the water, the sea became calm. It was obviously the Lord.

Now God had prepared a big fish to swallow up Jonah. Most likely that fish was not a whale but a shark, because in the Mediterranean there are extremely large sharks which can swallow even a horse: on at least one occasion, for example, people have opened up a dead shark and found a horse inside! Moreover, there was an instance in which a sailor had fallen overboard and a shark had swallowed him; the shark was caught and opened up and the sailor was found alive. It was miraculous, of course. And in the present instance with Jonah it was likewise a miracle, since God had prepared a shark at just the right time and at just the right place to swallow Jonah. And for three days and three nights God's prophet was alive in that shark. It was nothing short of a miracle; yet God is a God of miracles, such being a very common thing with Him. If you believe in God, miracles are common; if you do not believe in God, you probably will not believe in miracles. Yet our God can do anything.

God's prophet was in the belly of that fish for three days and three nights; and from chapter 2 of Jonah we learn that he set himself to praying. Now that he was in distress, he prayed and confessed; and in his prayer, he quoted psalm after psalm from the book of Psalms. It is good if we actually know the word of God by heart because, whenever we are in trouble, we will know how to express our feelings. Sometimes, though, we do not know how to express our inward feelings, and thus the book of Psalms can express for us the feelings of those who fear God. There in the belly of that fish, Jonah held his prayer meeting in faith; for he declared that salvation is of the Lord. He also voiced thanksgiving and made a vow that he would go back and do what God had originally wanted him to do. So after three days and three nights God commanded that fish to vomit, and he vomited out the prophet Jonah. Let us acknowledge that God is in control of everything.

GOD SPEAKS A SECOND TIME

The word of God came to Jonah the second time: "Arise, go to Nineveh, and preach what I have told you to preach." If God gives a word or command in Scripture and a person does not obey, or obeys only half of it, then to God it is not obeying Him and He will speak a second time. This we find true in the life of Abraham. When he was in Ur of Chaldea, God said to him: "Go out; leave your kindred, leave your land, and go to the place to which I send you." But when Abraham went out, his father went with him, Lot his nephew went with him, and also he stopped at Haran in Syria—only halfway. He thus did not obey God. So a second time God said to him: "Go, leave your kindred, leave your father's house, and go to the place to which I send you." We learn from this that when God gives us a word or command and we do not obey, there will not come forth from Him a new command but it will be the same word a second time; and thank God for this second time.

Jonah now obeyed. He went to Nineveh and took a day's journey into the city where he began to cry out and announced: "Within forty days Nineveh will be destroyed." Let us be reminded that Nineveh was a wicked city, so wicked that God threatened to destroy it in forty days. Why this number of days? We know that forty in Scripture is a number representing or signifying trial, testing or temptation. Recall that the children of Israel had wandered in the Sinai wilderness for forty years; the Lord Jesus had been in the wilderness for forty days being tempted by the devil. So forty is the number regarding trial or testing. In other words, God still gave Nineveh time to repent. He could have wiped the city out immediately without giving its people any warning, but God gave them forty days' time to repent.

Now when Jonah went into the city and began to preach, the people repented. In addition, when the news came to the king, he got down from his throne, put on sackcloth, placed ashes upon his head, and gave the order that everybody in Nineveh must do the same and that nobody could eat or drink—not even the animals. The Spirit of God was truly moving there. They sincerely repented of their evil before God, hoping that He would spare them. And thank God, He did spare them.

That does not mean, though, that their reformation in turning to God was permanent. As a matter of fact, the Old Testament tells us that after thirty or forty years, the king of Assyria went from his Ninevite capital to the northern kingdom of Israel and made her a vassal state to Assyria (II Kings 17:23-24). Later on, when Sennacherib became the Assyrian king, he, with arrogance, attacked Judah during the days of Hezekiah. The Assyrians had become a very powerful warrior nation. They even blasphemed God. They became arrogant and very wicked before God and man. A century and a half later, God raised up another prophet, Nahum, to prophesy the destruction of Nineveh. This time they refused to repent. So eventually Nineveh was destroyed by the Babylonian Empire and the Medes in the early seventh century B.C. They had combined together to destroy Assyria, and thus Babylon would now become the latest and greatest empire in the world of that day.

Thus we see that Nineveh's repentance in the time of Jonah was not a permanent turning to God. There had indeed been a reformation in Jonah's day for God to have spared them, but only for a hundred and fifty years. Ultimately, because of their resumption of arrogance and gross wickedness, the people of Nineveh were finally destroyed.

Jonah was very unhappy about Nineveh's repentance. He had preached and six hundred thousand people repented. This harvest of souls was even greater than that on the day of Pentecost when Peter preached and only three thousand repented. By comparison, therefore, would anyone not be very happy about such a great harvest? But, strangely, Jonah was very unhappy—not only unhappy but very angry with God. He could not believe what had happened. So he moved out of the city and established a booth on a high place overlooking the east side of the city. He wanted to observe what he thought and hoped would eventually happen. He was still hoping that Nineveh would be destroyed. Jonah was a most stubborn prophet.

God in His kindness towards Jonah, and knowing that the weather was going to be very hot, had prepared a gourd. In that part of the world there are some plants which can grow up very quickly, within a few short days; this particular plant, however, grew up overnight. At God's command a gourd rose up in the night and produced big leaves, thus forming a kind of shade for Jonah. God's prophet was very happy about this development because though it was hot he now had shade. Then God prepared a little worm to eat the gourd and in the following night the plant withered. In the morning God sent an east wind, and it became very hot. So Jonah cried out: "It is better for me to die. I do not want to live anymore." God responded by saying: "Are you right to be angry over a gourd?" He replied: "I am right even unto death." What a prophet!

Then God taught his prophet a lesson. God said to him: "You pitied that gourd which came up in the night and withered in the night, and yet, it was not of your making; but consider the fact that this huge city Nineveh has a hundred twenty thousand children unable to discern their right hand from their left [meaning, that they had not reached the age of accountability], and also many cattle. And these are all created by Me. Should I not have pity upon them?" God left that question with Jonah, and I believe He leaves that same question with us to ponder over today.

THE SIGN OF JONAH

Centuries later Jonah would serve as a most dramatic sign. When the Lord Jesus was on the earth, the Pharisees and the scribes came to Him one day and said: "Show us a sign from heaven"—as though to say that if they were provided with a divine sign, they would believe; but the Lord Jesus replied, as it were, as follows: "To this wicked and adulterous generation there will be no sign given save the sign of Jonah. As Jonah was in the belly of the fish three days and three nights, so shall the Son of Man be in the earth three days and three nights. One day, the Ninevites will rise up and judge this generation because they heard Jonah and repented, at least for a time, but this generation hears One who is greater than Jonah and refuses to repent" (see Matthew 12:38-41).

Jonah the prophet was a sign. He was a sign to Nineveh. What is a sign? A sign points to something. It points to the merciful character of God. Nineveh was a large and wicked city. In figure it represented the world. God who is the sovereign Ruler and Judge of this world, and who is just and righteous, had to punish this world because of its wickedness. Nevertheless, we see here that He is also a merciful God.

We may remember from Exodus 33-34 that when Moses pleaded before God to spare the children of Israel, He spared them; and then Moses said to God, "Show me Thy glory." In response the Lord said this: "I will pass by you and declare My name. You cannot see My face, but I will declare My name that you may know who I am." And when He passed by Moses, God's servant declared: "Jehovah, Jehovah God, merciful and gracious, slow to anger, full of goodness and tender mercies, forgiving iniquities and sins and transgressions."

Oh, our God is indeed a merciful God! He gives grace to those who do not deserve it. So far as Nineveh was concerned, they should have been destroyed, but God in His great mercy wanted to spare them. Fortunately, they repented and experienced His grace.

It is the same way with this current generation of today. This generation actually began with the time of Christ and has continued right up to our time today. A generation in Scripture may mean a generation of thirty or forty years or it may mean a certain period of time. Here the Lord Jesus inquired: "What is this generation like?" This generation, He observed, is characterized by two things—wickedness and adultery. It is wicked so far as human relationships are concerned; and it is adulterous so far as its relationship with God is concerned because it worships idols that are abominations to God; and in His sight that kind of conduct is spiritual adultery. So what characterizes this current generation is wickedness and adultery. Even up to our day this is still that same generation. And this generation will not pass away until everything shall have been fulfilled. This wicked and adulterous generation is still looking for a sign. And what is that sign? Is it not wonderful that the sign given it is the Son of Man? We would say that for this wicked and adulterous generation the sign shall be judgmental fire falling from heaven; but on the contrary, the sign which God continues to give to this wicked and adulterous generation is His Son.

When Jonah appeared in Nineveh, it was a sign that God was intent on showing mercy to that wicked city. Otherwise, He would not have sent Jonah there. And hence, the very presence of Jonah became a sign to the Ninevites that there was still an opportunity for them to escape God's judgment.

God sent His only begotten Son into this world. His very coming into this world is therefore a sign to this continuing wicked and adulterous generation. God wants to spare the world. God so loved the world that He gave His only begotten Son. Comparatively speaking, Jonah was a small prophet when viewed in relation to the Lord Jesus, for He is the Prophet of God. Jonah was a prophet from the northern kingdom of Israel sent to Nineveh, but Jesus Christ is the Prophet of God sent from heaven to the whole world. Jonah was an unwilling prophet, but Jesus was a most willing Savior. He came to this world willingly and voluntarily; but, strangely, whereas Nineveh listened to Jonah, this world as a whole refuses to listen to the Lord Jesus. But those in this world who listen to Him shall be saved. Such is the mercy of God.

THE LESSON OF JONAH

It can be rightly assumed that God wanted to teach Jonah and the children of Israel a lesson, since this book of Jonah is included in the Old Testament; therefore, it was for the Jews to read and from which to learn. The Jews have always had the attitude that they are the chosen people of God and that God's covenant is with them and with nobody else. Accordingly, over time a narrowness had developed within them. They thought God's blessing was only on them and not upon the other nations. Yet they forgot one aspect about their father Abraham. We read in Genesis 12 that when God commanded Abraham to go out from Ur and follow Him, God had declared to him: "I will bless you, and through you all the families of the earth will also be blessed." Furthermore, they likewise forgot that after Abraham had offered up Isaac, God with an oath gave him a promise, saying: "In thy seed shall all the nations be blessed." Somehow, the Jews forgot all of this. They gradually came to believe that the blessing of God was upon them and nobody else and thus they did not want to see anybody else obtain that blessing.

This narrow thought and belief was true at the time of Jonah, was true at the time of Christ, and was true even with Christ's disciples and His early apostles. We will recall that dramatic instance involving the apostle Peter. He was at Joppa on a rooftop one day and saw a vision of a sheet coming down from heaven towards him with various unclean animals in it; and God said to Peter: "Rise, kill and eat." Peter objected, saying: "No, Lord, I have never eaten anything unclean." This occurred three times in succession, and, finally, the sheet was drawn back up to heaven. At that very moment, emissaries from Cornelius the Gentile were knocking at the door of the place where Peter was staying, and the Spirit of God said to him, "Go with them." There was a kind of natural narrowness and exclusiveness in the hearts of the Jews throughout most of their history. They thought that God and His salvation were exclusively for them—a curse upon the nations but blessings upon them. Even with Peter, it took a repetitious vision to deliver him, and even later he was still not completely delivered (see Acts 10 and Galatians 2:11ff.). How seemingly impossible it was for the Jewish people to be delivered from such prejudice; nevertheless, in God's word we find that through Abraham and his seed all the nations—the whole human family—would be blessed. God wanted to bring all the nations to himself. So He taught Jonah a lesson here to the intent that he would know His heart more fully. The lesson: that Jonah should have a heart as broad as God's heart and be as merciful as He is merciful. It was, and still is, a transformative lesson for the children of Israel to learn—and, for us also to learn.

Now it can be said that the minor prophets, as God's spokesmen, had prophesied against the people of four different geographical entities: Judah, northern Israel, Edom, and Nineveh/Assyria/Babylon.

Yet in one very particular sense it can also be said that these same prophets had prophesied as well against what each of these physical entities represented, negatively, in spiritual terms. First, of course, we know that Judah represents the church of God, and we also know that, just as was unfortunately true with the people of Judah all through their history, things have similarly not always been right and true with the people in God's church throughout her history; nevertheless, they have still been considered by God to be His church.

Israel, on the other hand, represents the apostate church—the church as apostatized; and even as God had continually sent His prophets to northern Israel in an attempt to restore its people to himself, so God has continually sent His messengers to the apostate church in an attempt to do the same. But like Israel, the apostate church has obstinately refused to repent. Unfortunately, therefore, the fate of the apostate church, unless there be sincere repentance, will be similar to that of the northern kingdom of Israel, which was totally destroyed by Assyria in the seventh century B.C.

As for the third of these four physical entities, we find that Edom represents the flesh; and we know that certain of these minor prophets have revealed in their books how God utterly dealt with the Edomites. And thus we are provided a picture of how God will likewise deal with those people who live according to the flesh. Finally, there was the physical entity of Nineveh/Assyria/Babylon, against which God through His prophet Jonah had prophesied. This fourth geographical entity, as was pointed out earlier, represents the world—the people of the world; and here in the book of Jonah we clearly see revealed God's attitude towards the world. This I would now like to focus our attention upon by way of conclusion to this book of Jonah.

What exactly is God's attitude towards the world? The world is wicked, and becomes more and more wicked as time goes on. According to prophecy, one day this world will be judged at the return coming of the Lord Jesus. At His first coming He came as the Lamb of God to save the world (cf. John 1:29); but at His second coming He will come as the Lion of Judah and will judge the nations (see Revelation 5:5ff.). Ultimately, this world will be judged and even burned up, but in the book of Jonah we see the heart of God—how merciful and gracious He is, how He has suffered long through all these generations and centuries.

So far as the world is concerned, it has rejected God's only begotten Son; and what will God therefore do? We will recall the parable which the Lord taught, saying, that a man—a king—had a vineyard which he rented out to people. At the time of harvest he sent servants. They killed the servants and, finally, the king sent his son, whom he thought they would respect. But they killed the son; what, then, should the king do? He will destroy those people (see Luke 20:9-19).

From this parable we see that the world has been rejecting the Son of God for two thousand years. We would probably say that God should have wiped out this world long ago, but He is merciful and gracious. He is long-suffering, not wanting to see anyone perish but all to come to the knowledge of the truth (II Peter 3:9b; I Timothy 2:4). People will mock and say, "Where is the promise of the coming of Christ? Is not the world today as it was yesterday?" (cf. II Peter 3:3-4) They do not realize that His delay is due to the forbearance of God, He not willing for anyone to perish but that all should come to repentance (see II Peter 3:9b; Romans 2:4).

We need to see the heart of God towards this world. How He loves the world, how He wants to see its people repent and be restored—because He sees the preciousness of each living soul. Too often we do not have that heart. Too often we are too narrow. Our attitude is, if God blesses us, fine, we do not care about the rest of the world; but let us look at the world and all its sufferings and see God's heart towards this world. In His patience and mercy He sends warnings upon warnings to the people of this world. All the disasters which are occurring today are God's warnings to this world because of the wickedness of this generation. He desires that people would repent and return to Him. That is the heart of God. May the church today have God's heart of compassion. May we be filled with His mercy, just as He is so merciful and gracious towards this world, and may we not be like Jonah—an unwilling prophet—but may we be willing like the Lord Jesus was to tell people of the glad tidings of His salvation.

So I do believe that this is the preeminent lesson which God wants us to learn from this book of Jonah—the mercy and forbearance of God.

Let us pray:

> *Dear heavenly Father, we marvel at Thy mercy, at Thy compassion, at Thy love towards the world. We do acknowledge that, so far as we human beings are concerned, there is nothing for You to love. The world of man is full of sin, violence, corruption, wickedness, rebellion. But God, we do want to thank Thee for Thy long-suffering and forbearance. Truly, Lord God, if it were not because of Thy mercy and compassion, we already would ourselves have been consumed. But we thank Thee that Thou hast spared us. We thank Thee that Thou hast given us repentance and belief in Thy beloved Son. We do pray that Thy merciful heart will fill us so that we too may become a merciful, gracious and compassionate people, that we will truly love the world—not the things of the world but the people of the world—as Thou dost love them, and share with them Thy goodness. Oh God, we do pray that in these last days, as long as Thy judgment has not yet come, many in this world will turn to Thee, that Thou wilt have a people out of every nation, every tribe and every tongue to be gathered unto Thy beloved Son and to worship and serve Thee. We ask in the name of our Lord Jesus. Amen.*

MICAH

WHO IS A GOD LIKE UNTO THEE?

Micah 1:1-7—The word of Jehovah that came to Micah the Morasthite in the days of Jotham, Ahaz, and Hezekiah, kings of Judah, which he saw concerning Samaria and Jerusalem. Hear, ye peoples, all of you; hearken, O earth, and all that is therein: and let the Lord Jehovah be witness against you, the Lord from his holy temple! For behold, Jehovah cometh forth out of his place, and will come down, and tread upon the high places of the earth. And the mountains shall be melted under him, and the valleys shall be cleft, as wax before the fire, as waters poured down a steep place. For the transgression of Jacob is all this, and for the sins of the house of Israel. Whence is the transgression of Jacob? is it not from Samaria? And whence are the high places of Judah? are they not from Jerusalem? Therefore will I make Samaria as a heap of the field, as plantings of a vineyard; and I will pour down the stones thereof into the valley, and I will lay bare the foundations thereof. And all her graven images shall be beaten to pieces, and all her harlot-gifts shall be burned with fire, and all her idols will I make a desolation; for of the hire of a harlot hath she gathered them, and to a harlot's hire shall they return.

Micah 3:1-4—And I said, Hear, I pray you, ye heads of Jacob, and princes of the house of Israel: Is it not for you to know judgment? Ye who hate the good, and love evil; who pluck off their skin from them, and their flesh from off their bones; and who eat the flesh of my people, and flay their skin from off them, and break their bones, and chop them in pieces as for the pot, and as flesh within the cauldron. Then shall they cry unto Jehovah, but he will not answer them; and he will hide his face from them at that time, according as they have wrought evil in their doings.

> *Micah 6:1-5—Hear ye now what Jehovah saith: Arise, contend before the mountains, and let the hills hear thy voice. Hear, ye mountains, Jehovah's controversy, and ye, unchanging foundations of the earth; for Jehovah hath a controversy with his people, and he will plead with Israel. O my people, what have I done unto thee? and wherein have I wearied thee? testify against me. For I brought thee up out of the land of Egypt, and redeemed thee out of the house of bondage; and I sent before thee Moses, Aaron, and Miriam. My people, remember now what Balak king of Moab consulted, and what Balaam the son of Beor answered him, from Shittim unto Gilgal, that ye may know the righteousness of Jehovah.*

> *Micah 7:18-20—Who is a God like unto thee, that forgiveth iniquity, and passeth by the transgression of the remnant of his heritage? He retaineth not his anger for ever, because he delighteth in loving-kindness. He will yet again have compassion on us, he will tread under foot our iniquities: and thou wilt cast all their sins into the depths of the sea. Thou wilt perform truth to Jacob, loving-kindness to Abraham, which thou hast sworn unto our fathers, from the days of old.*

Let us pray:

> *Dear heavenly Father, as we gather together again in the name of Thy beloved Son, our Lord Jesus, we know that we are in Thy presence. We pray that Thy word will come forth from Thy throne to Thy people. We pray that Thou wilt open our ears and our understanding that we may hear Thy voice. We pray that we may repent and return to Thee as Thou wilt return to us. We pray that we may know Thee in a way that we have never known before. Lord, we want to know Thee. In Thy precious name. Amen.*

Micah's name is the combination of three Hebrew words which together mean "Who is like Jehovah?" He was a Morasthite from the village of Moresheth, in the plain of Judah near the border of the Philistine city of Gath. This is to distinguish him from the many Micahs one finds in the Bible, and especially from another famous one, Micah the son of Imlah. I wonder if we remember how, during the time of Ahab and Jehoshaphat, Micah son of Imlah, who at that time was the only true prophet of God, prophesied the death of Ahab; but he lived about one hundred and fifty years prior to the Micah of this book.

This Micah prophesied during the reigns of Jotham, Ahaz and Hezekiah, the kings of Judah the southern kingdom. His contemporaries were Isaiah in the south and Hosea in the north. We know the prophet Hosea began prophesying very early and prophesied for a long period, but he lived in the northern kingdom of Israel. Isaiah was prophesying in the southern kingdom of Judah. Micah actually began his prophetic ministry a little later than Isaiah began his and concluded his ministry earlier than did Isaiah. The reason we know this is because in reading the book of Micah we learn that he prophesied the destruction of Samaria; which destruction was for him an event yet to be realized—though it would occur in the near future. But we know from II Kings 17 that Samaria was destroyed by the Assyrian Empire in the fourth reign year of King Hezekiah. So that is the reason we know that his prophetic ministry closed earlier than did that of the prophet Isaiah. Nevertheless, in his prophesying he sounded together the dominant notes to be found in the ministry of both Isaiah and Hosea. For example, Micah agreed with Isaiah in denouncing the moral corruption of God's people and nation; and he also prophesied concerning the coming of the Messiah, something for which Isaiah was particularly noted. Moreover, Micah simultaneously exhibited in his ministry the compassion of the prophet Hosea.

Micah is mentioned in the book of Jeremiah. Towards the closing days of the nation of Judah the wicked King Jehoiakim, together with the priests, wanted to kill Jeremiah because he had been prophesying against the nation. But there were some princes there who were God-fearing, and they mentioned to Jehoiakim that during the time of Hezekiah Micah the Morasthite had prophesied that Jerusalem would be plowed under like a field and that Hezekiah had not killed him; rather, Hezekiah had listened to Micah's prophecy (see Jeremiah 26:18-19). The incident involving Jeremiah had occurred about a hundred and twenty years later. So we must acknowledge that the prophecy of Micah occupies a very important place in the word of God.

First of all, we would like to know what is the theme of Micah's prophecy. Some have thought that the theme is arraignment, that is to say, a calling of the people to come and hear the judgment of the Lord upon them. Now it is true that we do find in his prophecy the calling of his people to come and hear God's judgment; but if we read more carefully, we shall discern that the theme of Micah's prophecy is actually not negative at all; it is most positive. As a matter of fact, at the closing of his prophecy the last three verses in essence sum up all of his prophetic utterance, and these three verses therefore constitute the theme of this book: "Who is a God like unto thee?"

We mentioned at the very beginning that the name Micah means "Who is like Jehovah?" That was the prophet's name, and thus we shall see that Micah identified himself with his message. There is no one like the Lord Jehovah. He is incomparable; He is unique; He stands alone, all by himself; He is different; and that is Micah's message, whose very name reflects the message he continually declared. Such is the God whom Micah knew. He knew Him to be the God who is unique, who is different from all gods: wonderful, glorious, and loving. In one respect the messenger of God must identify himself with his message; otherwise, that message will not ring true. And here we behold a prophet whose whole life, as is represented by his name, is one with the message which he delivered. He not only delivered the Lord's message; he also himself was the very embodiment of that message. And that is why his message was so powerful: Who is a God like Thee?

Our God is the almighty God. He is the One who created the heavens and the earth, yet Micah did not present God in that regard. Instead, he presented God as the One who forgives iniquity; for that is the aspect of God he knew. Now, of course, our God is the almighty One, the Creator of the heavens and earth, He is the all powerful, almighty God; and yet, redemption is greater than creation. God as the One who forgives and redeems is greater than the God who creates. Forgiving iniquity makes our God unique because all the gods created by man are formed, defined, even confined according to human concepts. In the latter there is no thought of free, pardoning mercy, and that is the reason why all the gods which man creates are hard, harsh, cruel, demanding and vengeful. There is no mercy and no forgiveness because that is alien to human thought. We can therefore say that the Judeo-Christian God is unique because His very nature is mercy. Now it is true that God sometimes must judge, but He does not delight in judging. On the contrary, His delight is in expressing loving-kindness. And even when He does judge, it is His abnormal work, which He wants to accomplish very shortly and very quickly. God's normal work is to show mercy because that is what He really is. So here the prophet declares: "Who is a God like unto thee, that forgiveth iniquity [for He loves to forgive] and passeth by the transgression of the remnant of his heritage?"

How could God pass by the transgression of the remnant of His heritage? The duty of God, being just, is to punish, if there be any transgression. Most certainly God dislikes punishing His people because He loves to bless and not to judge. But if there be transgression, if there be any sin against His law, it is His duty as a just God to judge. How, then, can He pass by our transgression without in the process making himself unjust? He has to judge in order to vindicate himself, so how is it that He can pass by man's transgression? Thank God that He made a provision: He sent His beloved Son, the Lord Jesus, into this world to die for us, to pay our debts, and to receive judgment on our behalf. Only because of this can God pass by the transgressions of those who believe and repose faith in His beloved Son, the Lord Jesus.

Now the word remnant, in the prophet's statement that God "passeth by the transgression of the remnant of his heritage," refers to those who believe in what God has provided for them in the Savior. The prophet Micah further declared that "He retaineth not his anger for ever." Yes, it is quite true that God has to be angry with us because we have sinned against Him, but He will not retain His anger forever because that would not be like Him. On the contrary, He delighteth in showing loving-kindness; for that is what His nature verily is.

Moreover, said Micah, God "will yet again have compassion on us, he will tread under foot our iniquities: and thou wilt cast all their sins into the depths of the sea." To tread underfoot our iniquities means our iniquities have been judged and dealt with. And to cast our sins into the depths of the sea means that they disappear—not only are they forgiven, they are also forgotten altogether.

Furthermore, reads the prophecy, "thou wilt perform truth to Jacob, loving-kindness to Abraham." God demonstrated His loving-kindness to Abraham by having given him promises, and God gave truth to Jacob by His having made a covenant with him. All this, Micah announced, God "has sworn unto our fathers, from the days of old."

What in essence, therefore, is the message of Micah? It is one of forgiveness, of loving-kindness, of compassion. In short, it is a message of telling what a God we have! And if we truly see this, we cannot help but bow and worship Him.

The message of Micah is in three parts and one can very easily notice it because each part begins with the word "hear." The first part runs from 1:2 through 2:13: "Hear, ye peoples, all of you." The second part is again introduced by the word "hear" and is found in 3:1: "Hear, ... princes of the house of Israel." The third part runs from chapter 6 through chapter 7. Again we find that word "hear"—"Hear the mountains and the hills." In these three parts there are similarities. They all begin with a kind of indictment: an arraignment marked by judging, telling the people what is wrong with them. They each then follow with threatenings of judgment that will come upon the people, but all three parts end with promises.

GOD CALLS ALL TO COME AND HEAR

"Hear, ye peoples, all of you; hearken, O earth, and all that is therein: and let the Lord Jehovah be witness against you, the Lord from his holy temple! For behold, Jehovah cometh forth out of his place." Here in this first part of Micah's message the Lord is calling all people of the earth to come and hear; not just Israel, not just Judah, but God is calling all peoples upon the earth to come and hear the Lord Jehovah from his holy temple. Now it is true that what they would hear is God's arraignment of Israel and Judah, especially of

Samaria—the capital city of Israel—and Jerusalem—the capital city of Judah—because sins seem to mount up in the capital cities and then spread over the land of these two nations. But when God judged Israel and Judah, He wanted all the peoples of the earth to hear about it because Israel and Judah were to serve as examples to the entire world. The intent was to make clear that if God will judge His chosen people, will He spare the rest of the nations if they, too, sin against Him? But because Israel and Judah were God's chosen ones, therefore, God's judgment came to them first—and more severely—because they were supposed to represent God. So the whole world is to witness and hear what God was going to say.

To be in His temple was God's normal place, and that was the place of blessing. But here we read: "Behold, Jehovah cometh out of his place." In other words, He came out of His normal place of blessing; He came out to judge. Here we see Micah being more attentive to the moral corruption and social decay of the nations. The people were talking and planning during the night in their beds, and during the daytime they commenced doing the wicked works they had devised in their minds. It began with Israel, and then it influenced Judah. The people had departed from God to worship Baal; and because of their departure, religious and moral corruption quickly followed. People began to be immoral, to be greedy, and to gather wealth for themselves. In addition, they oppressed people and shed much blood; and all kinds of other wicked things happened. These two nations had thus fallen, and because they had fallen, God could not refrain from judging.

At the same time false prophets began rising up everywhere because the people's ears had been itching to hear what they liked to hear. And sure enough, there had been plenty of suppliers; so false prophets had emerged everywhere. The people did not hear the word of God and, because of this, Micah prophesied what the Lord had said: "Therefore will I make Samaria as a heap of the field, as plantings of a vineyard; and I will pour down the stones thereof into the valley, and I will lay bare the foundations thereof" (1:6).

This prophecy was very quickly fulfilled because in the fourth year of Hezekiah the Assyrian king came over and destroyed Samaria. As a matter of fact, what Micah prophesied here was literally fulfilled in that the stones were poured down into the valley; for the city of Samaria had been built on a hill; so when Samaria was destroyed, the stones from the walls were thrown down into the valley and the very foundation of Samaria was laid bare.

Even so, there were indications given in Micah's message of God's promise mixed with His judgment. In chapter 1, for example, we find Micah playing with words; he mentioned many cities and what happened to these cities. Yet, while doing so he made a play on words similar to what we might do when saying, for instance, that there is no brotherly love in Philadelphia. But let us notice that in this playing with words Micah was talking about destruction and yet, suddenly in verse 15, God through His prophet announces this: "I will yet bring unto thee an heir, O inhabitress of Mareshah; the glory of Israel shall come even unto Adullam." Thus, we can discern that in between pronouncing all the judgments of the Lord, suddenly Micah mentioned that an heir would be coming. Who is this heir that is to come? The Son of God, whom God has made heir of all things (see Hebrews 1:2). And God through Micah also mentioned "the glory of Israel." What or who is the glory of Israel? The Messiah is that glory. Hence, we see that even with Micah's pronouncement of God's judgment, he nonetheless interjects some encouraging hints—to the effect that God will yet bring in the glory of Israel.

We can detect this same phenomenon in chapter 2: "I will surely assemble, O Jacob, the whole of thee; I will surely gather the remnant of Israel; I will put them together as sheep of Bozrah, as a flock in the midst of their pasture: they shall make great noise by reason of the multitude of men. One that breaketh through is gone up before them: they have broken forth, and have passed on to the gate, and are gone out by it; and their king passeth on before them, and Jehovah at the head of them" (vv. 12-13). In short, amidst words of terrible judgment there can also be found the Lord's promises, and that is like our God.

GOD CALLS THE LEADERS TO HEAR

The second part of Micah's message again begins with "Hear"—"Hear I pray you, ye heads of Jacob, and princes of the house of

Israel." In this instance, however, instead of calling all peoples to come and hear His judgment as well as His promise for Israel, He now directly summons the rulers of Israel and Judah—the princes and the heads of the house of Israel. And, subsequently, in verse 5 we read that He also calls the prophets and mentions the priests. These all are the leaders of these two nations. The word further declares: "Is it not for you [leaders] to know judgment?" God does indeed raise up rulers and leaders, but these are to be God's servants. This we find spelled out in Romans 13—that rulers are God's servants, that they are supposed to serve His purpose, do His will, and judge with His judgment. Instead, these Jewish rulers and leaders had fallen terribly: we learn from Micah that the princes had judged for reward, the priests had taught for hire, and the prophets had divined for money. The very ones who were supposed to be rulers and leaders, leading the people to God to do His will, had so fallen that they had misrepresented Him completely. They were the very ones who had led the people away into corruption and decay. So God's judgment was upon these leaders: "Therefore shall Zion for your sake be ploughed as a field, and Jerusalem shall become heaps, and the mountain of the house as the high places of a forest" (3:12).

In chapter 1 there was prophecy pronounced against Samaria, and it was literally fulfilled in the fourth year of King Hezekiah. Here, however, is a prophecy against Jerusalem—that it would be plowed under as a field, that it would be completely destroyed. Now we know that about one hundred and thirty-six years after that prophecy, Jerusalem was destroyed by Babylon and the people were taken into captivity. But, strangely, we do not find that at that time Jerusalem was plowed under as a field. Yes, it was destroyed but not plowed under. Even so, eight centuries later, in A.D. 70, when the Romans under Titus laid siege to Jerusalem and finally broke into the city, they not only destroyed the temple—with not a stone upon a stone left standing; it being a literal fulfillment of Christ's prophecy (see Mark 3:2)—but history also tells us that at that time a Roman general, Rufus by name, under the order from the throne in Rome, actually plowed Jerusalem under as would one do so to a field. This was meant to give expression to the utter destruction of the conquered city.

Now why did God wait eight centuries for the prophecy to be fully fulfilled? It is because the sin of rejecting God's beloved Son is the fullness of all sin. Hence, actually, what Micah prophesied here was literally fulfilled concerning Jerusalem; nevertheless, we find God's greatest promise being given simultaneously. Is it not a wonderful prophecy which we read in Micah chapter 5:2?—"(And thou, Bethlehem Ephratah, little to be among the thousands of Judah, out of thee shall he come forth unto me who is to be Ruler in Israel: whose goings forth are from of old, from the days of eternity.)"

Within the very context of utter judgment being pronounced upon God's people there is that magnificent promise that One will be born in Bethlehem Ephratah who is the One who is from the beginning, whose goings forth are from of old, from the days of eternity. In other words, unto us a child is born, a Son is given. This is fulfilled as told of in the text of Matthew 2. Indeed, the Pharisees and scribes knew the Old Testament very well; for when Herod heard from the Eastern wise men that the King of the Jews had been born, he gathered these scribes and Pharisees and asked where the King of the Jews was to be born, and they revealed that they knew this very Scripture by heart. (By comparison, I think we should be ashamed of ourselves!) They did not need to search the matter out; they neither had nor needed a concordance in order to give an accurate response, for immediately they replied: "The Messiah shall be born in Bethlehem," quoting as they did so Micah 5:2. (Many of us today cannot even find the book of Micah in the Bible!) This promise of God was literally fulfilled.

Not only that, but we read in Micah chapters 4 and 5 that this One promised will lead the world; He will bring in peace because He is Peace. Let us acknowledge that there will not be peace upon this earth unless the Prince of Peace returns because His name is Peace.

There is also that very much quoted passage to be found in Micah chapter 4:1-3: "But it shall come to pass in the end of days that the mountain of Jehovah's house shall be established on the top of the mountains, and shall be lifted up above the hills; and the peoples shall flow unto it. And many nations shall go and say, Come, and let us go up to the mountain of Jehovah, and to the house of the God of Jacob; and he will teach us of his ways, and we will walk in his paths. For out of Zion shall go forth the law, and Jehovah's word from Jerusalem. And he shall judge among many peoples, and reprove strong nations, even afar off; and they shall forge their swords into ploughshares, and their spears into pruning-knives: nation shall not lift up sword against nation, neither shall they learn war any more."

Here in Micah we find an almost exact wording of Isaiah chapter 2:2-4 being used. All this will yet come to pass in this world. There will come a day when all the swords will be forged into ploughshares and all the spears will be turned into pruning-knives, and there will not be any war, for the people will not learn war anymore. There will be peace over this whole earth, and we know this will come to the earth when the One who is called Peace shall return. Again, how marvelous it is that, in the midst of judgment, there are such wonderful promises made to the world. This demonstrates, does it not, that our God is totally different from the gods of this world? Oh! Who, indeed, is like our God?

GOD CALLS THE MOUNTAINS AND THE HILLS TO HEAR

In the third part of Micah's message, once again it is introduced by the word "hear": "Hear ye now what Jehovah saith: Arise, contend before the mountains, and let the hills hear thy voice. Hear, ye mountains, Jehovah's controversy, and ye, unchanging foundations of the earth; for Jehovah hath a controversy with his people, and he will plead with Israel" (6:1-2).

The first summons to "hear" is "Hear all peoples of the earth what God has to say against Israel and Judah." The second summons to "hear" is "Hear, ye leaders of the nations." And now God is summoning the mountains and the hills to hear. It is as if human ears are quite deaf; that the ears of the earth's people do not hear, and that even the ears of God's chosen people do not hear. So God is compelled to call the mountains and the hills to hear what He has to say.

This is similar to what we find in Luke 19:40. When the Lord Jesus entered Jerusalem the last time—during the last week of His earthly life—and the disciples had witnessed what God had done through Him, they began to say, "Hosanna, glory to the King that has come in the name of the Lord." And upon hearing this the Pharisees told the Lord Jesus to silence them. But He replied: "If they keep silent, the stones will cry out." And here we find a similar circumstance. It is as though human ears were so deaf that God in Micah's day had to call out: "Mountains and hills, hear the controversy that I have with My people." Is it not sad that there should have been a controversy between Jehovah and His covenanted people? They ought to have been obeying Him, ought to have been doing His will, but there was an ongoing controversy between Jehovah and His covenanted people. And so God pleaded with His people, saying: "O my people, what have I done unto thee? and wherein have I wearied thee? testify against me."

Let us clearly understand that the Spirit of the Lord is not One of vengeance. Though He has to judge, though He has cause to be angry, the Spirit is One of grief. It is a Spirit of love being hurt and wounded. "O my people, what have I done? testify against me. If I have done anything wrong, testify against me." What humility! What love! Even though God had a controversy with His very own people, He reminded them how He had led them out of Egypt, how He had given them leaders like Moses, Aaron and Miriam, and how He had turned curse into blessing out of the mouth of Balaam. In other words, how God continued to love them and provide them with everything, and why, then, should they rise up as His enemies? And now there was no godly one among the people, not even one. Moreover, no one could trust his friends anymore, not even the one who lies in his bosom. Each one had become selfish to the uttermost. A person could not trust anybody any longer. Furthermore, the shedding of blood was present everywhere. Things had become so bad that the situation had forced God to judge, yet it was not His pleasure to do so; rather, it was His delight to show loving-kindness. Thank God, though, that His pleading seemed to have opened some ears, if not all ears, because we read in the book of Micah the following passage in response to God's pleading: "Wherewith shall I come before Jehovah, bow myself before the high God? Shall I come before him with burnt-offerings, with calves of a year old? Will Jehovah take pleasure in thousands of rams, in ten thousands of rivers of oil? Shall I give my firstborn for my transgression, the fruit of my body for the sin of my soul? He hath shewn thee, O man, what is good: and what doth Jehovah require of thee, but to do justly, and to love goodness, and to walk humbly with thy God?" (6:6-8)

His pleading had indeed touched some of the hearts of His people. These were the remnant of the people who now turned to the Lord, saying: "Lord, what should we do? Shall we bring offerings and sacrifices to Thee? What can we do?" And the Lord's response was that what He desired was not any outward display but the inward reality—to do justly, to love goodness, and to walk humbly with their God. What He desired was repentance. While it is true that He has to judge, nevertheless, those who really respond to God's pleading could now say: "But as for me, I will look unto Jehovah; I will wait for the God of my salvation: my God will hear me. Rejoice not against me, O mine enemy: though I fall, I shall arise; when I sit in darkness, Jehovah shall be a light unto me. I will bear the indignation of Jehovah—for I have sinned against him—until he plead my cause, and execute judgment for me: he will bring me forth to the light; I shall behold his righteousness" (7:7-9).

For those who repent and submit themselves under the mighty hand of God in humility until God's work in them is done, light will come upon them and salvation will come to them. And God will enlarge them and bring even their enemies to them, and thus the whole world will come under the reign of the King of kings and the Lord of lords.

This is the message which God gave to Judah and to Israel back then through the prophet Micah. Yet what is the lesson from Micah for us today? The study of prophecy is not only for the purpose of learning history and prophecy, it is also for receiving admonition because all Scripture is given to us for our admonition that we may learn something spiritually valuable (see II Timothy 3:16-17). What, then, are we to learn from Micah? Does it ring true to you when God says "Hear"? In Revelation 2 and 3, seven times God's word declares: "He that has an ear to hear, let him hear what the Spirit says to the churches." God is speaking to His people because He loves them so much. Unfortunately, however, His people's ears are stopped up with some foreign matter. They cannot hear. So the Bible repeatedly says: "He that has an ear, let him hear what the Spirit says to the churches." Not only in the olden days did the Spirit of God speak through the prophets, not only in the time of John the apostle did the Spirit speak to the churches in the province of Asia, but even today, God's Spirit is likewise speaking to us through His written word. And there is in fact a word for us in Micah.

Whereas the northern kingdom of Israel represents the apostate church the southern kingdom of Judah represents the faithful church. Yet today we can readily observe that not only the apostate church but even also the faithful church has fallen. In these last days, is it not true in Christianity that love for the Lord has grown cold not only among those who have altogether departed from the truth in apostasy but even also among those who have been faithful? Do we not see that the truth of God has been departed from? Do we not see that God's people have become worldly? The world has come in and taken over the church. Christianity has become a world religious system. Even among the faithful, how many have actually remained faithful to the Lord? How many have remained faithful to the testimony of Jesus? Are we not in the same position as were Israel and Judah in those olden days? Is it not obvious that God is angry with us? Judgment must therefore begin with the house of God (I Peter 4:17a) because His house—the church—is supposed to represent Him in this world. The world is looking to the church to know who God is, to know what kind of God He is. But how she today has misrepresented Him!

Who is like Jehovah? Does the world see that our God is different? Does the world know that our God delights in showing loving-kindness? Does it know that our God has compassion? He loves to forgive. His anger is but for a night. He is the faithful God who keeps His covenant and His truth. Yet does the world know about that? How do we represent God? Where is the testimony of Jesus to the world? The cry is: "Repent; return; return to the beginning; return to the simplicity that is in Christ"—"Those who have ears, let them hear what the Spirit says to the churches" (see II Corinthians 11:3b; Revelation 2-3).

It is quite true that judgment will come and not be spared. It will come to the church, and it will also come to the whole world; yet God is looking for a remnant among His heritage. In New Testament terms we can say that God is looking for overcomers. The Lord speaks and says, He that overcomes ...(see Revelation 2-3). Yet who is he that overcomes? Not so-called super Christians, but normal Christians. The latter are no better than anybody else, but they repent and return to God in humility. Such are the overcomers. They are willing to submit themselves under the mighty hand of God until "the indignation of Jehovah" passes over and light shines and salvation comes upon this earth.

So in these last days God is in need of many Micahs. God needs many brethren whose very name—whose very being—is a testimony to the world: Who is like our God? Our God is different. God needs many who will bring to this world the message which Micah brought. We want to tell the world that our God is incomparable, that He is the only One, that He is the only hope.

We will recall that when Israel sinned in worshiping the golden calf, Moses went up the Sinai mount to atone for the children of Israel, and God forgave them. Moses pleaded with God, "Show me thy glory." And God said, "You cannot see it. No man can see My glory and live. But I will let you see My back." So while Moses was still on the mountain, God passed by and covered Moses' sight with His hand until He had passed and then God declared concerning His name: "Jehovah, Jehovah God, merciful and gracious, slow to anger, and abundant in goodness and truth, keeping mercy unto thousands, forgiving iniquity and transgression and sin, but by no means clearing the guilty; visiting the iniquity of the fathers upon the children, and upon the children's children, upon the third and upon the fourth generation. And Moses made haste, and bowed his head to the earth and worshipped" (Exodus 34:6-8).

Now such as this is the message of Micah; this is what God declares concerning himself. And if we truly hear and know who He is, we will respond like Moses and bow down and worship God.

Let us pray:

> *Oh Lord God, You are all alone. There is none like You. You are merciful, gracious, You delight in showing loving-kindness, and love to forgive; and yet You are righteous and just. Oh how we praise and thank Thee. It is because of what Thou art that there is hope for us. It is because of what Thou art that Thou hast provided the Redeemer for us. It is because of what Thou art that we are here this morning. We do worship Thee. Thou art the only God. Thou art the one true God. There is no other. Praise the Lord. Amen.*

NAHUM

THE SEVERITY OF GOD

Nahum 1:1-15—The burden of Nineveh. The book of the vision of Nahum the Elkoshite. A jealous and avenging God is Jehovah: an avenger is Jehovah, and full of fury: Jehovah taketh vengeance on his adversaries, and he reserveth wrath for his enemies. Jehovah is slow to anger, and great in power, and doth not at all clear the guilty: Jehovah,—his way is in the whirlwind and in the storm, and the clouds are the dust of his feet. He rebuketh the sea, and maketh it dry, and drieth up all the rivers: Bashan languisheth, and Carmel, and the flower of Lebanon languisheth. The mountains quake before him, and the hills melt, and the earth is upheaved at his presence, and the world, and all that dwell therein. Who shall stand before his indignation? and who shall abide in the fierceness of his anger? His fury is poured out like fire, and the rocks are broken asunder by him. Jehovah is good, a stronghold in the day of trouble; and he knoweth them that trust in him. But with an overrunning flood he will make a full end of the place thereof, and darkness shall pursue his enemies. What do ye imagine against Jehovah? He will make a full end: trouble shall not rise up the second time. Though they be tangled together as thorns, and be as drenched from their drink, they shall be devoured as dry stubble, completely. Out of thee is gone forth one that imagineth evil against Jehovah, a wicked counsellor. Thus saith Jehovah: Though they be complete in number, and many as they be, even so shall they be cut down, and he shall pass away; and though I have afflicted thee, I will afflict thee no more. And now will I break his yoke from off thee, and will burst thy bonds asunder. And Jehovah hath given commandment concerning thee, that no more of thy name be sown: out of the house of thy god will I cut off the graven image, and the molten image: I will prepare

> *thy grave; for thou art vile. Behold upon the mountains the feet of him that bringeth glad tidings, that publisheth peace! Celebrate thy feasts, Judah, perform thy vows: for the wicked one shall no more pass through thee; he is utterly cut off.*

Let us pray:

> *Dear heavenly Father, as we continue in Thy presence, we do praise and thank Thee for Thy blessed word. We thank Thee that Thou art a God who speaks. Thou hast spoken and Thou dost still speak, and we do expect Thee to speak to us again through Thy word. We give this time unto Thee and ask Thy Holy Spirit to do the work for which Thou hast sent Him forth, to the praise of Thy glory. In the name of our Lord Jesus. Amen.*

The very name Nahum means "compassion," "comfort," or "be comforted." We are not given his background. Usually when a prophet in the Old Testament is introduced, we are told whose son he is, but not so with Nahum. We are only told "Nahum the Elkoshite," and even up to the present, we are not certain where Elkosh was located. Some say it was somewhere in Galilee and some say it was some place near Nineveh. The only thing we are sure of is that he was a prophet whom God had raised up in the southern kingdom of Judah.

Now usually, in the books of the minor prophets or even in those of the so-called major ones, the Bible gives the time during which the prophet prophesied—as in the days of king so and so—but in this book of Nahum, we are not even given that information. And yet from internal evidence I believe we can come quite close to knowing the time when the prophet Nahum was prophesying. This is because we know that by that time the northern kingdom of Israel had already been destroyed. We shall recall that it was destroyed in the fourth year of King Hezekiah by the king of Assyria, whereas the southern kingdom of Judah still continued to exist, though admittedly in a very weakened state.

At the time of King Hezekiah, Sennacherib, the king of Assyria, had come with his army over to Judah and had attacked its cities and had even sent his military chief to Jerusalem demanding surrender. Hezekiah prayed, and through the prophet Isaiah it was prophesied that God would do a new thing and destroy the army of the Assyrians; and God verily did so in a most miraculous way (see II Kings 19). But after Sennacherib returned to his capital of Nineveh, he was murdered by his sons. Then one of these sons, Esarhaddon, succeeded him, and he resumed the undertaking of Assyrian expeditions again. He came to the Mediterranean region where, according to II Chronicles 33, his captains captured Manasseh, the son of Hezekiah, and bound him with chains of brass and brought him captive to Babylon where at that time the king of Assyria resided. Now Manasseh, the son of Hezekiah, had been a most wicked king.

We will recall that there came a time when God told Hezekiah to set his house in order because his time on earth was coming to a close; but Hezekiah did not want to die, so he turned his face towards the wall and cried out to the Lord to spare him of death. God heard his cry and gave him fifteen more years. But during those fifteen years, two tragedies for the people of Judah happened. One was that Hezekiah's son Manasseh was born, and the other was when the king of Babylon came to comfort Hezekiah over God having spared his life—prompting Hezekiah to show off all his wealth to the Babylonian king. Eventually, Babylon would come and destroy Judah.

So Manasseh, having been born during that fifteen-year period, became one of the most wicked kings Judah ever had. He introduced all kinds of idol worship; he even set up idols in the court of the temple of God. He in his wickedness thus led the whole nation away from God. And because of that, God sent prophets to warn him and the people; but the king would not listen. Finally, God allowed Manasseh to be taken captive, to be bound and brought to Babylon. But thank God that while he was in deep trouble, he repented and cried out to the Lord; the Lord heard him and he was released. Manasseh returned to Jerusalem and began to build up the kingdom of Judah again. He destroyed all the idols and restored the true worship in the temple; however, people still worshiped in the high places—yet they did so only to Jehovah. So in King Manasseh's latter years, there was a kind of national restoration, and most probably it was during this restorative period that Nahum was raised up by God to be a prophet to the nation of Judah. Even so, Judah was very weak; there was only a remnant of Israelites there. Meanwhile, under King Esarhaddon, Assyria was approaching the height of its military strength. And hence, there was always a fear in Judah that at some point Assyria would come back and destroy the nation. In view of that, God sent Nahum to the nation of Judah.

JUDGMENT ON NINEVEH

We will recall that one hundred and thirty years earlier, a prophet by the name of Jonah had been sent from the northern kingdom of Israel to Nineveh by God to proclaim the same message that later Nahum was also to proclaim. Jonah actually went to Nineveh and proclaimed that in forty days the city would be destroyed; but the city and nation repented and God spared them. Then God raised up another prophet, Nahum, and the burden God gave him was that of Nineveh; and yet, he was not sent to preach directly to its people. Instead, he remained in Judah and prophesied to the nation of Judah. His prophecy concerned the destruction of Nineveh, and it was a real comfort to Judah because the people had been in fear and trembling that one day Assyria (that is, Nineveh) would come and destroy them. But the prophet said that God would destroy Assyria and that she would never come again. It was therefore actually an encouragement to God's people because the Israelites returned to Him. God comforted their hearts by indicating through Nahum that He would destroy their enemy and would save them.

At the same time, the prophecy served not only as an encouragement but also as a warning. A century and more earlier Nineveh had been set to be destroyed because of their many sins, but through repentance they were spared. But when much later they fell back into their sins, judgment eventually caught up with them. So now with respect to Judah, Nahum's prophecy would serve as a warning; the same thing could and would happen to the people of Judah if they, too, refused to repent. But if they returned to the Lord, the Lord might spare them; and if later they would fall back into sin, then God—being just—must mete out His judgment upon them. So the prophecy of Nahum was both an encouragement and a warning to the nation of Judah.

Now in order to understand Nahum better we must put the book of Jonah and the book of Nahum together, because the latter is actually the continuation of Jonah. Nahum is also a complement to Jonah, for the burden of both these prophets was the same concerning Nineveh. Jonah was sent directly to Nineveh and, through his preaching, the city and its people were spared: the nation of Assyria was preserved through repentance; but one hundred and thirty years later, Nineveh returned to its former violence, sins, pride and arrogance. Its people forgot what God had earlier done for them, what mercy He had shown them, and accordingly they began to believe in themselves and in their own strength. They even challenged God himself by plotting against Him, as it were, and because of that, the message of Nahum was that Nineveh would be utterly destroyed.

As was pointed out earlier, during this period, Nineveh was at the height of its military might. It was the capital of the mighty kingdom of Assyria, and it was called in Scripture a great city. Indeed, someone has pointed out that in the Old Testament this is the only city of which the Bible says, "the great city ..." We know, of course, that Nineveh had been founded ages ago by the rebel Nimrod, whose works ultimately led to the beginning of world empires. In essence he had become a dictator who attempted to build up a kingdom, and whose labors were connected with the tower of Babel. Such was the historical beginning of Nineveh.

Now in the time of Nahum the city of Nineveh had a wall one hundred feet high with a circumference of some sixty to ninety miles. Can you imagine that? Furthermore, the wall was broad enough at its top for three or four chariots to be driven abreast; it also had over 1,200 defensive towers, and it was totally surrounded by the waters of the Tigris River. It was impregnable, especially when one is aware of the methods of ancient warfare. In short, nobody could take Nineveh. So in the latter part of the seventh century B.C., when Babylon began to raise its head, she joined in with the Medes to lay siege to Nineveh. Nineveh successfully resisted that siege for over two years; her enemies could not break into the city. Even though Mede-Babylon had cut off all connections between Nineveh and the outside world and had completely surrounded the city, it stood its ground for over two years. However, during the third year of the siege, there arose such a violent rain storm that the river overflowed its banks. As a consequence, the city was inundated and part of the wall collapsed. Now there had been an old saying among the Ninevites to the effect that "no one shall take Nineveh unless the river first becomes the enemy of the city." And hence, when part of the wall fell down because of the swollen waters, the king thought that this saying was coming true; with the result that he gave up all hope. He accordingly gathered together in the palace his own people—that is to say, all his royal family—and all his wealth, and set fire and burned up everyone and everything. That is how Nineveh was finally destroyed, probably in the year 625 B.C. Even though Nineveh had been such a strong and mighty city, it ultimately was completely destroyed. The prophecy of Nahum was fulfilled.

THE CHARACTER OF GOD

I believe the most important matter to discern while studying this book of Nahum is the character of God. In the previous chapter we reviewed together the book of Micah, and we saw that its central message is: "Who is a God like unto thee, that forgiveth iniquity, and passeth by the transgression of the remnant of his heritage? ... he delighted in loving-kindness. He will yet again have compassion on us, he will tread under foot our iniquities: and thou wilt cast all their sins into the depths of the sea. Thou wilt perform truth to Jacob, loving-kindness to Abraham, which thou hast sworn unto our fathers, from the days of old" (7:18-20).

Indeed, our God is merciful, gracious, forgiving; He delights in showing loving-kindness. Moreover, He will cast our sins into the depths of the sea. He is a faithful God who always remembers His covenant with His people. What a merciful, loving, gracious, forgiving God He is. Such, then, is the God we know, and who can be compared with Him? He is the unique and only God.

But when studying Nahum, we are probably left with the opposite impression because this prophet declares: "A jealous and avenging

God is Jehovah: an avenger is Jehovah, and full of fury." Is there any contradiction here between Micah and Nahum? Let us look at a verse in the New Testament: "Behold then the goodness and severity of God: upon them who have fallen, severity; upon thee goodness of God, if thou shalt abide in goodness, since otherwise thou also wilt be cut away" (Romans 11:22).

Here we find the apostle Paul mentioning the two sides of God's ways of dealing with people. On the one hand, there is severity; on the other hand, there is goodness. Upon those who have fallen there comes severity; but upon those who abide in God's goodness there comes goodness. These two are not contradictory. They are but the two sides of the character of God. As a matter of fact, even when Micah declared that God forgives our iniquities and delights in loving-kindness, he also declared that God does not retain His anger forever. In other words, there is indeed His anger. And it is quite true in Nahum that God is portrayed as a jealous, avenging God who pours out His wrath upon both His adversaries and enemies; but the prophet also makes clear that He is slow to anger. We thus can see that these are the two sides of the character of God. On the one side, His character can be severe: He is not weak at all; nor is He indulgent and careless but strong, just, and right. Yet on the other side, God's character is merciful, gracious, good and faithful to those who trust in Him, who return to Him and abide in His goodness. So these are not contradictory but are complementary; and this is the God whom we know, whom we worship, and whom we serve. We need to know our God more fully, that He is not only merciful and gracious but is also jealous and wreaks vengeance upon those who oppose Him. To live a godly life is to know God as He truly is.

GOD IS JEALOUS

"A jealous and avenging God is Jehovah." We naturally do not like to hear the word "jealous" because in our minds it has a bad connotation. With respect to fallen man, of course, the word will always convey an unpleasant connotation. But we need to recognize that jealousy in and of itself is neutral, and consequently it really depends upon the context. Our God is a jealous God, but in a good sense. The first time we read in the Bible that God is a jealous God is in Exodus 20:5. We may remember that in giving the Ten Commandments to the children of Israel, God declared in the second commandment that they should not make an image of any kind nor worship any image, for "I am a jealous God. I will visit the iniquity of the fathers upon the sons to the third and fourth generation of those that hate me, and I will show mercy to the thousands of those that keep my commandments." So this is the first instance in God's word that we are told He is a jealous God.

JEALOUS FOR HIS GLORY

Now in what sense is He jealous? He is jealous for His glory. What is the glory of God? It is simply this, that our God is the only One; He is unique; He is above all. He is the only One who is worthy to be worshiped and served, and He is very jealous about His glory. In other words, He will not share His glory with anybody else. If anyone wants to share in His glory or attempts to rob Him of His glory, the divine response will be that God is a consuming fire. In Deuteronomy 4:24 we read that God declares that He is a jealous God and a consuming fire. No one can interfere with the glory of God, that is, with what God himself is. Let us realize that the glory of God is in reality what God himself is. He will not allow anything or anyone to interfere with that glory and, because of this, He is jealous—very jealous—about that. This is an issue about which we need to learn much. We need to see most clearly that our God is a jealous God. We also need to be very careful lest in some way we ourselves intrude into this divine area. God is very jealous and, whenever His glory is being interfered with, He will consume the perpetrator with His fire.

JEALOUS FOR HIS NAME

Not only with regard to His glory, God is likewise jealous for His very name. We read in Ezekiel this: "Therefore, thus saith the Lord Jehovah: Now will I bring again the captivity of Jacob, and have mercy upon the whole house of Israel, and will be jealous for my holy name" (39:25).

God is jealous for His name. He committed it to the children of Israel; nevertheless, they did not preserve the holy name of God. On the contrary, they brought shame and reproach to His name, whereas He is very jealous concerning it, and consequently punished the children of Israel because of it. He even raised up Gentiles as His chastising rod to discipline His people for His name's sake so that it would not be put to shame and that the people of the world would not say, "See! Look at this people called by the name of God; ha! that is what He is." We see that God had to vindicate His name with His people. But, then, the rod which God had raised up to serve as His instrument for chastising His people went beyond what He allowed them to do. For they began to trust in their own strength and thought they could do whatever they pleased, they even blaspheming God in saying to the Israelites: "See, the God whom you serve is nothing. We destroyed all the other gods and their kingdoms, so now we will destroy your God and your kingdom." In response, God targeted those Gentile nations and judged them out of His jealousy for His holy name by putting a stop to their blasphemy.

We will recall from the Old Testament record how certain of His people had pleaded before God. For instance, Daniel and Moses both knew that in themselves they had no right to plead; however, there was one thing they could do—they pleaded for God's mercy and grace on behalf of His name. For example, on one occasion Moses had said: "Lord, You have brought this people of Yours out of Egypt by Your mighty deeds and the surrounding nations have heard about it, but if You destroy your people, these unbelieving people will mock and say, 'You are not able to lead them into the Promised Land.' What, then, will happen to Your name?" And God heard Moses.

And Daniel pleaded concerning the same issue: "We have no right; we have sinned; but God, this is a people called by Your name. Think of Your name." And God heard him. So let us always acknowledge that our God is jealous for His holy name.

JEALOUS FOR HIS LOVE

"And the angel that talked with me said unto me, Cry, saying, Thus saith Jehovah of hosts: I am jealous for Jerusalem and for Zion with a great jealousy" (Zechariah 1:14).

Why is God jealous for Jerusalem and for Zion with a great jealousy? It is because of His love. God set His love upon Jerusalem and upon Zion. God has His purpose for Zion and for Jerusalem and is determined to see that what He has purposed out of His love will be fully realized. Whenever that purpose is interrupted, opposed, or interfered with, He becomes very jealous about it. In other words, God will see to it that out of His love His purpose will be fulfilled. We should thank God for such jealousy.

We often view jealousy as not being a very good emotion. But what is love if there is no jealousy? Love is so concentrated and so single in its manifestation that it will not allow anything to diminish it or dampen even a little of its ardor. Love wants to retain it all, and that for us is who God is. He loves us so greatly that He will not allow anything which would take us away from His love or take us away from what His love has determined for us. I say again that we ought to thank God continually for His jealousy. If He were not jealous, He would say this to us: "You can go your way. Even though you are Mine, if you drift away and fail to fulfill My loving purpose, that is all right; I will let go of you and let you be aborted." No; that is not our God. He is jealous and will see to it that His love will accomplish its complete work in those whom He has chosen.

GOD IS THE JUDGE

"An avenger is He." Once again, according to our fallen mind the word avenge conveys a very bad impression. If it were left to us to avenge or wreak vengeance, the result would be most ugly because we are not qualified to undertake such a task. God is the only Judge of all the earth. What would the earth be if there were no righteous judge? God is the Judge of the whole earth, and this Judge always does right. In fact, that is how Abraham could plead before God. When God decided to destroy Sodom and Gomorrah, Abraham pleaded with Him and inquired: "Will the Judge of all the earth do wrong and let the righteous perish with the sinful? Certainly not, for You are a righteous and just God. You are the just Judge of the whole earth." Because of his plea, God heard Abraham and saved Lot. God is the only One who has the necessary knowledge and the power and authority to judge. None of us is qualified to judge or to avenge.

From John 5 we learn that when the Lord Jesus was on earth, He declared: "I can do nothing of Myself; as I hear, I judge, and my judgment is righteous, because I do not seek my own will, but the will of my Father." And after our Lord died and was raised and ascended, God appointed Him as the Judge of all the living and the dead (see Acts 10:42). God in Christ is the only One who is qualified to judge and that is the reason why we are told in Romans 12: "Avenge not yourself, beloved." Do not give yourself to wrath but leave such to God, for "Vengeance is mine," says the Lord, and He will recompense (v. 19). So we know that the just and righteous God, being the Judge of the whole world, must surely avenge and wreak vengeance because if He does not do such work, who, then, will do it?

To show mercy is God's delightful work; to pour out wrath is His unpleasant work. On the one hand, He delights in loving-kindness. On the other hand, though He does not want to judge, nevertheless, because He is the just Judge of the whole earth, He has to judge when forced to; and He will do it. But we also learn from Nahum that He is slow to anger. How long-suffering God is. How He suffers over a long period, hoping that all would be saved and none would perish (II Peter 3:9b; I Timothy 2:4a).

Now upon whom will He pour out His anger? Nahum states here that "Jehovah taketh vengeance on his adversaries, and reserveth wrath for his enemies." If you are not His enemy, if you are not His adversary, He will not pour out His wrath upon you. On the contrary, we read even in this book of Nahum that "Jehovah is good, a stronghold in the day of trouble; and he knoweth them that trust in him" (1.7). Even in the time of trouble, if we trust in Him, He will be a stronghold to us because He is good. He only reserves His wrath for His enemies. So let us not become His enemy.

To repeat, we need to understand that there are two sides to God's character. On the one hand, we need to know of His severity; on the other hand, of His goodness. On the one hand, we need to recognize His love, compassion and mercy. On the other hand, we need to acknowledge His righteousness, justice, wrath and anger. Unfortunately, most people know only one side of God's character, and that is the reason our knowledge of Him is unbalanced. And if our knowledge of Him is unbalanced, it will affect our Christian life; it will be unbalanced. So we need to know our God as He truly is. Let us not think that God's severity and wrath are only to be found in the Old Testament. Not so. We also find this side of God's character in the New Testament. Yes, it is quite true that from the New Testament we know of the love of Christ: "The love of Christ constrains us"—that He loves us to the uttermost and to the very end (see II Corinthians 5:14). But we may overlook the fact that Paul also said in this same chapter of II Corinthians this: "knowing the terror of the Lord" (v. 11a). The Lord can be terrible and severe, and hence we need to know God's character in this way as well. We need to know not only the love of Christ that constrains us, but also the terror of the Lord so that we do not become careless and fall under the wrathful hand of God. Let us thank God that He "is good, a stronghold in the day of trouble; and [that] he knoweth them that trust in him."

NINEVEH REPRESENTS THE WORLD

When Nahum prophesied concerning Nineveh and its destruction, it was probably around the year 650 B.C., and we know from history that Nineveh was in fact eventually destroyed in about 625 B.C. Thus Nahum's prophecy was fulfilled; but if we know the nature of Biblical prophecy, we are aware that though there is always a near-term fulfillment, there is additionally a remote fulfillment. There is always a full fulfillment as well as a partial fulfillment. Such is the nature of Biblical prophecy. So even though, historically, the destruction of Nineveh was fulfilled in the seventh century B.C., it nonetheless has something to do with us today because Nineveh was more than just a city but also this Nineveh (or Assyria) in Scripture serves as a type of the world.

Indeed, the Bible uses different cities, kingdoms or nations to represent the world. For instance, Egypt was very much a type of the world—and more specifically a type of the wealth of the world: the place in the world where there was abundance. When there was famine everywhere else, there was food aplenty in Egypt. But this land also speaks of the oppression that was there, even though there had likewise been great wealth. And all of that is what the world is.

Moreover, Babylon, too, is a representation of the world. But in her case Babylon usually represents the world in its greatness and also in its confusion. This is especially true in the area of religious confusion because despite the fact that the children of Israel were delivered out of Egypt they were ultimately taken captive into Babylon. In other words, God's people were taken out of the world as it is but fell into the confusion of the religious world. Hence, we find that Babylon represents the great religious system of the world.

Here in Nahum's prophetic burden we read of the "wicked [Assyrian] counselor," who actually points to the antichrist. Hence, Nineveh represents the world in its greatness of strength and in its terrible violence. Nineveh represents worldly pride in its own strength—not only opposing God but even disdaining Him, not only rebelling against God but even fighting against Him. Now that is what the world is as represented by the Assyrian capital of Nineveh.

GOD'S BURDEN FOR THE WORLD

What is meant by "the burden of Nineveh"? God had a burden for this world; He created the world; He loved the world. But the world rebelled against God. It became a place of great violence, a place of opposition to, and the despising of, God—a fighting against God under the rule of Satan, God's adversary. Though the world had fallen in such a way God still loved the world. Having a burden for the world, He sent His prophets to the world, calling it to return and repent and He would spare it. At one time God had spared Nineveh through the prophecy of Jonah, whose message had been that if the world as represented by Nineveh repented, God would spare it; and God did spare.

Not only that, but two thousand years ago, God so loved the world that He sent His only begotten Son into this world to die for it, thus attempting to recall and bring back the people of this earth to himself; and yet, the world rejected Him and crucified Him. Even so, God's anger, we are told by Nahum, is slow. We know that the wrath of God is upon this world—upon all those who are impious towards Him and upon all those who are unrighteous; just as we find clearly spelled out in Romans 1. In one sense, the wrath of God is already here, but in another sense we realize that He still restrains His wrath: He is still giving the world opportunity to be saved, yet not because our Lord returns to the earth late; rather, it is because He does not wish to see anyone perish but that all may come to repentance and be saved. That is the long-suffering of God. But let us not think that because of this, the world will continue on without eventually being judged. The word of God tells us very clearly that the day of judgment is coming soon; Christ will return to judge this world. Judgment shall in fact come upon this world, and when the wrath of the Lamb shall come, who is able to stand?

Revelation 6 tells us that the wrath of the Lamb will ultimately come. We view the Lamb of God as only being very meek and mild, never becoming angry. People wrongly assume that they can do anything to the Lamb and that He will simply take it and suffer under it. But one day the Lamb will be full of fury and who can withstand it? People will cry out to the mountains, "Fall upon us, hide us from the wrath of the Lamb" (see vv. 16-17). One day judgment will indeed come upon this world because it refuses to repent, for God is just; He shall be most severe with those who have sunk into impiety towards Him and become unrighteous. But thank God that He is good; He is a stronghold in the time of trouble and knows those who trust in Him.

We recognize that actually the wrath of God is in part already upon this earth, for we are aware that there is so much trouble in this world today and that we are living in the midst of it. Do we think God has forgotten about us or that He will forsake us? To the contrary, we have been told here that He is good, that He will be a stronghold to us in these days of trouble because He knows those who trust in Him. So if we simply trust in God, we shall know that even though we live in a troublous time, we have the confidence that He is our stronghold. We hide in Him and He knows those of us who trust in Him. When the whole world is in fear and trembling, when they contemplate what is going to come upon this earth, they will be frightened to death (see Luke 21:25-26). Nevertheless, let us by faith look up, for our redemption draws near (see Luke 21:28).

Is not our God good? Thank God that we are enabled to live through this troublous time with faith and with hope, knowing that it will not be long. He who has promised to come is coming. "Come, Lord Jesus" (Revelation 22:20).

Let us pray:

> *Dear heavenly Father, we are comforted by the word of Thy prophet. We do praise and thank Thee that, even though the day of judgment is almost upon us, we know that Thou art our stronghold. We have our rest and peace in Thee. We do praise and thank Thee that Thou knowest how to separate the just from the unjust, even though in ourselves we are unjust; but Thou hast reckoned us righteous in Christ Jesus. So we are full of hope as we come to Thee this day. We know that Thou who hast saved us will save us to the uttermost. We thank Thee that we know whom we have believed and we are fully persuaded that Thou art able to keep that which we have committed to Thee unto that day.*[*] *Our Father, we thank Thee. In the name of our Lord Jesus. Amen.*

[*] II Timothy 1:12b

HABAKKUK

THE JUST SHALL LIVE BY FAITH

Habakkuk 1:1-5—The burden which Habakkuk the prophet did see. Jehovah, how long shall I cry and thou wilt not hear? I cry out unto thee, Violence! and thou dost not save. Why dost thou cause me to see iniquity, and lookest thou upon grievance? For spoiling and violence are before me; and there is strife, and contention riseth up. Therefore the law is powerless, and justice doth never go forth; for the wicked encompasseth the righteous; therefore judgment goeth forth perverted. See ye among the nations, and behold, and wonder marvellously; for I work a work in your days, which ye will not believe, though it be declared to you.

Habakkuk 2:1-4—I will stand upon my watch, and set me upon the tower, and will look forth to see what he will say unto me, and what I shall answer as to my reproof. And Jehovah answered me and said, Write the vision, and engrave it upon tablets, that he may run that readeth it. For the vision is yet for an appointed time, but it hasteth to the end, and shall not lie: though it tarry, wait for it; for it will surely come, it will not delay. Behold, his soul is puffed up, it is not upright within him: but the just shall live by his faith.

Habakkuk 3:1-2—A Prayer of Habakkuk the prophet upon Shigionoth. Jehovah, I heard the report of thee, and I feared. Jehovah, revive thy work in the midst of the years, in the midst of the years make it known: in wrath remember mercy!

Habakkuk 3:17-19—For though the fig-tree shall not blossom, neither shall fruit be in the vines; the labour of the olive-tree shall

> *fail, and the fields shall yield no food; the flock shall be cut off from the fold, and there shall be no herd in the stalls: yet I will rejoice in Jehovah, I will joy in the God of my salvation. Jehovah, the Lord, is my strength, and he maketh my feet like hinds' feet, and he will make me to walk upon my high places. To the chief Musician. On my stringed instruments.*

Let us pray:

> *Dear heavenly Father, oh how we do praise and thank Thee that through Thy beloved Son we are now in Thy presence, and in Thy presence there is fullness of joy and life forevermore. So as we come, we ask Thee that Thou wilt open Thy word to us and make Thy word life and spirit to us that Thou mayst be glorified. We ask in Thy precious name. Amen.*

The very name Habakkuk means "embrace," "strong embrace," or "the embracer." We do not know whether that name was given to him by God or the prophet took that name for himself, but we do know that this word Habakkuk—signifying "embrace" in its strictest form—is used in Scripture in relation both to God and to man. For instance, in Song of Songs 2:6 and 8:3 the beloved mentioned therein—who represents the Lord Jesus—puts his left hand under our head and uses his right hand to embrace us. And with respect to man, in Proverbs 4:8 we are exhorted to embrace wisdom.

In the particular case here in Habakkuk, probably the word is applicable to man. In other words, the prophet was embracing God with the arms of faith in the midst of trials. He held on to God just as did Jacob when while wrestling with the angel of the Lord his thigh was touched and he was thereby crippled. He embraced and held on to the angel and said, "I will not let you go until you bless me." That was the same experience which the prophet Habakkuk had: he embraced God with the arms of love and faith and refused to let go of God until he was instructed, blessed and established.

It was Martin Luther who said of Habakkuk: "He is the prophet who embraced the people of God, who took them into his arms, comforted them, and lifted them up before God, comforting them by assuring them that, if God wills, it would soon be better." Hence, this word "embrace" can apply in two ways to the prophet Habakkuk because, on the one hand, that was his personal experience, and, on the other hand, it can also apply to how Habakkuk had embraced the people of God at that time and tried to comfort them with the reassuring words that God was with them.

We are not provided with the genealogy of Habakkuk. We are only told that he is Habakkuk the prophet. Now of all twelve minor prophets, and even though they are all indisputably prophets, only three are specifically designated as being prophets. Habakkuk is one; Haggai and Zechariah are the other two. In other words, he was officially put in the place and position of prophet by God. He was to be His spokesman to His people in the particular period during which Habakkuk prophesied.

The last phrase in the final verse of this book reads: "On my stringed instruments." Many believe that because he said this, most likely it indicates this prophet was a Levite. We know from Scripture that in the temple service it was the Levites who participated in the music and played the musical instruments. So evidently Habakkuk was a Levite and participated in the temple worship by playing on his stringed instruments.

We are not given the time period of his prophesying, but from internal evidence within the book, I think we can come very close to determining the approximate time-frame for his prophesying. Various commentators on this matter have put forward different ideas, but probably Habakkuk had prophesied during the latter part of King Manesseh's reign, on through the two years of King Amon, and into the earliest years of King Josiah. This is because in 1:5 of the book the Lord is recorded as having declared: "I will work a work in your days, which ye will not believe, though it be declared to you."

Now we can correctly assume that the work which God was going to accomplish "in [their] days" was the Chaldean-Babylonian invasion of Judah; for when God said He was going to do this work in the generation of the people who heard this prophecy, it meant that they would actually experience that work and its consequences but would not believe it. We know that at that time Assyria—that is to say, Nineveh—was still the dominant world power, whereas Babylon was only just then beginning to ascend in power. Therefore, the remnant people of Judah at that time feared the Assyrians and not the Chaldean-Babylonians. As we learned earlier, they were afraid that the Assyrians would come again and destroy Judah. They never thought of or imagined the Chaldean-Babylonian threat because Nineveh was not destroyed until much later—in 625 B.C.—and Habakkuk's prophetic ministry dates from before the destruction of Nineveh and well before the full-fledged ascendancy of Babylon as the new dominant power in the world.

Furthermore, Habakkuk's contemporaries were Zephaniah and Jeremiah. Indeed, Zephaniah evidently adapted Habakkuk's words in his own ministry. For instance, in Zephaniah 1:7 we read: "Be silent at the presence of the Lord." This is similar to a fuller version to be found in Habakkuk 2:20: "The Lord is in his holy temple. Let all the earth keep silence before him!" And we definitely know that Zephaniah prophesied during the reign of Josiah. Then, too, in the writings of Jeremiah, there are a number of passages which express similar sentiments to those of Habakkuk, and we know that Jeremiah began his prophetic ministry in the thirteenth year of King Josiah. So from this historical evidence we can conclude that Habakkuk must have commenced prophesying before Zephaniah and Jeremiah. Even Zephaniah prophesied the destruction of Nineveh; and hence, this further confirms that Habakkuk must have prophesied earlier than that historical event.

Habakkuk employed the language of the earlier prophets like Isaiah and probably Micah; and he also employed the language of Deuteronomy and the Psalms. His prophesying is therefore more in the style of the older prophets than the later ones. Hence, scholars tend to believe that he prophesied during the latter part of Manasseh's reign and into the earliest part of King Josiah's.

Habakkuk prophesied of the Babylonian or Chaldean invasion of Judah. We know that because of the sins of Manasseh, God was determined to destroy Judah, but we also recall how Manasseh repented and we remember the prayer of Josiah. So God postponed his judgment and hence the Babylonian invasion did not come until the reign of Jehoiakim. So even though the invasion was not immediate, it was not too remote, either. So the work of God's judgment would ultimately occur in the times of the generation of the people who actually heard the prophecy of Habakkuk.

The book of Habakkuk is most unusual because it is not strictly a prophetic writing in the manner of the other prophetic books wherein their entire texts consist of one prophetic message after another aimed towards the people. Instead, we find that the text of Habakkuk is cast in very dramatic form: a conversation between the prophet and God. Accordingly, there are two main speakers in the book—Habakkuk the prophet and Jehovah God. They are engaged in a colloquy, a conversation, a dialogue; and this constitutes the essential nature of the book of Habakkuk. Even so, it is still classed as a prophetic writing.

Of all the prophetic books Habakkuk is different in that it reveals the deep spiritual exercise of the prophet himself; whereas the other prophets simply prophesied what was going to happen; but here we find Habakkuk was deeply exercised inwardly by the content of his prophecy, and that is a most unusual characteristic among the prophets.

This book of Habakkuk is divided into three chapters, and we can very clearly identify them by the use of three different words. The first chapter is comprised of the burden; the second chapter is marked by the vision; the third chapter is a prayer. First, there was a burden; and out of that burden the prophet saw a vision; and because of that vision, he offered up a prayer.

THE BURDEN

This book begins with the burden which Habakkuk the prophet saw. What was that burden? And from whence did that burden come? We read: "The burden which Habakkuk the prophet did see." He definitely saw something. Yet who made him see it? It was Jehovah God.

There are things around us, too, which we may see, and yet, spiritually speaking, we do not see. To put this another way, things are there for us to see and we cannot say we do not see them; yet, strangely, we have not seen them. They do not create a burden within us. For instance, on one occasion in the days of the Lord Jesus, He went into the outer court area of the temple where merchants were selling and also exchanging currencies; and this had been going on for years and years and years. Everybody was aware of it. So when people went into the temple, and even though they saw these things taking place, they took them for granted. Some people even thought that these were highly beneficial activities since they made it more convenient for the people because whenever they came to the temple to offer up animal sacrifices, the latter had to be without blemish and had to be approved by the priests. If you brought your own lamb to the temple, the priests might not approve of it because even if it was almost perfect, there was nonetheless some blemish in it. Because the priests wanted their own business, they would not approve of a given sacrifice. And hence, you had to buy—from the established sellers—the kosher lamb, sheep or bullock which had already been approved by the priest. That is why there was the buying and selling of these sheep and cattle in the temple outer court area. It made it easier for those who came to sacrifice. Similarly, the same could be said concerning the money-changing activity. Jewish people coming from foreign countries had to exchange their currency for the required temple money, and this activity was therefore very convenient for them because the exchange could occur right there in the temple area. All this had been going on for decades and people simply acquiesced in these commercial enterprises and took them for granted. Nobody had a burden concerning these activities; but when the Lord Jesus entered the outer temple area and observed all this commerce, He was so deeply burdened and offended that He had to cleanse the temple thoroughly.

Now the same kind of burden was true with the prophet Habakkuk. The nation of Judah at that time was nearing its last days, and the moral and spiritual condition had become so mean and low. There was violence, strife, contention and injustice; the unjust prevailed over the just. Moreover, the law had been twisted to such a degree that the righteous suffered greatly. The whole society was corrupted to its core and this had been the situation for quite some time; nevertheless, the people saw all these things around them but submitted themselves and lived under it all. But here was this man Habakkuk, whose eyes God opened—yet not only to see these things with the natural, human eye, but to see them all with the eyes of the Lord himself; and what a great difference that is! If one observes things as they are with one's natural eyes, that is one thing; but if one observes the same things with the eyes of God, then a person will view the situation quite differently.

Essentially God called Habakkuk to see iniquity. It was not that the prophet would now purposely try to find fault with his nation, but God had opened his eyes and caused him to easily see iniquities everywhere. He now discerned the corruption which was all around him: he now discerned how the righteous were suffering and the wicked were prevailing, and he beheld all this with the eyes of God, or, to describe it more succinctly, the burden of God had now come upon him. Indeed, the burden of God became his burden. God was burdened by the multiplied corruption and degradation of His people. God saw all this and could not tolerate it any longer; and so He shared His burden with the prophet; with the result that the prophet saw the same situation as did God; and when the prophet discerned it all, he was deeply distressed. He cried out: "Lord, how long shall I cry and thou wilt not hear? I cry out unto thee: Violence! and thou dost not save. Why dost thou cause me to see iniquity, and lookest thou upon grievance?" In other words, why do you not do something about it, Lord?

God is righteous and holy. And one would naturally assume that when God beheld with His holy eyes and with His righteous character all these iniquities in His people, would He not do something about it? Surely God would not allow these things to go on forever! So when the prophet became burdened with the burden of the Lord, he began to pray, "God, do something. You should not allow this evil situation to continue. You should not let the righteous suffer any longer; rather, You should punish the wicked; You should change the whole situation. Why, therefore, do You not do it?" Let us understand, here, that this very burden of the prophet's came from the Lord himself. The Lord was going to do something about it but He first wanted His people—especially His prophet—to pray concerning it. Strange to say, this in part defines and explains the long-suffering of God.

Is it not true that when we see something which in our eyes does not measure up to God's standard, we want it to be judged and punished right away. God, with holier eyes than we have, cannot even look upon these corrupt things—He cannot bear them; and yet here is being manifested the long-suffering of God. Why is this? It is because He wants to show mercy. He hopes that people will repent. Yes, He will judge; but He waits and delays, wishing to provide even further opportunity for people to repent.

On the other hand, when the prophet Habakkuk was burdened with God's burden, he in his humanity could not stand it any longer but cried out, saying: "Lord, do something. Why do You not put an end to this?" He could not understand God's delay. So in chapter 1:5 we read God's response to the prophet's cry: "[Look] ye among the nations, and behold, and wonder marvelously; for I work a work in your days, which ye will not believe, though it be declared to you." In other words, God was saying here: "Yes, I am going to do a work; I am going to raise up from among the surrounding nations the Chaldeans to chastise My people. You cry out for Me to discipline My people. I will, but I will use the Chaldeans to be the rod of My chastisement by which to correct My people." Now the Chaldeans were very wicked, bloody and violent—even more wicked, violent and corrupted than the remnant of the people of Judah. In fact, here is how God assessed the developing attitude and mindset of His chosen chastising instrument: "Then will his mind change, and he will pass on, and become guilty: this his power is become his god" (v. 11).

God is sovereign, and in His sovereignty, He raised up as His vessel of wrath the Chaldean-Babylonian kingdom. He would use it to correct His people; but the king of Babylon, instead of humbly acknowledging that it was God who had raised him up and given him the power to destroy nations, began to assume that it was only his own power. So he commenced passing over the boundary which God had set for him. Instead of acknowledging that he was but a servant of the Lord being used by Him as His chastising instrument, he began to worship his own power. In fact, he made his power his god, having become proud of himself and having overstepped the boundary which God had set for him; and that is always the result with the natural man.

God revealed to His prophet that this selected chastising vessel was more wicked than the wicked people of Judah. When Habakkuk realized that the Chaldeans had crossed over God's set boundary and began to make their power their god, the prophet discerned that there was hope and in essence said, "We will not die." Now in the natural order of things, if the more wicked are used to punish the less wicked, we would assume that the less wicked will die; but because the more wicked had overstepped the set boundary, therefore, the prophet concluded that a remnant of God's people would not die. He came to realize that the Chaldeans were but a rod in the hands of God, that God was simply using them to correct His people. Nevertheless, Habakkuk still could not understand why God used the more wicked to punish the less wicked. It did not seem right to him nor did it make any sense. Furthermore, he did not understand why God did not do this chastising work quickly. God had answered His prophet's first question, but he had a second, more serious one. Habakkuk was greatly puzzled.

G. Campbell Morgan once commented: "This book of Habakkuk is one of contrast. It opens up with 1:2 and ends with 3:19." That initial verse opens with a question, and additional questions follow. At this juncture things are a puzzlement and a mystery to God's prophet. But 3:19 ends with certainty and assurance. The book's text begins with a wail and a cry of despair in chapter 1, but it concludes with a shout of confidence at the end of chapter 3; and the key to understanding this dramatic change is to be found in 2:4.

But before going further I would like to point out again that Habakkuk was told by God, as recorded in 1:5: "I work a work in your days, which ye will not believe, though it be declared to you. [For, behold, I raise up the Chaldeans.]" In other words, the work which God would do in the nation of Judah's day, and which they would not believe, would be the raising up of the Chaldeans as His rod of chastisement. But I would like to point out further that this same verse is quoted in the New Testament—in Acts 13:41. When

Paul was preaching at Antioch of Pisidia, he presented to his hearers the whole counsel of God with respect to His plan of salvation. He spoke to them of the death and resurrection of the Lord Jesus, that God had made Him the Savior of the world, and that through Him comes repentance and remission of sins. Then Paul quoted in its essential wording the verse from Habakkuk 1:5: "I work a work in your days, a work which ye will in no wise believe if one declare it to you."

What exactly is that work to which Paul made reference here? We have already seen that in relation to the time of the prophet Habakkuk the work was the Chaldean invasion of Judah; but in relation to what Paul was preaching in his day, the work referred to was the first coming of Christ. Moreover, in Habakkuk's day that work was one of chastisement and correction; but in the time of Acts, it was and continues to be a gracious and merciful work of salvation. Such is the distinctive way the Holy Spirit handles the word of God. Thank God that He is continuing to do a salvation work today. Indeed, He says: "I am doing the work of forgiving people's sins through the finished work of My Son, Christ Jesus the Lord."

THE VISION

As we indicated earlier, the prophet Habakkuk was still puzzled; he therefore announced the following: "I will stand upon my watch, and set me upon the tower, and will look forth to see what he will say unto me, and what I shall answer as to my reproof" (2:1). Because he did not understand, he went to a particular tower and waited for God to reveal to him what it was all about. Let us see here that a prophet is also a watchman. "And Jehovah answered me and said, Write the vision" (2:2). In response God gave His prophet a vision: "For the vision is yet for an appointed time, but it hasteth to the end, and shall not lie: though it tarry, wait for it; for it will surely come, it will not delay. Behold, his soul is puffed up, it is not upright within him: but the just shall live by his faith" (2:3-4).

What, then, was the vision which God had shown His prophet? If you read chapter 2 in its entirety you will learn that the vision was nothing less than the destruction of the Chaldeans. Because their souls had become puffed up and were not upright, God would consequently destroy the chastising rod which He had raised up. Such was the vision. Nevertheless, the hour for this vision's realization was for an appointed time yet to come. The destruction of Chaldea-Babylon would most surely come, for God does not lie; but it would occur at His appointed time. And from history we know that Babylon was ultimately destroyed by the Medo-Persian Empire.

Let us notice that in this second chapter of Habakkuk there are five "woes" cited. God pronounced five of them over the Chaldean people—that is to say, over the Babylonian nation; and interestingly each "woe" is three verses in length. Verses 6-8 provide the text of the first "woe." The Chaldeans were an ambitious people. They were so full of ambition that they attempted to conquer the whole world. Such gross ambition sowed the seed of their ultimate destruction. The second "woe" is found in verses 9-11. It was pronounced over Babylon because of its imperial covetousness. They were so greedy that they could never be satisfied with their many gains and conquests. The third "woe" was expressed due to their unrestrained violence and bloodshed (verses 12-14). The fourth "woe" came forth because the Chaldeans were terribly insolent: they treated those whom they conquered most cruelly—in short, they were shockingly inhuman (verses 15-17). The fifth and final "woe" was provoked due to idolatry. The Chaldean-Babylonian people worshiped their natural power as their god (verses 18-20). Now because of these five sins, God had determined to eventually destroy Babylon.

Yet this frightful vision God gave to the prophet in order to comfort him. There are two passages in chapter 2 which are quoted in the New Testament for the same purpose: to encourage believers to persevere in the midst of difficult circumstances. The first passage quoted is verse 3: "For the vision is yet for an appointed time, but it hasteth to the end, and shall not lie: though it tarry, wait for it; for it will surely come, it will not delay." This is quoted in an adapted form in Hebrews 10:37: "For yet a very little while he that comes will come, and will not delay." Notice that in this verse of Habakkuk 2 there appears multiple times the pronoun "it." It—the content of the vision—hastens to its end; it delays its fruition, yet wait for it; for it will surely come; it will not delay itself forever. Hence, "it" repeatedly refers to the destruction of Babylon.

But quite differently from how we ourselves would quote this Old Testament verse for a New Testament purpose, the Holy Spirit, when quoting this verse from Habakkuk, changed the pronoun "it" to the pronoun "he." Now we must acknowledge that when the Spirit inspired the New Testament writer of Hebrews to quote and adapt this Old Testament verse in the way he did, the Spirit knew very well what He was doing through that writer. And so God's Spirit changed the "it" of Habakkuk 2:3 to "he" in Hebrews 10:37. Now to whom does "he" refer? To answer that, one must consider the context of Hebrews 10. There we learn that the writer of Hebrews was exhorting and encouraging God's people to be patient and press on and not be disappointed or fall into despair. By faith and patience inherit the promises because "he" is coming back soon. Now the "he" here obviously refers to Christ at His second coming. The Lord Jesus is coming back soon; therefore, do not give up hope. Continue on and you will inherit the promises. He is coming back; He will not tarry forever.

The second passage quoted from Habakkuk 2 is this: "Behold, his soul is puffed up, it is not upright within him: but the just shall live by his faith" (v. 4). This was the message which lay behind the vision given to God's prophet. The vision pertained to the destruction of Babylon; but the message behind that vision was that the wicked will eventually die, the proud will ultimately perish, but meanwhile the just shall live by his faith. Yes, it is quite true that the proud must die, that Babylon will be destroyed, but this would not occur immediately. On the contrary, history tells us that the Babylonian Empire existed for about a hundred years and, during that time, Babylon ruled over the entire world. The issue for the righteous among God's people therefore becomes: How are they going to live through that difficult time? The answer: "the just shall live by his faith." That is the only way the righteous can live through such a time. And that is the needful message which lay behind the vision.

Now this very sentence, "the just shall live by his faith," is quoted three times in three different New Testament books. It is to be found, first of all, in Romans 1:17: "the just shall live by faith," and there the emphasis is on the just; secondly, in Galatians 3:11: "The just shall live on the principle of faith," and the emphasis there is on faith; finally, in Hebrews 10:38: "The just shall live by faith," and the emphasis there is on live.

So this one verse was planted by God there in the Old Testament book of Habakkuk; and much later the Holy Spirit referenced it in three different books of the New Testament in order to develop a very important spiritual principle for God's people. And hence, we can see that this is a very significant verse.

The issue before us today is the same as was true in Habakkuk's day: How are we going to live through our own distressing times when we see the wicked prevail but the righteous suffer? Moreover, we know that God is going to judge, but when? Why is judgment of the wicked delayed so long? It is because of the long-suffering patience of God who is not willing that anyone should perish but that all would come to repentance. In the meantime, how are we going to live through this difficult period? Only by faith. We can only live through such bewildering and terrible circumstances by faith. And such is the vision and the message for us today.

A PRAYER

Heretofore we have learned that after the prophet had received God's burden and had begun to seek Him about that burden, God gave him a vision, showing him what He was going to do. But then we read that the prophet responded with a prayer, and that is how it should be. If you have a burden from the Lord, you should seek Him about it and He will reveal His mind to you in a vision. But when you see the vision, you are not simply to sit back and do nothing; you must respond with prayer. So in the third chapter of Habakkuk we learn that the prophet began to pray.

"A Prayer of Habakkuk the prophet upon Shigionoth." This prayer is a psalm. In the book of The Psalms there are several psalms which are also defined as prayers. For instance, Psalms 17 and 86 are prayers of David. Psalm 90 is a prayer of Moses. Psalms 102 and 142 are likewise called prayers, most likely written by David because in

Psalm 102 it reads: "by the afflicted"; and that is probably an allusion to David himself. So a psalm is sometimes couched in the form of a prayer, and the psalm here in the book of Habakkuk is a prayer of the prophet himself. It is a prayer which flows out of a burden and a vision. Now a prayer which arises out of a burden and a vision is real prayer, and here it states that it is "upon Shigionoth." We are told by scholars that Shigionoth is probably a term which has an association with analogy, and, further, that the word has a root which conveys the idea of "reeling." Hence, it is a reeling song; by which is meant that it is a song to be sung with excited motion and rapid change. Interestingly enough, only verse 2 of this chapter is actual prayer. All the rest of this chapter's text is either praise or worship; even so, we know that praise and worship are the higher forms of prayer. So the prophet prayed: "Jehovah, I heard the report of thee, and I feared. Jehovah, revive thy work in the midst of the years, in the midst of the years make it known: in wrath remember mercy!"

The prophet heard God's report; he heard what God was going to do: raise up the Chaldeans to chastise His chosen people; but He was also going to punish the Chaldeans themselves. These were fearful reports, and when the prophet heard, he was afraid. He was afraid of what he had heard because it was judgment—judgment upon His very own people, judgment upon the nation of Judah, and judgment also upon the nations. It was a distressing report full of fearful news; and yet Habakkuk was in full sympathy with God. For he as it were cried out: "Revive thy work, O God, in the midst of the years. Perform it! In spite of how fearful it is, O Lord, do it! Revive thy work; execute it! Yet, in wrath remember mercy!" God's prophet knew the wrath of God. He knew that without mercy all would perish, everyone would be consumed. Not only would the Chaldeans be consumed, even the remnant of the Jews in Judah would be consumed because no one—not even among God's people—is righteous before Him. Therefore, Habakkuk added most meaningfully: "In wrath remember mercy!" That was his prayer. And God heard his prayer: He saved a remnant out of Judah for himself.

Verses 3-16 actually present to us a glorious picture of theophany: that is to say, the glorious appearing of the Lord. The Lord comes forth in glory and He is delivering as well as punishing. To all these verses there is a narrative background, and that narrative tells how God delivered His people out of Egypt and led them into the Promised Land to inherit it. The prophet of God refers to the Red Sea, he also refers to the Jordan River. So the waters were miraculously divided and/or held back on behalf of the children of Israel. God delivered His people; and within the Promised Land itself, the sun and the moon at one point stopped. That is a reference to Joshua, who prayed and the sun and the moon ceased in their motion so that the people might inherit the land (see Joshua 10:12-13). In other words, God was judging the nations in order to deliver His people, and it is a glorious picture of the mighty hand of God.

Then Shigionoth ends with the last three verses that are worship. The prophet looked at his circumstances and described to his readers the worst circumstances that can possibly be: "The fig-tree shall not blossom, neither shall fruit be in the vines; the labour of the olive-tree shall fail, and the fields shall yield no food; the flock shall be cut off from the fold, and there shall be no herd in the stalls." In other words, figs, grapes and olives are the things which the people enjoy, whereas the food in the field, the flocks of sheep and the herds of cattle are the people's very sustenance. And all these things shall fail. Everything will fail. Now when everything fails, what does one do? The answer: the just shall live by his faith. When everything fails, said the prophet, then "I will rejoice in Jehovah, for He never fails. I will joy in the God of my salvation. Indeed, He himself is my salvation. Jehovah Lord is my strength. And he makes my feet like hinds' feet, and He will make me to walk upon my high places" (see vv. 18-19). In short, He will enable me to leap to the highest place—in victory.

Now this that is being described is true faith. What in reality is faith for the believer? Faith is a looking away from circumstances. Faith is a looking straight towards God. Faith does not look at oneself but looks off to Jesus (see Hebrews 12:2a). And when you fix your gaze upon the Lord, you will find that the Lord is your rock; He is also your salvation, your strength, and your victory. And that gives you joy in the midst of distress. The prophet Habakkuk, having learned that lesson, shared it with the people of his time.

Now in our study of Habakkuk, do we receive a burden as the prophet had himself received God's burden for the Jewish people of his time? His burden was: What would happen to his countrymen? Yet he also received a burden for the Chaldeans—What would happen to them? Or we may put it another way, that Habakkuk was burdened concerning the holiness and the righteousness of God.

Are we today burdened with a like burden? When we look at the people of God today, what do we see? Do we see the apostasy of the church—how the church has fallen from the truth and grace of God? Where is the testimony of Jesus in His church? Do we see this? Or are we so familiar with this flawed scene that it does not bother us or trouble us anymore? Are we concerned with the holiness and the righteousness of God? Are we burdened with the testimony of Jesus in this world? And are we also burdened as to whether God is going to do anything about it? We find that those among God's people who love the world and go along with the world seem to prosper and have a good time, whereas those who want to follow the Lord seem to suffer, and are perhaps even despised by those who love the world. Furthermore, why does God allow such things to happen to His people? For God is righteous and holy, and thus a person would naturally assume that if he follows the Lord faithfully, he should be blessed. Why is it, then, that he suffers? Why is it that those who deviate from the truth of God prosper in this world while those who follow the Lord become very small and insignificant and are even despised? Where is the holiness and righteousness of God in all this? And how are the righteous ones going to live through such a troubling time? If we do not have faith, we will fail. But the just shall live by faith.

One day, the Lord Jesus is coming; and at His coming and at His judgment seat, everything will be made clear. Tears will be wiped away; there will be no scorching of the sun; and He will shepherd His people. Such is our faith. However, when we look at the world, we find that it is so wicked and that its wickedness and perverseness seem to go on and on and on. And so people are moved to say that there is no end to it. Indeed, it verily appears to be that way. Is there, then, no justice? If there is a God, where is He? Is He going to do anything about it? How the world persecutes the church! And furthermore, it seems as though God does not even hear the cry of the church.

Let us by faith wait for the coming of the Lord Jesus. At His first coming He came to save; but at His second coming He will come to judge the world, and who can withstand that judgment?

Hence, today we, too, need to have a burden: a burden for the church and a burden for the world. We also need to have a vision, and our vision is the coming back of the Lord Jesus. But, additionally, we need to pray that God will revive His work of judgment in the midst of the years and make it known; and yet, in His wrath let mercy be remembered.

Let us pray:

> *Lord, give us burden; show us Thy vision; and give us prayer. Oh Lord, revive Thy work in the midst of these years. Yet in Your wrath remember mercy. In Thy precious name. Amen.*

ZEPHANIAH

JUDGMENT

Zephaniah 1:1-7—The word of Jehovah that came unto Zephaniah the son of Cushi, the son of Gedaliah, the son of Amariah, the son of Hezekiah, in the days of Josiah the son of Amon, king of Judah. I will utterly take away everything from off the face of the ground, saith Jehovah: I will take away man and beast; I will take away the fowl of the heavens and the fishes of the sea, and the stumbling-blocks with the wicked, and I will cut off mankind from off the face of the ground, saith Jehovah. And I will stretch forth my hand upon Judah, and upon all the inhabitants of Jerusalem; and I will cut off the remnant of Baal from this place, the name of the Chemarim with the priests; and them that bow down to the host of the heavens upon the housetops; and them that bow down to Jehovah, that swear by him, and swear by Malcham; and them that turn back from after Jehovah, and that do not seek Jehovah, nor inquire for him. Be silent at the presence of the Lord Jehovah; for the day of Jehovah is at hand; for Jehovah hath prepared a sacrifice, he hath hallowed his guests.

Zephaniah 1:14-18—The great day of Jehovah is near, it is near, and hasteth greatly. The voice of the day of Jehovah: the mighty man shall cry there bitterly. That day is a day of wrath, a day of trouble and distress, a day of ruin and desolation, a day of darkness and gloom, a day of clouds and gross darkness, a day of the trumpet and alarm, against the fenced cities and against the high battlements. And I will bring distress upon men, and they shall walk like blind men; for they have sinned against Jehovah; and their blood shall be poured out as dust, and their flesh as dung: their silver and their gold shall not be able to deliver them, in the day of Jehovah's wrath; but the whole land shall be devoured by the fire of his jealousy: for a full end, yea, a sudden end, shall he make of all them that dwell in the land.

Zephaniah 2:1-3—Collect yourselves and gather together, O nation without shame, before the decree bring forth, before the day pass away as chaff, before the fierce anger of Jehovah come upon you, before the day of Jehovah's anger come upon you. Seek Jehovah, all ye meek of the land, who have performed his ordinance; seek righteousness, seek meekness: it may be ye shall be hid in the day of Jehovah's anger.

Zephaniah 3:14-20—Exult, O daughter of Zion; shout, O Israel; rejoice and be glad with all the heart, O daughter of Jerusalem: Jehovah hath taken away thy judgments, he hath cast out thine enemy; the King of Israel, Jehovah, is in the midst of thee; thou shalt not see evil any more. In that day it shall be said to Jerusalem, Fear not; Zion, let not thy hands be slack. Jehovah thy God is in thy midst, a mighty one that will save: he will rejoice over thee with joy; he will rest in his love; he will exult over thee with singing. I will gather them that sorrow for the solemn assemblies, who were of thee: the reproach of it was a burden unto them. Behold, at that time I will deal with all them that afflict thee; and I will save her that halted, and gather her that was driven out; and I will make them a praise and a name in all the lands where they have been put to shame. At that time will I bring you, yea, at the time that I gather you; for I will make you a name and a praise, among all the peoples of the earth, when I shall turn again your captivity before your eyes, saith Jehovah.

The very name Zephaniah means "whom Jehovah hides" or, "treasure." We are told that he was the great-great-grandson of Hezekiah; and I think without doubt that that Hezekiah was King Hezekiah, the good king of Judah. Thus, this man Zephaniah was raised up by God from Judah's royal family to be His prophet. God is sovereign and so He is able to raise up prophets from all walks of life and from different levels of social status. Wherever He can find someone whose heart is towards Himself, God will apprehend that one for His purpose. And we do thank God that this man of the royal family was one who sought after God and was used by Him to be His spokesman.

Zephaniah prophesied in the days of King Josiah. He denounced the sins of Judah that were prevalent in the days of both wicked Kings Manasseh and Amon. Strangely, however, Zephaniah did not mention in his book the reformation or revival which came in the eighteenth year of the reign of Josiah. Hence, we believe that most likely he prophesied in the early days of Josiah before that reformation; nevertheless, the word of God which came through him to the remnant of Judah helped towards the reform which King Josiah inaugurated in the eighteenth year of his reign.

This man Zephaniah prophesied shortly after the prophet Habakkuk. It is therefore assumed that he and Habakkuk were contemporaries. They prophesied more or less about the same issues. They denounced the sins of Judah, and they also foretold the future restoration. But as you read these two books you will find that there is a great difference between them. Habakkuk's prophesying was more an expression of the deep spiritual exercise of his soul. As he looked at his circumstances and beheld the wickedness among God's people, his heart was profoundly troubled and concerned. He was deeply exercised because he was concerned about seeing that the justice, righteousness and holiness of God would be upheld. So he cried out to God that He would do something about it. But when God answered him and said He would raise up the Chaldeans as the rod of chastisement upon His people, that created a further problem for the prophet Habakkuk because he knew that the Chaldeans were even more wicked than the remnant people of Judah; and hence, he wondered why God would use the more wicked to punish the less wicked. So he went to a watchtower and with expectation waited for an answer from God. And God answered him and said He would punish the Chaldeans but that in the midst of it all the righteous ones were to live by their faith. Therefore, the book of Habakkuk was the outflow of the prophet's deep spiritual exercise in view of the coming judgment of God.

With Zephaniah, it was quite different. Even though these two were prophesying about the same matters, Habakkuk was more subjective in his reaction whereas Zephaniah was more objective in his. That is to say, Zephaniah contemplated the glory of the justice of God and, further, he beheld the great love of God. So he was more drawn to the objective side of things.

Jeremiah was also a contemporary of these two prophets. And it seems to me that in his prophetic ministry Jeremiah combined the two different characteristics of these other two prophets. Because of the deep exercise of his soul, Jeremiah was called the weeping prophet; and that characteristic in him was similar to what we found in Habakkuk. On the other hand, Jeremiah was likewise one who revealed the judgment of God and God's ultimate restoration of His people through the new covenant which He promised He would make with His chosen people; and thus the character of his prophetic ministry was like that of Zephaniah. Hence, we can say that these three prophets actually worked together as God's spokesmen.

At the beginning of this book we read: "The word of Jehovah that came unto Zephaniah the son of Cushi." So the whole book reveals the word of the Lord which came upon this prophet. And what was that word? To sum it up most briefly, it was *judgment*. The great day of the Lord was that of judgment. Now we naturally do not like to hear this word because it does not connote spiritual help and sounds to us quite negative. But as a matter of fact, judgment is considered to be one of the greatest works of God. Our brother Watchman Nee, for example, once said: "Besides the work of creation, judgment is the other great work of God."

THE GREAT WORK OF JUDGMENT

Now we all recognize that the work of creation was a great work. God created the heavens and the earth and all things therein, including us human beings. That was a tremendous work. But let us realize that God created man with a purpose. He created him for His glory. He created man that he might cooperate with Him. God created man that he might be used by Him to restore the earth back to himself. Unfortunately, because of man's fall, sin entered this world. Man became flesh—carnal, and because the devil was able once again to thrust himself back into this world—this time through man—God's purpose of creation was not fulfilled. How, then, is the purpose of God in creation—especially with regard to man—to be fully realized?

Now we know, of course, that because of this world's sin, God sent His only begotten Son to this world; and with the coming of the Lord Jesus Christ there occurred the work of redemption. So salvation has been presented to this world in order to rescue man from his fallen state and to eventually restore the whole earth back to the glory of God. That was a glorious action taken by God; but unfortunately, even though salvation has been prepared, not all men will receive the salvation which God has provided. What is He going to do, then? How is He going to fulfill all of His glorious purpose? We shall realize that the very last work which, in a sense, will sum up all the work of God in completing His purpose is the work of judgment; and this is because, after judgment, all the work of God will be finished.

We are told in Genesis 1 that when the earth was in ruin and in emptiness and without purpose as a result of the devil's first entrance into the world, the Spirit of God brooded upon the face of the earth's waters and God then said, "Let there be light," and there was light. And in six days God restored this earth to be habitable once again. On the sixth day He created man; and after everything was created, on the seventh day God rested. We do not know how long He rested because, not too long afterward, as we read in Genesis chapter 3, God started to work again. He had to come into the Edenic garden and cry out and say, "Adam, where are you?" God had to do something to rescue man and, ultimately, the world. In other words, even with the great work of creation, sin nonetheless entered this world. What, therefore, was to be God's remedy? The answer: another great work. For in Revelation 20 we are told of this other great work of God—His great judgment—and how it comes to completion. And, then, in Revelation 21 and 22, we read of the new heaven and the new earth with the holy city, the new Jerusalem, descending upon this new earth; and there is neither any more sin, death, tears, nor darkness. God's great work is done—all is finished. Hence, let us not think that judgment is so terrible; on the contrary, it, too, is a great work of God.

Why, though, is judgment necessary? What does it do? First, by means of judgment God glorifies himself. He vindicates His righteousness and holiness. How people greatly misunderstand God!—just as we find in the book of Zephaniah, for people were saying: "God will do nothing good, God will do nothing bad" (see 1:12). In other words, they were asserting that He did not care. But God does care. He is holy and righteous; and through judgment God glorifies himself, showing us who He is.

Second, by means of judgment God exposes, reveals and unveils all the hidden things. It exposes the real situation in all things so that through judgment we may be able to know our true situation. Without judgment we would never discern our actual personal and collective situation; but with judgment it shall be revealed as to exactly who we are, where we are, and where we stand. In short, all is exposed.

Third, through judgment God puts sin to an end. It has to be judged; but after sin is fully judged, it comes to an end.

So we believe that judgment is a very great work of God. We do thank Him that He does indeed judge because through judgment He shows us who He is. What a God we have! Moreover, it is only through judgment that we can come into full salvation and recovery. And it is also through judgment that the world will eventually be rid of sin.

GOD WILL HIDE HIS TREASURE

We may sometimes think that both judgment and mercy (or loving-kindness) are contradictory; but let us recall that in Psalm 101:1 it says: "I will sing of loving-kindness and judgment." The psalmist sings of the loving-kindness and the judgment of the Lord together because these two acts of God are not contradictory; they are complementary: God judges because He loves; and He loves, therefore He must judge. And through judgment He will bring everything back to what He had originally designed all of creation to be, and this, in reality, is an act of love.

In this book of Zephaniah the word of God which came to the prophet was: God will judge. He will judge the whole world; He will also judge His own people. Yet that was not all of God's word which came to the prophet because along with the word *judgment* God gave His spokesman another word, and that was, *Zephaniah*. This word, as we learned earlier, means "whom God hides." That is to say, in the day of judgment, God will hide some whom He considers as treasure (see 2:3b). Hence, even in the midst of wrath there is mercy.

In the context of God's judgment, if we were to consider His holiness and righteousness, we would all be consumed. For who among us can actually stand before the judgment of God? Who of us is so holy and who of us is so just that he can stand in the presence of the holiness and justice of God? Do we not sometimes look in judgment upon other people and others' situation; and even though we are not so righteous nor so holy, yet when we look at all the corruption which surrounds us, do we not also render judgment upon all such things? We feel that these things ought to be completely wiped out and done with. If such is the feeling of us who are not so holy and just, therefore, when God—who is justice itself and holiness itself—shall judge according to His righteousness and holiness, can we possibly imagine that there would be any human being able to stand before that judgment? When God shall judge, who among us can stand, indeed? Without His mercy we would all be consumed. But thank God that, along with the word judgment which came to Zephaniah from Jehovah, there came forth another word: "He will hide." There will be some people whom God will consider to be treasure, and in the days of wrath He will hide them under His wing. How comforting such a word is!

The prophet Zephaniah's name is the very word of God to His people. Similarly, in Psalm 27:5 we read that in the day of trouble He will hide us in His pavilion, He will hide us in His tabernacle, He will put us in the cleft of the rock. God verily hides His people in the time of trouble.

Why does God hide them? It is because He considers them to be His treasure. If for us something is merely trash, our reaction would be to simply let it be burned; but if it be something of value, we would keep it and hide it during the time of burning. So even though God says, "I will judge," He also declares, "I will hide." He will judge all wickedness but will hide those who seek meekness and those who seek righteousness (see 2:3a). Now that in essence is the word of Zephaniah.

This short book has three chapters and as to their content they can be very clearly distinguished. Chapter 1 is the announcement of judgment. Chapter 2 is the call to seek meekness. And chapter 3 tells of restoration through love.

THE ANNOUNCEMENT OF JUDGMENT

Zephaniah opened his prophecy by prophesying that God would utterly destroy the world. He will remove everything from off the face of the ground. Saith Jehovah: "I will take away every man and beast; I will take away the fowl of the heavens and the fishes of the sea, and the stumbling-blocks with the wicked, and I will cut off mankind from off the face of the ground."

There is to be a general judgment upon the whole world because it is so wicked. A few of the opening verses of Zephaniah may immediately remind us of how God had done this once before. Chapter 6 of Genesis relates the fact that when the population began to increase, gross wickedness began to prevail, corruption was present everywhere, violence came upon the earth, and the very imagination of man's mind was continuously wicked and evil. So God looked upon man and upon the earth, and He repented that He had ever created the earth and man. God therefore said, "I will destroy everything." He did so because what He observed had offended His holiness and because what He had created did not serve His purpose nor had brought Him the glory for which He had created it. God therefore declared: "I will destroy everything by water." And we remember how God destroyed the world with a universal flood. At that same time, however, there was one man who had found favor in the eyes of God—Noah. So when the flood came, God as it were hid Noah and his family within the ark; He preserved that one family. Let us see, then, that through judgment God was able to bring this world to a fresh beginning.

Similarly, in the time of Zephaniah the world was once more becoming increasingly wicked and ever more corrupted, so much so that God once again looked upon the world and was forced to announce a second time: "I will destroy everything." But let us notice that from this general judgment, God immediately turned His attention to His chosen people. We know that some time after the flood there had been a people chosen by God through Abraham to be His testimony on earth concerning His holiness and righteousness in a world that once more was becoming corrupted. However, the people whom God had chosen were now themselves corrupted; for they had become wicked and had even become idol worshipers. And, eventually, only a remnant of that chosen people was left: only Judah remained. By this time the northern kingdom of Israel had already been destroyed and the southern kingdom of Judah was now in a very weakened state. Only the leftovers were there, and even those who were the leftovers had themselves become so wicked and corrupted that God was ultimately compelled to declare: "I have to judge." He will not spare even His chosen people if they sin against Him. In fact, God is even stricter with them.

Accordingly, God announced: "I will stretch forth My hand upon Judah." Why, specifically, had it come to that? It was due to the fact that they, like the nations around them, had adopted the practice of worshiping idols. Some of God's people in Judah worshiped idols; some others did worship God but at the same time swore by Him and also by these idols; and still others did not care about God at all. So God announced: "Because of this, I will bring judgment upon this nation of Judah." Furthermore, those in higher society at that time had sought for pleasure and luxury, with the result that gold and silver became their gods. They went about accumulating all such objects made of these precious metals; but God said, "I will search [throughout] Jerusalem with lamps" (see 1:12a). In other words, He would destroy most thoroughly and completely; and when judgment time came, silver and gold was of no help whatsoever to save them (see 1:18a). They could not even dwell in the luxurious houses which they had built.

Now we know, of course, that this prophecy was fulfilled not too long afterwards when the Babylonians came in and destroyed Jerusalem and took the people away into captivity. But it cannot be said that at that particular time God by means of the Babylonians had searched throughout Jerusalem with lamps. Some five hundred years later, though, when in 70 A.D. the Romans destroyed Jerusalem, history tells us that that was precisely what they did. These Romans went into every house, searching in every cave and every basement, and found people and destroyed them. So the word of God is accurate and exact. Jerusalem was utterly destroyed.

Immediately after issuing this prophecy concerning Judah and Jerusalem, the prophet Zephaniah spoke forth about the great day of Jehovah: "The great day of Jehovah is near, and hasteth greatly" (1:14a). The great day of Jehovah is a direct reference to the day of God's wrath. One can readily find this term employed in the Old Testament as well as in the New. It is a special term in the Bible and refers to the day of God's wrath in general: it not only is applied to the destruction of Jerusalem by the Babylonians but is also applied to the destruction of Jerusalem by the Romans and applied to all the destructions which have occurred in this world throughout human history. Nevertheless, all these are but parts or preludes; the complete fulfillment of the great day of Jehovah still lies in the future. In other words, there will come a day—called the day of the Lord or the day of Jehovah—when the whole world will be fully judged. Every judgment which we find in past and present human history is but a prelude to the full judgment which will be meted out upon this earth in the future—and which is called the great day of Jehovah or the great day of the Lord. This first chapter of Zephaniah thus speaks of judgment.

THE CALL TO SEEK MEEKNESS

Zephaniah's second chapter begins with a call. God is calling His people: "Collect yourselves and gather together, O nation without shame, before the decree bring forth, before the day pass away as chaff, before the fierce anger of Jehovah come upon you, before the day of Jehovah's anger come upon you. Seek Jehovah, all ye meek of the land, who have performed his ordinance; seek righteousness, seek meekness: it may be ye shall be hid in the day of Jehovah's anger."

The day of Jehovah's anger was unquestionably coming; it was coming upon His very own people; nevertheless, God would still give His people an opportunity to repent. Hence, He said to them: "Collect yourselves; gather yourselves." But God knew that this people of His as a whole would not repent, so He focused on those who were meek. On the one hand, God called the whole nation to change course and repent, and if they had repented, He would have spared them before the day of His anger came; yet it seems as though their situation was irreversible because the people persisted in their wickedness (see 3:18); therefore, on the other hand, God would now focus His call upon those in the nation who were meek.

What is meant by "the meek"? It is those whose hearts are tender towards God. When the hearts of the people in general are hardened, thank God that there are nonetheless some among them whose hearts are tender towards Him; and because of this He can still speak to them and they can still receive His word. Hence, God spoke to them, saying: "You who are meek, continue to seek meekness and to seek righteousness." Meekness is a trait which is in relation to God. In our relationship with God meekness is the right attitude to have. He is gracious to those who are humble and meek, but He is against those who are proud, arrogant, or stubborn. We in our day need to seek meekness. We need to learn to be humble, open and tender before God, allowing Him to work in our lives. We also need to seek righteousness, which is a trait which is in relationship with our fellow human beings. We need to do things which are right in the sight of man. And if we do seek both meekness and righteousness, then God will say to us: "In the day of My anger and of My judgment, I will hide you." Such is the way of escape.

Let me illustrate this matter this way. We learn from Jeremiah that before Jerusalem was destroyed by Babylon, there was a scribe, Baruch by name, and he wrote down all the words of the prophecy of Jeremiah. He was a good man, but he was also an ambitious man. Before Jerusalem was destroyed, God spoke to Baruch through Jeremiah and said, "Seek not great things for yourself. This is not a time to seek after great things." So because he sought the Lord instead, God said to Baruch: "I will spare your life. I will give your life as a prey to you" (see 45:5). In other words, when destruction would finally come, Baruch's life would be preserved. So he is an example of those who seek meekness and God hides and protects them.

Another illustration of this was when the Babylonians came and took the children of Israel into captivity; actually, it had occurred in three stages. At the time of the second stage, the king of Babylon took away a number of people—King Jeconiah, the royal family, and a number of other people—to Babylon and subsequently he set up Zedekiah to be the king over Judah. Humanly speaking, it can be said that those people who were taken into Babylon were taken into captivity; but in actuality and speaking spiritually, they were preserved by God. For in Jeremiah 24 we read that God gave Jeremiah a vision of two baskets of figs—one basket of good figs and one basket of bad ones. In the vision God said that the good figs were those who were already taken into captivity, whereas the bad figs were those who had remained in Jerusalem and who would ultimately be completely destroyed. So those people who were taken away into Babylon would be preserved and some of them would later return to Jerusalem. Hence, it can truly be said that God hid them.

These are historical illustrations, yet we know that the spiritual principle is always true, no matter who, when or where. In the day of judgment—whether past, present, or future—God always hides those who seek after Him. And how does He hide them? We do not know. He may take them to himself early on in the period of judgment or else He may preserve them throughout the period. We simply do not know, but He certainly knows how to hide His own in the day of judgment. For that is the trustworthy word of God.

The remainder of the chapter reveals how one by one God would destroy all those people around Judah—those neighbors who were on the west, the Philistines; those on the east, the Moabites and the Ammonites; those to the south, the Ethiopians; and those to the north, the Assyrians and their city of Nineveh. And God as it were said to Judah that since He was going to destroy all *these* nations, do you people of Judah still think you will be spared if you do not repent? (see 3:6-8)

RESTORATION THROUGH LOVE

Chapter 3 is a wonderful chapter because though it begins with the word woe it ends with the word love. "Woe to her [Jerusalem] that is rebellious and corrupted, to the oppressing city! She hearkened not to the voice; she received not correction; she confided not in Jehovah; she drew not near her God. Her princes in the midst of her are roaring lions; her judges are evening wolves, that leave nothing for the morning. Her prophets are vain-glorious, treacherous persons; her priests profane the sanctuary, they do violence to the law" (vv. 1-4).

"Woe" was pronounced upon that oppressing city of Jerusalem. In the city as a whole, in fact, there was nothing good. It and its inhabitants should have been destroyed. But suddenly Zephaniah's prophetic content changes to something positive in verses 8 and 9, yet not because of the city's inhabitants but because of the love and faithfulness of God. For God now declared: "I will do something. I will use judgment to purify My people. I will use judgment even to save the world. The whole world will be judged, including My very own people. Thus, all the wickedness will be destroyed and only the poor and the afflicted (that is, those who are humble and meek before the Lord) shall be My people; and I will restore them to be a name and a praise in the world." At the same time, God, in destroying the world, shall purify it of all wickedness and give all peoples a pure language. "For then will I turn to the peoples a pure language: that they may all call upon the name of Jehovah, to serve him with one consent" (v. 9).

That is what judgment has done in the past and will continue to do in the present and in the future. Judgment is therefore not all negative. It does get rid of all that is wicked, not of God, and does not serve His purpose; but judgment also brings in that which will glorify God. One day, He will judge the whole world; and, of course, we know that the fulfillment of this still lies sometime in the future. Nevertheless, we read prophecy—whether in Zechariah or Daniel or Revelation—wherein we learn that all the nations will one day be gathered together in the Middle East, Jerusalem will be broken into two, and there will be the last war—the war of Armageddon, with the Lord Jesus having returned to the earth. He will judge the whole world, purify everything, bring in the millennial kingdom, and all peoples will have a pure language. Having a pure language simply means that all peoples will speak of God, glorify God, and worship God. This is what judgment will do.

Zephaniah provides us with the sweetest love song of God to be found in the entire Old Testament: "Jehovah thy God is in thy midst, a mighty one that will save: he will rejoice over thee with joy; he will rest in his love; he will exult over thee with singing" (3:17).

Whenever we read in Scripture about love or singing or rejoicing, we usually think of ourselves: how we rejoice in God or how we sing to God. That is the way we usually think when considering these activities. But in this particular passage it is clearly not the case of our rejoicing in God or of our resting in His love or of our exulting over Him with singing. In the natural order of things that would be very much expected. Here, though, it is God who is stated as engaging in such emotional activities. God is the One who will rejoice; He is the One who will rest in His love; He is the One who will exult over man with singing. Think of that! It is as though God is adopting the position of a mortal being and who is expressing His love towards man, and in a sense He is left speechless in His attempt to do so. For the word rest here can be accurately translated as "silent in His love." Indeed, God's spokesman Zephaniah is at a loss in explaining God's heart, so he simply reports that God will rest or be silent in His love!

Now we human beings consider love to be something very audible and verbal in its expression; but Zephaniah states here that Jehovah God will be silent in His love, as if He has no words to utter. In other words, God loves us so much that He does not know what to say—that there is too much love in Him for Him to say anything. Have we not experienced this ourselves? Sometimes when love has become so deep, a person does not have any words; just being together causes love to flow without any words being uttered. One simply rests in love. What kind of rest is that? It is very restful, is it not? Such love is more than just talking. As the saying goes, talk can be cheap, but silence is golden; and here we are told that God says: "I will rest in My love." In other words, when God looks at us, He embraces us, caresses us, thinks constantly about us and admires us; and not knowing what to say, He ends up saying nothing; indeed, He ends up expressing everything in silence—He will rest and be silent in His great love for us. And, then, after a period of rest, God will burst out with singing in exultation over us! Now *that* is the great love which God has towards us. Our God is truly quite emotional. Praise Him for that!

So from this we can see that the book of Zephaniah is not that depressing. Some have thought Zephaniah to be a very depressing book. Even the great Bible expositor G. Campbell Morgan confessed that before he began to study the minor prophets, he expected to read about all the solemn, severe and harsh judgments of God. And when he actually commenced the study, he found it to be even more severe and more solemn. Nevertheless, he also discovered that a tremendously tender love and compassion of God was to be found as well in these minor prophets. Can we also see this aspect here in Zephaniah? It is there because God judges in love. He loves, therefore He judges. And through judgment, God brings us back to His love. That is essentially Zephaniah's message to God's people.

Now as earlier mentioned, the day of Jehovah or day of the Lord is a very special term in the Bible. In the Old Testament we can find it in such places as Isaiah 2:12, Joel 2:31, in the latter chapters of Amos and the last chapter of Malachi; and likewise in the New Testament we can find it in II Thessalonians 2:2. This term signifies the day of the wrath of God. There is also another term used in the New Testament which is called the day of Christ. The day of Christ and the day of the Lord signify two different events. Let us not be confused by mixing them up. The day of Christ or Christ's day is actually related to the church—to us. It can especially be found in three books of the New Testament: Philippians 1:6, 10; 2:16; I Corinthians 1:8; 5:5; and II Corinthians 1:14. These are very different terms: the day of the Lord is the day of God's wrath, but the day of Christ is the day of glory.

What are we who believe in the Lord Jesus looking forward to? We as the people of God do not look forward to the day of the Lord. We as God's people look forward to the day of Christ. The latter simply refers to the day when Christ returns and we shall all appear before Him and when all of God's faithful ones among His people shall be glorified. Yes, in the day of Christ there shall also be judgment, for it is the judgment seat of Christ before which all God's people shall appear. But if we want to receive glory in that day, we must seek meekness today and then we shall not be put to shame in that day. So it is a day which the church—God's people—is looking forward to. Those faithful ones of His are looking forward to the coming of Christ when they shall appear before Him, see Him face to face, and be rewarded: indeed, it shall be the day of their glory.

On the other hand, the day of the Lord mentioned in Revelation, refers, in its strictest application, to the seven bowls or vials. We may recall that there are mentioned in chapter 16 seven seals, seven trumpets, and then seven golden vials or bowls. Seven angels have these seven golden bowls given to them, signifying the seven plagues of God's wrath. This coming day of the Lord shall be a terrible day, but you and I—if we have been obedient and faithful to God—will not be there. We shall already be gone. And hence, the day of the Lord has nothing to do with us, but woe betide the world in that day and even betide God's chosen earthly people who remain because there will be judgment meted out upon them in order to purify them. That is why the Thessalonian believers, being aware of all this, were greatly troubled because some people had told them that the terrible day of the Lord had already come, prompting these believers to say: "If the day of the Lord is now here, then this means we have missed out on the rapture completely." Hearing of their troubled hearts, Paul wrote them, saying: "No, the day of the Lord has not come yet, because before that day arrives, the man of sin must first be revealed in the midst of great apostasy" (see II Thessalonians 2:1-12). So if we are faithful to God, we shall not be looking forward to the day of the Lord but to the day of Christ.

THE CALL FOR OVERCOMERS

Finally, let us take note that there is a spiritual application to be explained here. Israel, as the chosen earthly people of God, serves as a type of the church. In this world God has chosen the church to be His vessel or instrument to bear the testimony of Jesus to the world in showing the world who Jesus is and to bring salvation to the world. Unfortunately, the church has not fulfilled its mission. Already by the latter years of John the apostle at the end of the first century, the Lord Jesus as High Priest found it necessary to walk among, and critically observe, seven lampstands, representing seven churches in the province of Asia as represented by these seven golden lampstands that appeared to John by revelation; and the Lord Jesus was judging these churches (see Revelation 2 and 3). In other words, judgment—as we are told elsewhere in Scripture—begins with the house of God (I Peter 4:17a). As a matter of fact, the Lord has been judging His church from the first century even right up to our day. But let us be aware that when He judges His church, He does so as a priest—even as God's High Priest. Yet priestly judgment is quite different from kingly judgment. And the priestly judgment which we find the Lord Jesus engaged in, as prophetically described in Revelation chapters 2 and 3, symbolically presents a picture of the Lord tending and trimming lamps; that is to say, He is engaged in His High Priestly work of judging His church in an attempt to recover and restore His vessel of testimony to this lost world.

Throughout all of church history the Lord has been judging His church and calling her to repentance in an attempt to restore the church's testimony; but the church as a whole has not listened. Down through the centuries, therefore, the Lord has been calling for overcomers. Yet let us be clear that overcomers are none other than those who seek meekness and righteousness, and who are willing to accept His discipline; and these the Lord will hide. In fact, concerning this matter of His hiding and preserving His faithful ones, the Lord has promised this: "I will keep you away from the hour of trial that is to come upon this whole earth (the Great Tribulation), if you keep the word of my patience" (see Revelation 3:10). In other words, even before the Great Tribulation that is to come upon this earth (which, let it be understood, is not the great day of the Lord, but occurs prior to that terrible day), He will hide His faithful ones. And on another occasion the Lord gave further indication to His people of the hope of being hidden away during the very troublous times to come: "Watch and pray that ye may escape all these things and stand before the Son of man" (see Luke 21:36).

God's word tells us clearly that He will hide those who keep the word of His patience (Revelation 3:10). Those who watch and pray God will take to himself even before the Great Tribulation comes upon the earth. Moreover, even those who are left behind during the Great Tribulation, He will hide; for let us notice that after the manchild (representing collectively the overcomers) is to be taken up to heaven, God will take care of the woman (representing the greatly flawed church) (see Revelation 12:6). Furthermore, let us also notice that God will seal a hundred and forty-four thousand of the twelve tribes of Israel (see Revelation 7). He will seal them so as to keep them through the Great Tribulation. In short, He will hide and spare them.

Yes, indeed, God must and will judge; but thank God that He will hide His treasured ones. During the days of declension, when there shall be some who fear the Lord and talk one to another about Him, God will observe, listen, and note down in His book; and by this means God will remember them (see Malachi 3:16). And then, concerning the day of preparation of His treasured possession God has declared this: "I will spare them as one spares his only begotten" (see Malachi 3:17). In other words, He will hide them. So may the Lord help us that we may be a peculiar treasure to Him and thus He will hide us in the days of wrath.

Let us pray:

> *Dear heavenly Father, we do thank Thee that Thou dost have a word for us today. Lord, we thank Thee that though the day of judgment is coming, Thou wilt hide those whom Thou wilt consider as treasure to Thyself. Lord, we are unworthy, but we do want to humble ourselves before Thee and seek meekness and righteousness so that we, by Thy grace, may be hidden in the days of wrath. In the name of our Lord Jesus. Amen.*

HAGGAI

REBUILDING THE HOUSE OF GOD

Haggai 1:1-15—In the second year of Darius the king, in the sixth month, on the first day of the month, came the word of Jehovah by the prophet Haggai unto Zerubbabel the son of Shealtiel, governor of Judah, and to Joshua the son of Jehozadak, the high priest, saying, Thus speaketh Jehovah of hosts, saying, This people say, The time is not come, the time that Jehovah's house should be built. And the word of Jehovah came by Haggai the prophet, saying, Is it time for you that ye should dwell in your wainscoted houses, while this house lieth waste? And now thus saith Jehovah of hosts: Consider your ways. Ye have sown much, and bring in little; ye eat, but are not satisfied; ye drink, but are not filled with drink; ye clothe yourselves, but there is none warm; and he that earneth wages earneth wages for a bag with holes. Thus saith Jehovah of hosts: Consider your ways. Go up to the mountain and bring wood, and build the house, and I will take pleasure in it, and I will be glorified, saith Jehovah. Ye looked for much, and behold it was little; and when ye brought it home, I blew upon it. Wherefore? saith Jehovah of hosts. Because of my house that lieth waste, whilst ye run every man to his own house. Therefore over you the heavens withhold their dew, and the earth withholdeth its fruit. And I called for a drought upon the land, and upon the mountains, and upon the corn, and upon the new wine, and upon the oil, and upon that which the ground bringeth forth, and upon man, and upon cattle, and upon all the labour of the hands.

And Zerubbabel the son of Shealtiel, and Joshua the son of Jehozadak, the high priest, and all the remnant of the people, hearkened to the voice of Jehovah their God, and the words of Haggai the prophet, according as Jehovah their God had sent him, and the people feared before Jehovah. Then spoke Haggai, Jehovah's messenger, in Jehovah's message unto the people, saying, I am with you, saith Jehovah. And Jehovah stirred up the spirit of Zerubbabel the son of Shealtiel, governor of Judah, and the spirit of Joshua the son of Jehozadak, the high priest, and the spirit of all the remnant of the people; and they came and worked at the house of Jehovah of hosts, their God, in the four and twentieth day of the sixth month, in the second year of Darius the king.

We know that there are altogether twelve so-called minor prophets, and the prophecies of these twelve cover approximately four hundred years, from 800 B.C. to about 400 B.C., and they can be divided into three periods. The first is what we would call the Assyrian period—roughly from 800 to 625 B.C., the latter date being when Nineveh was destroyed. The second is what we would call the Babylonian period; and it was from 625 to around 538 B.C., the latter being the date of Babylon's destruction. The last period was the Medo-Persian, which was the period following the destruction of Babylon, from 538 to around 400 B.C.; and we sometimes call this the postexilic period. With the time of the prophet Haggai we are entering the third of these periods—the Medo-Persian or postexilic period. We learned earlier that because of their unfaithfulness to God, the children of Israel were taken into Babylonian captivity; but God was faithful to His promises and faithful to His covenant. So after seventy years, God stirred up the spirit of King Cyrus of the Medo-Persian Empire to allow the children of Israel, who were his captives at that time, to return to Jerusalem to rebuild the house of God.

In order to better understand the necessary background, we need to recognize that there are altogether five Old Testament books which deal with this postexilic period—that is to say, the period following the Babylonian exile. Two of these five books are historical: Ezra and Nehemiah. Ezra deals more with the religious aspect—the rebuilding of the temple and the beautifying of the temple service. On the other hand, Nehemiah deals more with the civil aspect of the people of God—the rebuilding of the wall and how to strengthen the life of the people together as the city of God. Hence, these two books deal with the history of that time.

The three other books deal with the prophecies during that period—Haggai, Zechariah and Malachi. So, actually, in our discussion here we are entering into a new period or stage, and Haggai was the first one who was raised up by God to speak to the remnant people who returned from Babylonian captivity to rebuild the house of God.

We know from history that the captivity began in 606 B.C. when Nebuchadnezzar, the king of Babylon, came and took some of the children of Israel captive into Babylon. And thus the seventy-year period of captivity began in 606 B.C. and ended with the return to Jerusalem of the remnant from Babylon in 536 B.C. They came back under the leadership of Zerubbabel and Joshua. The next year, 535 B.C., they laid the foundation of the temple; but after the foundation was laid they were attacked, accused and threatened by their neighbors the Samaritans; and because of this persecution and oppression, the work of building the temple ceased for some fifteen or sixteen years. It was therefore not until 520 B.C. that the rebuilding was resumed under the prophetic ministry of Haggai, and by 515 B.C. the second temple was finished. This, then, is the background of the book of Haggai.

A REMNANT STIRRED BY GOD

The children of Israel who came back from Babylon to Jerusalem were only a remnant, which meant that most of the Jews who had been taken captive to Babylon simply remained behind in captivity after seventy years. They did not bother to uproot themselves and return to Jerusalem with the others who did return. Only a remnant, a small number whose spirits were stirred by God, were willing to give up what they had built for themselves during that seventy-year period and return to Jerusalem, which was still a most barren and ruined place. Yet they returned for one reason only—to rebuild the temple of God.

We know that during this time of captivity the temple in Jerusalem was destroyed. And if we read the Scripture carefully, we will find that during that period, God was no longer called the God of the heavens and the earth. Indeed, from this time forward He was almost always addressed simply as the God of the heavens and not also as the God of the earth, because there was now no testimony of Him on the earth anymore. The children of Israel were supposed to have been the vessel of the testimony of God on earth; but because Jerusalem and the temple were now destroyed and the Israelites were now in captivity, God had no testimony on the earth. He was called the God of the heavens but no longer referred to as the God of the earth, even though He most assuredly still was.

The remnant of God's people had returned to Jerusalem to rebuild the temple in order that God might have a name upon this earth. They had returned solely for His testimony. They did not return for their own interest, for if they had been concerned with their interest, they—like the others—would have remained in Babylon because through the years they all had built houses and businesses for themselves. In fact, everything seemed to be permanently built up. But thank God that despite all of that, a remnant of them were stirred up to return to rebuild God's temple.

The only reason for this minority remnant's return was to rebuild the temple of God; however, upon arriving back, they encountered opposition, oppression and troubles of all kinds when their enemies began to surround and attack them; with the result that their hands were weakened and the work for which they had returned to accomplish ceased for fifteen or sixteen years. But, of course, during those years of cessation they had to be occupied with doing something; so instead of continuing to build the house of God they began to build houses for themselves. Yet they did not build simple huts or cabins; they built expensive wainscoted or paneled houses. In short, they spent all their money, energy and time on building houses for themselves.

Interestingly, during that entire fifteen-year period they never said they would *not* build the house of God; on the contrary, they said: "One day we shall still build the house of God, but this is not the time; we will simply wait until a more opportune moment comes, and then we will resume building His house." Consequently, that kind of mentality postponed the building of God's house for some fifteen or sixteen years. Nevertheless, as time went on, and even though they had not forgotten their commitment, they entered into a period of passivity in regard to the building of the temple of God.

GOD RAISED UP A PROPHET

So in response, God raised up a prophet by the name of Haggai. Haggai means "festive" or "the festivals of God." In other words, God raised up this particular man to bring in the festivals of God—that is to say, to bring in a happy atmosphere and the fullness of joy in the Lord among His people. We do not know much about Haggai's background but we do know that he was an old man. He probably was one of those who had seen the old Solomonic temple when but a boy. By the time of his being raised up by God, however, Haggai must have been in his eighties or even beyond; even so, God raised up this old man as His spokesman for a short time. As a matter of fact, this prophet's total period of ministry did not last longer than four months, and he only delivered four brief messages. Yet in that brief period of four months, with only those few messages, the heart of God's remnant people at Jerusalem was stirred up and the temple was finally rebuilt.

We will recall reading in Ezra that when this remnant came back and laid the foundation of God's house, the old men among them who had seen the former house *wept* for joy, whereas the young men among them who had not seen the former house *shouted* for joy. So Haggai must have been one of those old men who had wept for joy, and he was the one raised up by God to stir up the remnant to resume the building of this second temple.

GOD'S NAME ON EARTH—THE CHURCH

Here we need to pause and draw from all this a spiritual analogy for ourselves, because we believe that the book of Haggai has much to do with us today. Let us, first of all, clearly understand that the prophecy of Haggai was not directed towards the children of Israel in general nor towards those who had remained in Babylonian captivity.

Rather, it was aimed exclusively at the faithful remnant of Israelites who had returned from Babylon to Jerusalem to rebuild the house of God. And secondly, let us also understand that they had not forgotten why they had returned, but because of difficult circumstances they had failed to fulfill what they had returned to accomplish. Instead, they soon became occupied with building their own houses. Hence, in drawing the spiritual analogy for our time from this prophetic book, these are the things for which we need to have a clear understanding.

Now we know that the church of God is His chosen vessel. God in Christ puts His name there; for did not Jesus say: "Where two or three are gathered together unto My name, there am I in the midst of them"? In essence, therefore, the Lord is saying here: "I give My name to you" (see Matthew 18:20). And thus the church is the vessel for the name of the Lord Jesus and is the vessel of the testimony of Jesus. How will the world know the Lord Jesus except through the church? She is to present Christ Jesus to the world as He is. This has always been the calling of the church; but unfortunately, when the Roman Emperor, Constantine the Great, adopted Christianity in the early fourth century A.D., the world came into the church and began to rule over her. Christ, not Constantine or anyone else, is the head of the church. Yet history tells us that after Emperor Constantine adopted Christianity and called the Council of Nicaea together, he himself presided over it. Which signified that the world had entered the church and now governed her.

Gradually the church situation changed further. By the time of the sixth century the Roman Empire had already collapsed, and now it was the Roman Catholic Church which began to rule over the church of God. Which meant that instead of the church being governed by the *secular* world, it was now under the control of the *religious* world. In short, the church of God was in captivity.

Except for the first few centuries of her history God's church has been in captivity—if not in captivity under the rule of the secular world, then under the rule of the so-called religious world. But thank God that in every generation, in every century, God has always raised up a remnant. They might be few in number by comparison—and despised, persecuted and misunderstood—nevertheless, God has always had some believers to maintain the testimony of Jesus. There have always been some who returned, as it were, from Babylon to Jerusalem: from confusion to simplicity, purity and peace that are in Christ (cf. II Corinthians 11:3). And down through the centuries these few have always maintained the testimony of Jesus in the world even though they were persecuted by the secular Roman world and later on by the religious world of the Roman Catholic Church and still later even by certain segments of the Protestant Church. Many were martyred, many were killed; but thank God that throughout the centuries there have always been those who were faithful to God, to His word, and to the testimony of Jesus.

In the sixteenth century A.D. there occurred what we call the Reformation; and, historically speaking, the recovery work of God concerning His testimony occurred more intensely at this time, even though we know that before the Reformation there had been instances of recovery all along the way. But with the Reformation there occurred a new beginning because it was more worldwide in scope and of a far more extensive nature. The most important development which happened during the Reformation was the recovery of the teaching and reality of "justification by faith." Yet even more important than that was the recovery of the open Bible—a Bible which was for all peoples in their own languages and in their own tongues so that everybody could read it or hear it read.

Unfortunately, however, we find it eventually became clear that the Reformation did not bring Christians back to God's original purpose for His church; so instead of there only being the international or worldwide Catholic Church, national churches sprang up in different lands and countries. And in time so-called dissenters and independent churches emerged. Even though there was indeed a recovery during the Reformation, it was not one in its fullness; and because of that, in the ensuing centuries since the Reformation there could always be found a faithful remnant. God was continually calling a remnant to return, as it were, to Jerusalem; and there were always a faithful few who responded in returning to the purity and simplicity of Christ, to the maintenance of the faith, to the keeping of the truth, to refusing to deny the name of the Lord Jesus, to a return to the Bible, and to a return to God's original purpose. In researching the matter we discover that there were always some people who made serious attempts to return, even during the time of the Reformation. These people had fervently wished to return fully to the Bible and its teachings and practices; yet, strangely, they ended up being persecuted by the Reformers and some were even martyred for their faith. Such, then, is the general history of what has occurred concerning the recovery of the testimony of Jesus on the earth.

GOD CALLS EVEN NOW

Now as we come to the close of this present age, we do believe that God is even more earnestly calling His people out of the so-called church that is in captivity and captured by a religious system. He is calling people to return to Jerusalem and to the simplicity of Christ where they can maintain the testimony of Jesus. And by analogy we can readily say that this book of Haggai is especially addressed to such people. Thank God, that in our day there are people all over the world who are not satisfied with remaining in captivity and being bound by the religious systems of this world. They truly seek the Lord, wishing to experience the fullness of Christ; and because of this, they want to return to the simplicity and sincerity which are in Christ, and they also want to be gathered together simply to the Lord. They do not want to be divided but to be open to all of God's people for fellowship. They desire to build up together the temple or house of God as the testimony of Jesus. Throughout the world there are people like that who are in different stages or degrees in experiencing all of this; but thank God that there are such people who exist all over the world. They are unknown to the world, unknown even to the religious world, but are certainly known to God. Yet, oddly enough, these are the people who are being misunderstood, persecuted and despised; nonetheless, they are maintaining the testimony of Jesus. Their task is to rebuild the house of God so that He may have a place to put His name and dwell among His people and do His work through His people.

RETURN TO FIRST LOVE

Such people have been called to do but one thing, just as the Jewish remnant had returned to Jerusalem back in the time of Haggai for but one purpose—not two purposes, only one. They returned specifically to build the house of God. That was their purpose. Is it not true that our call today from God is for just one purpose? He has called us out of the secular world and He has called us out of the religious world. For what reason? It is for one purpose only—to build the house of God and that we may be built together as His house for Him to dwell in by His Spirit in order that the name of Jesus may be lifted up and glorified. Indeed, that is the whole purpose for why we ourselves are gathered here.

During those days in Haggai's time a remnant of God's captive people came back to Jerusalem and started to build; but, then, oppression arose, attacks began, difficulties came, and problems developed; and because of these things, the work stopped. Even so, they did not give up completely, yet they did not go on building the house of God; instead, they began to build their own houses.

Do we not today have the same temptation? We frequently forget why we are here. We are here for only one purpose—to build the house of God. But sometimes because of some difficulties, we begin to build our private houses instead. Let us look at the condition of the Jewish remnant at that time in Haggai's day. Why did they cease building God's house? Yes, it is quite true that the Samaritans attacked them and tried to weaken their hands. They even got the king to give an order that the work should cease; yet these are not the true reasons for the stoppage because when they finally did resume the building of the temple, those adverse situations were still present. Hence, the explanation for their ceasing to build the house of God was actually due to an inward reason. For when the Jewish remnant had returned to Jerusalem there was the initial thrill and excitement of their souls: "We have come back to build the house of God out of ruin!" It was something very heroic, even bold, and an event to excite their souls; but when these people actually got down to the business of laboring daily, it was a different matter altogether. Very quickly, the zeal and enthusiasm began to fade away. Or, to put it in stronger terms, they began to leave their first love. When they had that first love, there was strength and motivation; but when their first love gradually began to fade, naturally, the work commenced to dwindle until it came to a complete stop. So the problem had to do with this matter of first love.

When we read the letters of the Risen Lord sent to the seven Asian churches mentioned in Revelation, do we not discern the same development? There God's controversy with His people was that the believers had left their first love. We can therefore see that what God is really desiring is that first love towards Him; but oftentimes, when the thrill of revelation and the excitement of a new vision starts to fade away, somehow the first love of God's people begins to dissipate.

CONSIDER—"SET YOUR HEART ON"

Now as we carefully read the prophecy of Haggai, we shall discover a key word there. It is a word which God specifically addressed to His people who were marked by one particular condition—they were a people who had returned from Babylon to Jerusalem to rebuild His house but who in time were no longer building it. For such a people God has a very special word: *consider*. Five times in this short prophetic book God had said: Consider.

What is meant by this word? It actually means to "set your heart on." Given the particular condition of God's people back then, this word Consider conveys the following thought: You people have been engaged in building your own houses; indeed, so busily engaged that you no longer think correctly anymore. You now take things for granted. You have accepted the notion that the circumstances you find yourselves in are too difficult for you to build My house any longer. And therefore, you say: "We have to wait for a better, more auspicious time; so how are we going to occupy the time we have on our hands? Well, now, let us build our own houses." Consequently, as they built their houses for the next fifteen years, they all along thought they were doing the right thing; But they did not realize what was happening to them. In other words, their spirits had begun to grow dull, even, as it were, to have gone to sleep. So God had to say to His people: "Consider, think correctly once again, give careful thought to, set your heart upon, ponder over, what is happening in your lives, and repent and return to doing the first work."

Do we not at times need the same word today? As time goes on, things can begin to become very routine, and gradually, our spirits become dull. We may even take everything for granted and think that everything is all right, that all is fine; but at times God may have to send a minister of His word to us to stir us up and say to us, as He did to that Jewish remnant: "You say it is not the time to build the house of God. Is it time for you to build your own houses?"

Time is a very big problem for God's people. God is the God of eternity; and thus He is timeless. But He created time in order that a certain work of His may be done on the earth. He gave us—His people—time so that, in time, we may do His work. Time is opportunity given to us by God, time is His gift to us for accomplishing His work. Yet how do we use this gift of time? There is only this time; but the question is, How do we use the time God has assigned to us?

The Jewish remnant had said: "It is not the time to build the house of God." Why did they say this? It was because in their minds it had become too much trouble to build God's house. But God's response was: "Is it time for you to build your own houses? You allow My house to lie waste while you run to build your own houses. Is it time for you to do this?" We today can either use our time to build the house of God or use our time to build our own house and further our own affairs. Which house are we building?

When the Lord Jesus was on earth, He said on one occasion to His brothers in the flesh: "My time is not yet come, but your time is always ready" (John 7:6). When Jesus was on earth, time was a very important factor to Him. He always waited for the timing of His Father. Whenever His Father's time had arrived, He did the work. He never used the time for himself but always used the time God gave Him—thirty-three-odd years—according to His Father's timetable. But Jesus had said to His brothers in the flesh, "Your time is always ready." Instead of seeking to do the will of God in the time apportioned to them, they took time into their hands and used it for their private purposes. Therefore, time for them was always ready. They could go anywhere they wanted to go, do whatever they wanted to do, whenever they wanted to go or do—because it was always their time.

God had apportioned the time to the Jewish remnant to build His house, but they said: "No, it is not the time to build the house of God." They took time into their hands and declared: "It is time for us to build *our* houses." Their time was always ready.

If you are trying to use God's gift of time for Him, the enemy will try every way to frustrate you and make it so difficult that you end up believing it is not the time. But if you use the time to build up your personal interests or to build your private house or to build your personal kingdom, you will find that the time is always right for you because the enemy will help you along. There will be no opposition to such self-centered activities. Your time will always be right. Do we not discover the same thing? Time is indeed something everybody is fighting for. God is fighting for the time He has given us, but the enemy is also fighting for the same time.

When God delivered His message through Moses to Pharaoh and said, "Let My people go that they may serve Me," Pharaoh replied: "All right, I shall have the children of Israel do hard labor to such an extent so as to occupy all their time and energy that they will not think of going away to serve God."

Is not the enemy trying to do the same thing with us today? We who wish to be faithful to God are not just a people of the world. We are not even merely God's people. On the contrary, we are God's people who have come out of captivity to build the house of God, and the enemy is doing his very best to rob us of all our time by attempting to have us all so occupied with our private personal interests that we have no time to build the house of God. Where, for example, are God's people when the time for prayer comes? Where are His people when the time of fellowshipping over His word is present? If we are able to be present with God's people once a week and spend two hours, we think we are the best Christians in the world; but are we building the house of God? Such conduct is not building God's house. Building His house should be our occupation; He and

His house should have priority over all things. Too often, however, we have given up building the house of God and thus we say, "This is not the time." Yet the Lord responds by saying: "Is it time for you to build your own houses?" Yes, we each need a house in which to live, but we do not need a paneled house. We do need to be occupied, but if we are not occupied with building the house of God, surely we will be occupied with building our own houses. So the controversy among God's people today is a contention over time.

CONSIDER YOUR WAYS

God repeatedly said, "Consider." The first instance of this is found in chapter 1 of Haggai: "Consider your ways." Give careful thought to what you have been doing: "Ye have sown much, and bring in little; ye eat, but are not satisfied; ye drink, but are not filled with drink; ye clothe yourselves, but there is none warm; and he that earneth wages earneth wages for a bag with holes" (1:6).

In brief, God was saying here that nothing is satisfying, nothing of My purpose is being fulfilled. Why was that? You need to stop and think about what has been happening to you! During the past fifteen or sixteen years, while My house has been lying waste and you have been occupied with building your own houses, you have been putting much time, energy and resources into it, but how much satisfaction have you obtained and how much of My purpose has been fulfilled?

Let me inquire: Are you satisfied? Or are you still spiritually hungry? Having put much time and labor into building up your personal interest, have you gotten much out of it in return? Or do you now realize that though you have been earning wages, you have actually been putting them in purses which have holes? Have you at last realized that nothing you have been doing has been satisfying, that nothing has been fulfilled? Let us ask ourselves, are we, spiritually speaking, still in hunger and thirst, are we in spiritual poverty? If so, we may wonder, Why is it? In essence, the Lord is saying to us here, through His prophet Haggai, that the reason for this is because we are under discipline: "When you are out from under My ways, you are under My discipline. In response to your field labors I make sure you bring in little. And even when you bring this little home, I blow upon it." You are under the discipline of the Lord. Therefore, think, give careful thought to your ways!

CONSIDER YOUR MATERIALS

The second "Consider" is mentioned in 1:7-8. This second instance was not the same as the first one. The first was a looking backward, a looking at what the people had been doing during those fifteen wasted years. The second, on the other hand, was a looking forward to the fulfillment of God's purpose: "Go up to the mountains and take the wood, bring it down, build the house, and I will be pleased, I will be glorified."

If we want to build the house of God, we must go up—we must go to the mountains. This command signifies spiritual elevation. We simply cannot gather materials for the building of God's house on the plains. If we mix ourselves with the world, we are unable to gather the proper materials for the building of God's house. We have to be set apart in spiritual elevation in order to avail ourselves of the heavenlies; and there in communion with God we shall receive all the spiritual materials necessary for the building of His house. And if we do that, then the Lord will say: "I shall be pleased, I shall be glorified."

Whom are you pleasing? Whom do you want to glorify? For whom are you living? For yourself? Are you living to please and glorify yourself? Or are you living for God, wishing to please and glorify Him? It glorifies God to build His house. It pleases Him because this is what He wants. He wishes to dwell among His people and put His name there. He wants to grant His peace there (see 2:9b).

These are the first two "Considers" which the prophet brought to the attention of the returned Jewish remnant. And thank God that Zerubbabel, Joshua, and all the people feared God. They were stirred in their spirits and the word came to Haggai, God's messenger, and the message of God to the people was: "I am with you" (see 1:13b). This same message of God, "I am with you," would even come forth a second time later (see 2:4b).

There is no promise of God more precious than this: "I am with you." If God is with us, who can resist us? If He is with us, we can work to build His house. In spite of all opposition, it shall be done. So God promised the Jewish remnant: "I am with you." He stirred the spirits of Zerubbabel, Joshua, and all the people and thus they began the work of building the house on the twenty-fourth day of the sixth month of Darius the king's second year. So the work resumed. Thank God that they had listened and obeyed.

I do believe God is challenging us today on this matter of time. We often say we have no time. Yes, we are busily occupied, but we have to make time for the Lord. He must have the first place in our lives. We are here for the building of God's house, for He has given us time for that one and only purpose. If we do not use it for that purpose, then we have wasted the time which God has apportioned to each one of us.

Haggai was an old man who would soon pass away. Because of this, he was very burdened that the building of God's house should be finished.

THE SECOND MESSAGE

Let us notice that each message which Haggai brought forth begins with "the word of Jehovah." The second message (see chapter 2:1ff.) came on the twenty-first day of the seventh month. This was less than a month after they had resumed building from the foundation up. So God sent Haggai to them again and said: "You have been working for about a month, and what do you see? Who is left among you who saw this house in its former glory, and how do you see it now? Is it not as nothing in your eyes?"

Now Haggai was one who had seen the glory of the former house, that is, of Solomon's temple. So he asked the people: "What do you see now?" Of course, they had barely resumed the construction of this second temple; yet even with this new beginning, they could already discern what the new temple of God would look like when it was finished. And, outwardly speaking, God knew it could not be compared in any way with King Solomon's temple. Today's resources were so limited; today's people were so few in number; and also, they were not in a peaceful situation as was the case in Solomon's day when there was an era of peace. (Even when actually finished, this second house of God could still not be compared with Solomon's temple.)

Now because of this preliminary dismal comparison, some people were discouraged: "It is so small, so what is the use of continuing to build it?" Very quickly, despair and disappointment surfaced in the hearts of the people. So Haggai was sent by God this second time to tell them: "Be strong. What I covenanted with you when I brought you out of Egypt still stands. I have not changed and My Spirit is still with you. Therefore, do not fear." In other words, God was strengthening them through His word which came forth from Haggai. So God said: "I am with you. My covenant is with you. My Spirit is with you. Do not be afraid. Be strong. Continue on, and work; because one day I will shake the heavens and the earth, the sea, the land, and all nations, and the Desire of all nations shall come; and I tell you now that the latter glory of this house shall be greater than the former one" (see 2:4-9).

How many houses does God have? Some people have a winter house, a summer house, a house here, a house there; but God has only one house. Solomon's temple was His house, and it was destroyed. When the second temple was built by the Jewish remnant, outwardly, it was another house. But God said: "You think you are building a second temple; no, I have only one house. This little structure which you see being built is but a part of the one house that I am after. Though by comparison with the former temple it is very small, even so, it is Mine. It is part of what I am ultimately after and I shall continue to work on it until, one day, everything will be shaken and the Desire of all nations shall come." Of course, that is a reference to the Messiah who is to come again. Christ shall again come, and meanwhile He is building the house. For when first on earth did He not declare that He would build His church and the gates of Hades would not prevail against it, and that it shall be a glorious church without spot or wrinkle? (see Matthew 16:18b; Ephesians 5:27). So God through His prophet was essentially saying to the people of the remnant that the little edifice which they were at that moment laboring to build was part of that. It was not apart from God's one house but was very much an integral part of it. And that it would be in there—in this present but far less imposing temple—that His glory would come and fill once again (see 2:7b). Indeed, God promised that "the latter glory of this house shall be greater than the former glory." In other words, the glory of Solomon's house cannot be compared with the glorious church that is being built without spot or wrinkle or any of such things—holy, and without blemish—and which is to be presented to Christ as His bride.

Now this is the house which God is truly after. And if we are able to see *this*, we will not be discouraged. Yes, it is true that when we look around, we may at times feel that there is so little to show for all our labors, even, almost nothing. So we may be inclined to say, Why bother to labor any further? It is more comfortable and satisfying to enter a grand cathedral, listen to wonderful music, and be soothed by pleasing words. Why bother, indeed, to mix one's sweat with one's tears and undertake any longer to build something which to most human eyes is absolutely nothing?

Oh, if we can only catch a vision of God's glorious church, would that not be enough to satisfy us and to dispel any discouragement, despair or disappointment? For it is about *that* church—as small and insignificant as it may presently appear to man—that the Lord God has said: "*That* is what I am building, and it is here—in this place, in this small part of the one glorious dwelling place which I am ultimately after—where I shall grant My peace" (see again 2:7b, 9a, 9b).

THE THIRD MESSAGE

Three months had now passed since beginning to build. On the twenty-fourth day of the ninth month, in the second year of Darius, the word of God came once more to Haggai, but this time in the form of a parable (see 2:10ff.): Concerning what the Law says, ask the priests if when one carries holy flesh in the skirt of his garment and that holy flesh, being offered as a sacrifice, touches other things—bread, pottage, wine, oil, or any food—will they become holy? In other words, when holy flesh touches anything, will that make the thing touched holy? And the priests answered, "No." Signifying that holiness does not spread like that. But next, the priests were asked that if someone touches a dead body and then touches any of these aforementioned things, do they make those things defiled or unclean? "Yes," came the priests' reply. Uncleanness contaminates.

After three months of putting their hands to the building of the house, the remnant people's economic situation had not changed. They were still under discipline as manifested in the fact that they had sown a lot but had gotten very little back in return. Likewise, the temple-building program, even with their renewed labor and intensified energy, had yielded very little results to show for it. They were still under God's discipline but they could not explain why. The remnant people had thought that when they hearkened to God's word and had resumed building His house, everything would change for the better and that God's rich blessing would come upon them. But their three months of obedience to God's word found them still under His discipline, as is evident from this verse in 2:16: "When one came to a heap of twenty measures, there were but ten; when one came to the [wine] vat to draw out fifty press-measures, there were but twenty."

They were still under discipline. They could not understand why the blessing had not come. "We have obeyed God, we are now building His house. Why has His blessing not come?" So the prophet told them, "It is because that at the time when you sowed the seed you were still unclean, so everything is unclean; but from this day forward, from this twenty-fourth day of the ninth month, you must again *consider*; before this new temple foundation was laid, you were under discipline, and you are still under it because what you sowed was unclean." This explanatory word of God had come to Haggai in the ninth month, which would have been in our month of November or December. This meant that the spring sowing-time had not arrived yet, and thus the Lord said, "What you are currently reaping is the past, you are still under my discipline; but from this day onward, My blessing will come; I will bless you." Here we find three more instances of God telling His people to "consider": twice in 2:15 and once in 2:18. God was saying to His people to give careful thought about all this, and the blessing will surely come. What a comfort this must have been to this people.

Sometimes we think: here we are doing the will of God, and yet, why is it that the blessing does not come? Let us realize that it requires a little time, but God's promise always remains true.

THE FOURTH MESSAGE

On that very same twenty-fourth day of the ninth month in King Darius's second year, a final message from God came to Haggai. It was a wonderful message: "Speak to Zerubbabel, governor of Judah, saying, I will shake the heavens and the earth; and I will overthrow the throne of kingdoms, and I will destroy the strength of the kingdoms of the nations; and I will overthrow the chariots, and those that ride therein; and the horses and their riders shall come down, every one by the sword of his brother. In that day, saith Jehovah of hosts, will I take thee, Zerubbabel son of Shealtiel, my servant, saith Jehovah, and will make thee as a signet; for I have chosen thee, saith Jehovah of hosts" (2:21-23).

Here Zerubbabel serves as a type of Christ. Just as Zerubbabel was chosen and used by God to build the so-called second temple, Christ is the Chosen One who will build the house of God to perfect completion. God will shake the heavens and the earth and everything therein in order that Christ may become all and in all. The Lord Jesus is *the* signet of God: He will put His stamp of approval upon everything. And in that coming day every knee shall bow and every tongue shall confess that Jesus is Lord (see Philippians 2:10-11). All things in heaven and earth and beneath the earth shall be under His feet. So we are looking forward to that day of the second coming of Christ.

Let us pray:

> *Dear Lord, we do believe that Thou dost have a word for us today. Lord, we are before Thee, exposed, laid bare, nothing hidden. Oh, do shine Thy light upon us. Speak to each one of us. Deliver us from running to build our own houses. Rather, turn all our hearts to Thee that we may together build Thy house. All our desire is that the house shall be built, that Thou shalt have a dwelling*

place, a place of rest among Thy people. Do not allow us to rest until Thou canst enter into Thy rest among Thy people. Lord, we do praise and thank Thee that even though what we can see is so little—almost nothing—yet Thou dost comfort us, for this little is nonetheless within Thy house. Lord, we are looking forward to the day when Thy house shall be completed and Thou shalt come back and claim it to be Thine own. Lord, we want to give it to Thee. In the name of our Lord Jesus. Amen.

ZECHARIAH

RETURN TO THE LORD

> *Zechariah 1:1-6—In the eighth month, in the second year of Darius, came the word of Jehovah unto Zechariah the prophet, the son of Berechiah, the son of Iddo, saying, Jehovah hath been very wroth with your fathers. And thou shalt say unto them, Thus saith Jehovah of hosts: Return unto me, saith Jehovah of hosts, and I will return unto you, saith Jehovah of hosts. Be ye not as your fathers, unto whom the former prophets cried, saying, Thus saith Jehovah of hosts: Turn ye now from your evil ways, and from your evil doings; but they did not hearken nor attend unto me, saith Jehovah. Your fathers, where are they? and the prophets, do they live for ever? But my words and my statutes, which I commanded my servants the prophets, did they not overtake your fathers? And they turned and said, Like as Jehovah of hosts thought to do unto us, according to our ways and according to our doings, so hath he dealt with us.*

As was mentioned earlier, there were three prophets who prophesied during the postexilic period, that is, after a remnant of the children of Israel had come back from Babylonian captivity. And these three prophets are also called prophets of restoration. We have already discussed Haggai; God raised up this old man to stir up the hearts of the returned remnant to resume the work of building the new temple in Jerusalem.

Today we would like to consider together the second prophet, Zechariah. He was a young man raised up by God to reinforce the prophecy which Haggai had brought forth. It is very interesting to notice that Haggai, being an old man, had seen the temple built by Solomon; which meant that he was acquainted with the glory of that temple. No wonder, therefore, that his heart was very much burdened for its rebuilding.

On the other hand, Zechariah was a young man. Actually, he had been born in Babylon and was brought back to Jerusalem when he was but an infant. Thus, he had never seen the old temple, and yet the Spirit of God gave him such a burden for the rebuilding of the temple that he was used of God to prophesy and to help towards its rebuilding. We can consequently see from this that God can use both old men and young men. He can put His burden upon those who have seen something which He has done before, and He can likewise put His burden upon those who have never seen anything which He has done previously but who can discern with spiritual eyes what He is going to do in the future. And hence, armed with the same vision, these two prophets together bore the same testimony to the people of God. In our day, therefore, may the Lord raise up for himself young men and old men having the same burden and having the same vision which God has given so that His house may be built.

Zechariah's name means "Jehovah remembers" or, "whom Jehovah remembers." We are told that he was the son of Berechiah, the son of Iddo. Now in the books of Ezra and Nehemiah, which narrate the history of recovery, Zechariah is simply referred to as the son of Iddo, whereas here in the book of Zechariah he is identified as the son of Berechiah, the son of Iddo. Why is this? We know that Iddo had been one of the priests who had returned to Jerusalem from Babylonian captivity with Zerubbabel and Joshua. He had also been a chief priest, and Iddo therefore had been a chief father among his family. And evidently Berechiah had returned with his father together with an infant grandson. Most likely Berechiah himself had died young, and because of this, and in accordance with Jewish custom, it was not unusual for the grandson to be identified after the grandfather. Hence, that is the reason why we read in Zechariah that he is called the son of Berechiah, the son of Iddo, whereas in Ezra and Nehemiah he is simply called the son of Iddo.

Zechariah began to prophesy two months after Haggai began prophesying. Haggai prophesied a very short period—altogether only four months, whereas Zechariah continued to prophesy; and from

Nehemiah 12 we learn that during the high priesthood of Joiakim, who was the successor to Joshua the high priest, there was a priest called Zechariah. If this be the same Zechariah now being discussed, then that would mean that this grandson of Iddo prophesied over a rather long period.

Another interesting point to note is that because he was an old man, Haggai's words were few, though most powerful. He was a cautious man but there was depth in him. By contrast, Zechariah, being a young man, was full of vitality and imagination, and his words were many. Now whether a person is cautious or whether he is vigorous, God can use that one if all has been surrendered to Him and dealt with by Him by means of the cross. From this, then, we realize that God can use a young man and He can use an old man; God can use the gifts and talents which He has given to each so long as there is a surrendered life and the dealing of the cross upon that life.

Now some Jewish traditions claim that Zechariah had been one of the members of the great synagogue who prepared the liturgical service for this second temple. Moreover, some Biblical scholars have ascribed to Zechariah the authorship of Psalms 137 and 138. Psalm 137 is today quite familiar to Jewish people because of its famous lines which read: "By the rivers of Babylon, we hanged our harps on the willows there; how then can we sing a song of Jehovah's in a foreign land?" Psalm 138, however, is a song of praise and worship to be sung in the temple of God. Probably these are the reasons why some have ascribed these two psalms to Zechariah. Additionally, there are those who believe that some of the Hallelujah Psalms were written by both Zechariah and Haggai, but we do not know for sure.

Even though this young man had been born in Babylon and his return had not been the result of his initiative—his father having brought him back to Jerusalem—nevertheless, Zechariah had caught such a vision of the glorious house of God and His majestic plan for the future that he could be used by God at this very moment in the history of the Jews. As a matter of fact, it was the prophesying of both Haggai and Zechariah which made possible the rebuilding of God's temple.

RETURN

In the book of Zechariah, its first six verses actually serve as a preface to the entire text. Or to put it another way, the theme or key to the whole book is found in these six verses; and if we would want to condense their content into but one word, that would be the word return. In the book of Haggai the key word there is consider. God called His people to consider—that is, to give careful thought to their past actions, to review their present condition, and to ponder over what was going to happen. In this book of Zechariah, however, the key word is return. The Lord is quoted in these opening verses as saying: "If you return to Me, I will return to you." The Lord also said that He had been very angry with their fathers because they had not heeded the words of His prophets to turn away from their evil ways and evil doings and turn back to Him. And because of this, God in His justifiable anger with them had allowed them to be taken away into Babylonian captivity. God concluded by saying: "Where are your fathers now? Where now are those prophets who prophesied to them at that time?" They are all gone. But the prophetic word of God had proven to be true.

God therefore used this to encourage the returned Jewish remnant who were now living in Jerusalem. In fact, they had just begun to rebuild the house of God. We will remember that after they had come back from Babylon they had erected the altar; and then they had laid the temple foundation. They had been intent on building God's house but, then, because of the opposition and persecution around them and the pressure being put upon them by their neighbors, the work ceased for some fifteen years. And during those years of stoppage, instead of continuing to build God's house, they each undertook to build their own house. They expended all their energy, resources and time to construct their own houses and pursued their private interests. These were paneled houses which they had constructed for themselves to dwell in—beautiful and elegant homes, they were—while all that time the house of God continued to lie in waste.

So in the sixth month of the second year of Darius, which was eighteen years after their return, God raised up Haggai to stir up the hearts of the remnant of the people, and once again they began to put their hands to the work of building the house of God. Interestingly, this people had not only returned from Babylon but had also resumed the building of the house of God; and yet the word of God to this people through Zechariah now was, "Return unto Me and I will return unto you." Given the positive circumstances just mentioned, one would naturally think this word from God to be totally unnecessary; whereas if this word had been spoken to those Jewish people who had remained in Babylonian captivity, that would be considered most suitable. Moreover, had this word been spoken to those of the remnant in Jerusalem who had been building their own houses after having left off building God's house, then that would also have been appropriate. Yet this word through Zechariah was directed towards the returned remnant who had most recently *resumed* the building of the house of God!

Would we not naturally think that that word was quite unnecessary? Nevertheless, God thought otherwise. Why? Let us review the situation more deeply in attempting to answer this intriguing question. Let us first notice that this word was brought to them in the eighth month of the second year of King Darius. Haggai had prophesied in the sixth month, and by the seventh month it could accurately be said that the remnant people had been actively building for a month. But, then, in the eighth month such a word from God came to the remnant. Hence, outwardly speaking, it appears rather strange that God through Zechariah should say such a thing to this people whose hands had already resumed the building of His house. Strange, indeed, is it not? Yet not so to God, simply because He knows the heart of every man. Even though these remnant people had resumed the building of God's house, yet by the end of the seventh month into the eighth, doubts had apparently begun to surface; apparently, there were some who now thought of giving up once more because it appeared as though, as they observed the results of the work of their hands thus far, they deemed it to be quite insignificant. They thought that even if they were to finish the temple, it could never be compared with the glorious temple which had been built by Solomon; so, they mused, why bother? Such negative thinking had already been manifested. So Haggai, we will recall, was used of the

Lord to encourage them by saying: "The Lord is with you. Do not be afraid. Continue to work even though the outline of the temple in your minds may not appear to hold much promise when finally finished; nevertheless, it is part of the grand plan of God."

So as we learned from the book of Haggai, in the eighth month they were still engaged in building, and yet it is evident from both the books of Haggai and Zechariah that their hearts were weak. It is evident that there were some doubts in their hearts and that their hearts were divided; for we learned from Haggai that by the ninth month, when he had again begun to prophesy, the remnant people had been expecting that from the moment they would resume laying their hands to the work of building God's house the heavens would be opened, rain aplenty would fall upon them, and that crops, wine, oil, and cattle would be in abundance. In other words, they had been expecting God's abundant blessing to be upon them from the day they did resume rebuilding His temple: "Now that we are once more doing God's will, He will certainly bless us." So they were shocked and bewildered when the blessing did not come (see Haggai 1:9-11). Outwardly, these people were certainly building the house of God; but in their hearts, they were wondering where were His blessings.

Let us pause for a moment and inquire: Were these remnant people interested in the building of God's house? Or were they interested in receiving His blessing? Suppose you had been one of them building the house of God back then and you were not blessed; would you have continued to do it? Where would have been your heart—focused on the house of God or on the blessing of God? No wonder God, who knew and read their hearts most accurately, sent the young man Zechariah to challenge the people. Through His prophet He now said: "Examine your hearts. Outwardly, you are definitely doing the work, but your heart is not right; it is not pure. You are not occupied with My interests; rather, you are more interested in My blessing, not in Me Myself. You must return to Me. If you return to Me, then I will return to you." Such was God's message delivered by Zechariah to this remnant people at that moment.

HIS-STORY

Zechariah is sometimes called the Apocalypse of the Old Testament. Revelation is the Apocalypse of the New Testament. He was a prophet of hope and promise. His book contains fourteen chapters, and there are two divisions. Chapter 1:7 to the end of chapter 8 is the first division. Chapters 9-14 comprise the second division. We can discern these divisions very easily because the first division, unlike the second, is dated. All prophecies in the first division are given dates, whereas those in the second have no dates attached whatever. Moreover, in the first division the name of the prophet is mentioned, but in the second, his name is not. Additionally, the first division's prophecies have about them a local, current background; for example, there is given the background of the returned remnant and that of the rebuilding of the temple, even though the pertinent prophecies go beyond these current local matters. The prophecies in the second division, however, appear to be shorn of any dated local environment, they entering instead into the long-term future and providing a panoramic view of the history of the kingdom of God in contrast to the kingdom of the world.

Nevertheless, though there are these two contrasting divisions in the book, they are nonetheless very closely related to each other. They are not only related in terms of the subject matter of the prophecies; they are also especially joined together with regard to the various prophetic utterances concerning a Man—one particular Person who is the Messiah. Whether He has been mentioned in the first or in the second division, the Person of the Messiah is always present.

For the Christian, what essentially is history? Is it not His-story? Is it not the narrative of the Messiah, the story of the Christ? That is the essence of history. So we who believe in Christ cannot deal with history and neglect the One about whom history is centrally written.

What, then, is the nature of prophecy? "The spirit of prophecy is the testimony of Jesus" (Revelation 19:10). Even though the content of prophecy includes many things, people, and events, and therefore covers a wide realm of subject matter, nevertheless, the spirit of prophecy is but one thing—the testimony of Jesus.

Hence, we find that Zechariah prophesied a great deal. Furthermore, his prophecy is much richer and broader and more enlarged than that of Haggai. Yet there is a center to all of Zechariah's prophecies, that which connects all of them together. Instead of here a little, there a little, all the seemingly isolated events are gathered together in manifesting the history of one Person—the Messiah, Christ the Lord.

Indeed, there are numerous references to the Messiah throughout the book of Zechariah. For instance, in 3:8-9 the prophet mentions the Branch and the stone having seven eyes. And we know that that Branch is none other than the Messiah, the Christ. In chapter 6 we find the Branch again. It is none other than the King-Priest or Priest-King—even Jesus—who sits upon the throne. In chapter 9 there is mentioned the One who comes in humility and rides upon the colt of an ass. He will also bring peace to the world. Then, in chapter 11, there is this same One mentioned who is the good Shepherd who is rejected and given the wages of thirty pieces of silver. Back then, thirty silver pieces was the price of a slave, and we know how all this was literally fulfilled in the life of the Lord Jesus Christ when Judas sold Him in betrayal for thirty pieces of silver as a slave. We are then told in chapter 12 that this Messiah is the One whom people pierced in crucifixion but who is to bring salvation to His people. Then, chapter 13 tells us about the sword being awakened and which strikes down My Fellow (see v.7)—thus signifying how God himself crushes this precious One on the cross. And, finally, chapter 14 narrates how the Messiah will return to the earth, with His feet touching the Mount of Olives and how this Mount will be broken asunder into two. Therefore, this whole book of Zechariah presents us with the coming of the Messiah who is the hope of the world.

ZECHARIAH'S VISIONS

Now the first division of Zechariah can be divided into two sections. The first section runs from 1:7 through to the end of chapter 6, and the prophecies to be found therein were brought forth on the night of the twenty-fourth day of the eleventh month in the second year of King Darius. The prophet Zechariah must have had a very busy night for the word of God came to him in a series of many visions; altogether, some say seven, others say eight—I wonder how much sleep he got! We can only touch upon each briefly. The first vision was of a man riding a red horse among the myrtle trees in a low valley. The man on the red horse is believed to have been none other than Messiah-Christ, the second Person in the Godhead, even the angel of Jehovah as we find mentioned quite frequently there and in various other places in the Old Testament. Here, then, we find that the Lord is riding among myrtle trees in a low valley, and we know that myrtle trees only grow in low places. These therefore represent or speak of the low condition of God's people. Instead of it being the elevated cedar trees in Lebanon being presented here, these were myrtle trees situated in a low valley. Though the people were thus pictured as being in a very low state—and regardless whether such was meant in a physical or spiritual sense, the Lord was nonetheless there; this vision thus signifying that God is in control of all world situations. God knows what is going on everywhere and here He was bent on doing something which would further serve His purpose. And in the vision this Man on the red horse among the myrtle trees in the low valley, and three other horsemen, were going through the whole earth to take note of everything occurring throughout the world.

Let us not think that God is unaware of what is taking place in this world. He knows, and He is concerned. When God's people were in trouble and the whole world was at rest and in peace (see 1:11b), the angel of the Lord cried to the Lord God Almighty and said to and through Zechariah that the Lord Almighty is jealous for Jerusalem and Zion—that is to say, for His people—and that He is bent on doing something about it; which was that He would return to Jerusalem with mercy where His house would be rebuilt. This vision laid the foundation for the rest of the visions to follow. God is in control. Let us not forget that when God said through Zechariah, "Return unto Me, and I will return unto you," He had already returned to His people. Indeed, if God had not already returned to His people, how could they have returned from Babylonian captivity? It was God who had stirred the heart of King Cyrus. So their returning to Jerusalem was not because the hearts of the people in captivity had turned back to God.

Rather, it was because God, out of love for His people and because He is faithful to His covenant, stirred the heart of King Cyrus to allow His people to return to Jerusalem to rebuild the house of God. And, thus, the stirring of the heart of King Cyrus was what God had been bent on doing to bring all this about. For God had promised: "I will return to Zion, I will return to Jerusalem." And He always fulfills His promises.

This vision was followed by another one—that of the four horns. Horns in Scripture symbolize power; so these horns represent the world powers which were to arise on the world scene. The content of this vision was the same as that of the huge image which Nebuchadnezzar had seen—four world empires—and we know that all world empires are at enmity with the kingdom of God as represented by Judah, Israel and Jerusalem which these empires at one time or another will have scattered. Yet in this second vision God is seen as raising up, in response, four craftsmen, and these four craftsmen are representative of whatever or whoever God will employ to break the four horns. In short, God has His provision to break and destroy the kingdoms of this world in order that the kingdom of God may be established upon the earth.

The third vision was of a man holding a measuring rod, and he was measuring Jerusalem. Jerusalem will be a city without a wall. Whenever there is a wall, limitation is present; but when there is no wall, there is no limitation; and God said in this same vision: "I Myself will be a wall of fire around Jerusalem and I will be its glory within." Here God promised He would restore Jerusalem to glory and return to His people.

Following this third vision, there is a fourth one—found in chapter 3—concerning the recovery of priesthood. Not only the house of God must be recovered, the priesthood must likewise be recovered. Then in chapter 4 we find the recovery of kingship. And in the recovery of kingship the testimony of God is recovered as typified by the golden lampstand.

Following these fourth and fifth visions there comes forth the vision of the flying scroll containing curses upon the entire earth. In other words, there is to be judgment. God is righteous; therefore, judgment must come. It first comes to the house of God and then to the whole world (I Peter 4:17).

This was followed by a seventh vision—this one of an ephah (or basket-shaped container). An ephah is a unit or vessel of measurement, and here was beheld a woman sitting in the ephah, and she was called Wickedness. Now there was a lead covering upon this ephah and the ephah was itself brought to Shinar—that is, to Babylon. In other words, wickedness in great profusion will be present on this earth, but God places a restraint over it as symbolized by the lead cover.

Lastly, there is the vision of four chariots coming out between two brass mountains. Brass in Scripture always speaks of judgment. And hence, these four chariots with their powerful horses straining to rush forward were sent out to judge the world. Judgment is coming upon the entire world, and the kingdom of God is going to be established on the earth.

These visions thus comprise the first part of the book of Zechariah's first division.

INWARD REALITY

The second part of the first division is found in chapters 7-8. What is described here occurred during the fourth year of King Darius when some of the returned remnant who had relocated themselves from Jerusalem had now come back and began living around Jerusalem in different villages. Some people from other villages like Bethel came up to Jerusalem and asked a question of the priests and prophets there. It will be recalled that Zechariah was not only a prophet but also a priest, as was the case with Nehemiah and Ezekiel. Their question was: "Should we continue to mourn and fast in the fifth month of each year as we had been doing for so many years past?" Now it had been the habit of the people during the seventy years of captivity in Babylon to mourn and fast in four different months of the year. They fasted and mourned in the fourth month because it was the month when the city of Jerusalem had been broken into. They also did so in the fifth month, which was the time the temple had been burned. They mourned and fasted in the seventh month as well because that was the time when Gedaliah, appointed by Babylon as governor, had been murdered; and because of this, the people had fled into Egypt. And, finally, they did the same thing in the tenth month in remembrance of when Jerusalem had been besieged. So in these four months they had observed the habit of mourning and fasting.

So upon their return to Jerusalem they had inquired: "Should we continue with this practice?" And here the word of the Lord to them was: "When you mourn and fast, do you really do so as unto Me? When you eat and drink, do you do so for My sake? Or is it not all for yourselves?" In other words, God was saying: "If you do not do righteously by others, if you do not deal kindly with your neighbor, if you do not show mercy and compassion towards one another, if in your hearts you think evil of each other, then what is the point of fasting or eating?" God is not interested in these outward practices; He is interested in the inward condition—in His people's true moral state—rather than in such outward formalities as mourning, fasting, eating and drinking. So God responded to their inquiry by saying through Zechariah: "No, during all these years in which you have been fasting, it has been for you, not for Me. But now, since I have brought you back to Jerusalem, these four occasions should be times of joy and feasting. These times should now be happy festivals in remembrance of what the Lord has done for you."

Let us therefore always bear in mind that God is not interested in outward appearances. He is interested in inward reality.

THE BURDEN OF THE WORD OF JEHOVAH

As stated earlier, the second division's content is all undated. This has given rise to speculation that the prophecies in this book's second division were given to Zechariah during his later years. We may recall that the greatest prophecies which Daniel had prophesied were when he was in his later years. His knowledge of God and his life with Him was by that time so deep that God was able to give him a greater view of His plan. Probably the same was true with Zechariah. The dating which appears in his book dates from his earlier period of prophesying, but the second division to which we now come is totally undated. So, most likely the prophesies to be found in this prophetic book's latter division came forth during Zechariah's later years when by that time his horizon had been greatly broadened. For God now gave the prophet a panoramic view of the outward history of the children of Israel as it related to the kingdom of this world; even so, inwardly speaking, it is actually a history as well of the kingdom of God coming upon this world. Such is the true nature of the prophecies to be found in this book's second division.

WORLD HISTORY

The central description of this book's second division can be summed up in one word: burden—the burden of the word of Jehovah. Whereas the primary description of the first division's prophecies is the word of Jehovah, that of the second division is the burden over Jehovah's word. And this burden is divided into two parts. Chapters 9-11 present the burden concerning Hadrach, Damascus, and so forth. (Hadrach was a place near Damascus.) This was a prophesying about the Gentile world in relation to God's people. By contrast, the second part, chapters 12-14, covers the prophesying concerning Israel in relation to the kingdom of God. This division's first part describes in its prophecies how various places and lands—for example, Tyre, Zidon, and Damascus of Syria—would be destroyed and how Jerusalem would be spared. What Zechariah was actually prophesying about here were the conquests of Alexander the Great. When Alexander's forces swept over the eastern Mediterranean region, he destroyed the important strategic cities of Tyre and Zidon. How Jerusalem was spared is a most interesting story from history. The high priest in Jerusalem at that time had marched out clothed all in white to meet Alexander, and the general was so impressed by this that he did not destroy Jerusalem but bypassed it. All these events, as prophesied by Zechariah, we will find in the history books of the period, especially if one reads Josephus, the Jewish historian, who gives a detailed account of what eventually happened to Jerusalem, in particular.

Even the dramatic history of the Maccabees, which was to unfold during the period of the Greek Empire under Alexander, was prophesied by Zechariah. And intertwined with all this are this prophet's various allusions to the Messiah and how He would come as a gentle King and be rejected by His people. Following that, the Romans are prophetically brought into view by Zechariah; and they, too, would be destroyed. All these events prophesied by Zechariah are found in this first part of his book's second division.

THE DAY OF MESSIAH'S COMING

The most wonderful section is to be found in the second part of this prophetic book's second division, to be found in chapters 12 to 14. It is centered upon the day of the second coming of the Messiah. The Messiah first came some two thousand years ago, but the chosen people of God failed to recognize Him and rejected Him; and because of this, the Jews were scattered throughout the whole world. But the Messiah is coming back again, and when He does, the Jews will see and finally recognize the One whom they have pierced in crucifixion (see 12:10b). The whole house of Israel will repent. Moreover, all the nations of the world will be gathered in the particular area prophesied for the last battle between the forces of evil and good—the battle of Armageddon (see 14:2ff.). When Christ returns the second time, His feet shall touch Mount Olive, which at that very moment will break in two. Indeed, scientists have told us that there is a seismic fault line there and, thus, if an earthquake occurs there, the Mount of Olives can easily be broken in two. Christ will come, followed by the aforementioned last battle, and then Satan will be bound and thrown into the bottomless pit. God will judge His people and the nations, and then He will establish His kingdom upon the earth. And the prophecy of Zechariah is that there will be only one Jehovah, one God (see 14:9).

Now this, in summary, is the book of Zechariah.

MESSAGE TO THE CHURCH

What is the message for us today from this book? Let us bear in mind that Israel is the *earthly* people whom God had chosen, and she is actually a type of the church of God as His *heavenly* people. Consequently, whatever has happened to the children of Israel is something for us from which to learn. So what is the lesson God wants to teach us through Zechariah? Again, let me emphasize that the prophetic message in Zechariah was not addressed to God's people who remained in Babylon. Hopefully, they may have heard about it, but it was not directed at them. So as we look at the church today, we do realize that, even up to this present hour, spiritually speaking, the church in general is still in Babylonian captivity. She is being held captive to a religious system. She is not free but is in confusion, just as ancient Babylon had been in a Babel of confusion. Today's house of God has not been built; in fact, it has been destroyed; and the testimony of God is no longer there. Just as God had no longer been addressed, during the captive period of the Jews, as the God of the heavens and of the earth because there was no longer any testimony on earth at that time, even so, one could make the same observation regarding God's people today.

Spiritually speaking, sadly, we find the church in general lies today in ruins. She is still in confusion, she is still in captivity, and there is no house. God's people are like wandering Jews who have no home. As I travel here and there I hear cries from many believers: "We are homeless. Where is our spiritual home? We have none." In sum, there is no testimony of the Lord Jesus on earth. But thank God that throughout the centuries He has been calling His people out of Babylon: "Come out of her and return to Jerusalem. Return to singleness of heart; return to simplicity, to sincerity, to purity; return to live for the Lord alone and to build the testimony of Jesus."

Unfortunately, many today are still living for their own benefit and for their own interests, but who will live for the interests of God? Many are occupied with their businesses, but who will be occupied with God's business? Thank God that a remnant, only a few by comparison, had stood up by the Spirit of God and had returned to Jerusalem. And according to the findings of thorough research into church history, the very same thing has continued to occur down through the ages ever since. Throughout church history—in every age, in every century, in every generation—there have been a few who have returned to the simplicity of Christ and have tried to stand for the testimony of Jesus in building the house of God. And, sad to say, they have been a people nearly always despised; but thank God that there have been such people.

Let us review again the condition of the returned remnant in Jerusalem. Yes, they had returned, but their condition was pitiful. Not only was Jerusalem in ruins, not only were the remnant people oppressed by the surrounding enemies, but there was weakness in their hearts; so that the work ceased for a number of years, during which period they reverted to their old way of life—building their own houses—yet not in Babylon but now in Jerusalem.

Are we in the same situation today? Have we been called out of Babylon to return to Jerusalem? Are we a people now in Jerusalem? Are we a people who stand into the simplicity and sincerity that are in Christ? Are we a people who are supposed to have returned to live for God, to live for His testimony, to build His house? What are we actually doing today? Are we like that remnant who returned but not long afterwards began to build their own houses while the house of God still lay in waste?

Is there not a message for us here? Have we forgotten why we returned? Have we forgotten what we are here for? What is our occupation? Are we here to build the house of God or are we here to build our own houses? Even though, by the grace of God, we have begun to put our hands, as it were, to the work of building the house of God, there is nonetheless much doubt, fear, and trembling lurking in our hearts. Furthermore, our hearts are divided. We, like the returned Jewish remnant, may be wondering why the blessing of God has not come. If we are for Him, why is He not for us? Why is it that the blessing is still being withheld? Is it any longer worthwhile to continue on in the work of building God's house? What if there is no blessing? Is it therefore a waste of our time? Are we harboring such thoughts as these? God truly knows our hearts whereas we do not know our hearts; for man's heart is deceitful above all things: who can truly know it? Nobody (see Jeremiah 17:9). We ourselves do not know; but God knows. For this reason, there is a word for us today: "Return, return unto Me," says the Lord.

If this be our current situation, then we need to return. If this be our current state, we have probably left our first love. When we returned to Jerusalem, as it were, we had a first love. And though our *hands* are still there moving and laboring, where is our *heart*? The word of God says, "Remember from where you have fallen, and repent, and do the first works" (see Revelation 2:5a). Probably, we have fallen from simplicity, having become too complex. Perhaps we began to look at our surroundings; perhaps we began to look critically at our brothers and sisters; perhaps we began to complain of this and to complain of that, instead of setting our eyes upon the Lord and thus allow ourselves to be built up together. Where exactly are we spiritually? We truly need to return to the Lord with our whole heart. If we return, He will return to us. As a matter of fact, where we today are—in having found a spiritual home with those saints of like mind—is because He has returned to us in His mercy; but ought we not to return to Him with our whole heart? Let us see no one but Jesus only. Let us see the Lord Jesus in our brothers and sisters. Let our hearts be occupied with Him alone; let us love Him with a pure heart and not out of any ulterior motive. We love Him not because of His blessing but because of who He is. If we return to Him, we know He will return to us. He will return with abundant blessings, and all these blessings will contribute to the bringing in of the kingdom of God upon this earth. And what will be the greatest blessing of all? That we shall see Him face to face and not be put to shame (see I John 2:28).

So there is indeed a message for us today from Zechariah. Briefly put, it is the word return.

Let us pray:

> *Thou who searchest the heart of man, search us. Speak to each one of us. If there is a departure, Lord, turn us that we may return to Thee so that Thou mayst return to us in the fullest way in order that all Thy glorious plan for Thy Son may be fulfilled. We ask in the name of our Lord Jesus, our King. Amen.*

MALACHI

REPENTANCE

Malachi 1:1-6—The burden of the word of Jehovah to Israel by Malachi. I have loved you, saith Jehovah; but ye say, Wherein hast thou loved us? Was not Esau Jacob's brother? saith Jehovah, and I loved Jacob, and I hated Esau; and made his mountains a desolation, and gave his inheritance to the jackals of the wilderness. If Edom say, We are broken down, but we will build again the ruined places,—thus saith Jehovah of hosts: They shall build, but I will throw down; and men shall call them the territory of wickedness, and the people against whom Jehovah hath indignation for ever. And your eyes shall see it, and ye shall say, Jehovah is magnified beyond the border of Israel. A son honoureth his father, and a servant his master: if then I be a father, where is mine honour? and if I be a master, where is my fear? saith Jehovah of hosts unto you, priests, that despise my name. But ye say, Wherein have we despised thy name?

Malachi 3:16-18—Then they that feared Jehovah spoke often one to another; and Jehovah observed it, and heard, and a book of remembrance was written before him for them that feared Jehovah, and that thought upon his name. And they shall be unto me a peculiar treasure, saith Jehovah of hosts, in the day that I prepare; and I will spare them as a man spareth his own son that serveth him. And ye shall return and discern between the righteous and the wicked, between him that serveth God and him that serveth him not.

Malachi 4:4-6—Remember the law of Moses my servant, which I commanded unto him in Horeb for all Israel, the statutes and ordinances. Behold, I send unto you Elijah the prophet, before the

> *coming of the great and terrible day of Jehovah. And he shall turn the heart of the fathers to the children, and the heart of the children to their fathers, lest I come and smite the earth with a curse.*

Let us pray:

> *Dear heavenly Father, as we wait in Thy presence, we look to Thy Holy Spirit to breathe upon Thy written word and make it living and operative in each of our lives. We do commit ourselves to Thee for Thy word. We ask, Lord, that by Thy word we would be sanctified, that we would be transformed and that we shall be those who will truly satisfy Thy heart. We commit this time into Thy hands. In the name of our Lord Jesus. Amen.*

Malachi is the last book in the Old Testament. From the very beginning with the creation of man, God has continually spoken to him. In fact, it is said in Hebrews 1:1 that in the former times God spoke to the fathers in many parts and in many ways through the prophets. Our God is One who speaks. He loves to reveal himself to His people in order that they may be blessed; however, how dull His people have been in hearing and obeying Him.

The Old Testament opens with the book called Genesis—the book of beginnings; and Genesis commences with the creation of man. God put him in the Garden of Eden, the garden of pleasure, and placed him before the tree of life. But at the end of Genesis there is mention of a coffin resting in Egypt. This last book of the Old Testament now before us opens with a marvelous, glorious statement by God: "I have loved you." I think there is no announcement more glorious than that, and yet when we come to the end of Malachi, there is that awful, terrible word—curse.

Throughout the history of mankind God has always been faithful; whereas man has unfortunately always failed Him. As a matter of fact, there could really never be any hope reposed in that first man, Adam, and in all who have ever been of Adam. Our only hope, therefore, lies in the second Man—even our Lord Jesus Christ—and, of course, that leads us to the New Testament.

In order to understand this book of Malachi we need to know something of this prophet's background. Malachi means "my messenger." We do not know if that was the actual name of this prophet—probably it was—or whether he simply took that title as a way of hiding himself and allowing the message which he was to deliver to be really known unhinderedly by the people. But there is one point which we clearly do know about Malachi, and it is this: that the burden of the word of the Lord to Israel came profoundly upon him. God spoke to His people Israel through His burdened prophet.

Malachi prophesied about a hundred years after the remnant had returned to Jerusalem and Judah from Babylonian captivity. We know that in His mercy God had allowed His people who were in captivity to return from Babylon to Jerusalem to rebuild His temple. Sadly, however, most of the children of Israel chose to remain in captivity. There was only a minority remnant of them whose spirits were stirred by God and who were willing to be uprooted and return to Jerusalem, a city still in ruin at that time, in order to build God a house. As noted previously, this had occurred around 536 B.C. This remnant had returned under the joint leadership of Zerubbabel and Joshua. And we know that with the help of the two prophets Haggai and Zechariah that temple was finally rebuilt.

Then, after some seventy more years, Ezra also came back with some people from captivity for the purpose of beautifying the temple—that is to say, of strengthening the temple service and also for the purpose of teaching the people the law of God. About thirteen years after the return of Ezra, Nehemiah, too, came back—in his case for the purpose of rebuilding the wall of Jerusalem. That happened around 455 B.C. Nehemiah served as governor of Judah for some twelve years, and during that period the wall of Jerusalem was rebuilt. Not only that but also, the priesthood was strengthened and, in addition, the people entered into a new covenant with God. Moreover, there occurred quite a revival during the time of Nehemiah because the remnant people not only gave what God had commanded them to give but they even gave additionally what God had not commanded (see Nehemiah 10). They brought up the wood-offerings and so forth. It was quite a revival, indeed.

After his twelve years of governorship, Nehemiah went back to the imperial palace. We do not know exactly how long he would remain absent from Jerusalem, but probably it was around ten years. And during that brief period the spiritual condition of the remnant who were settled in Jerusalem and in the Promised Land beyond Jerusalem had greatly declined: the priesthood had become polluted; marriages were continually being dishonored; tithes had long since been discontinued. Religiously, they were guilty of sacrilege and profanity. Morally, they were guilty of sorcery, adultery, perjury, fraud and oppression. Socially, they were guilty of unfaithfulness in their family responsibilities. And materially, they were unfaithful in bringing to the temple—and therefore to God—their tithes and heave-offerings. Within a very short period a great corruption and degeneration had set in among the children of Israel who were in the Promised Land.

Eventually God, out of His great love, raised up Malachi in about 433 B.C. for the purpose of stirring the hearts of the remnant who were still there. At the same time, Nehemiah returned to Jerusalem from the palace once more after an absence of probably ten years; and, taking stock of the corrupt situation, he dealt drastically with the degenerated conditions of the people (see Nehemiah 13:4-31). It can therefore be said that Malachi dealt with the cause while Nehemiah dealt with the effect, and through the combination of their work, there seemed to have been some restoration. Yet we do not know how effective that restoration was. We only know that, after that, God fell silent, and remained so for the next four hundred years: He did not speak a single word to His people. Only after these four hundred years did a voice suddenly break God's silence, it coming from out of the wilderness. That was the voice of God's messenger John the Baptist calling His people to repent, "for the kingdom of the heavens is drawing near" (Matthew 3:2). Such, then, is a summary background for the book of Malachi.

This book is unique, in that it is cast in a very strange form. For the entire text is presented as a debate—even a series of debates. There were two parties to this debate: God on the one hand and Israel—as represented by the returned remnant—on the other. Interestingly, the prophet spoke both for God and for the people. The word of God, of course, came to the prophet, who simply delivered it to this remnant people of Israel. But as for the people themselves, the prophet through the Spirit exposed their hearts at that very time: he put their thoughts into words which they probably would never have spoken—words which were abrupt and cast in the most naked language: both blatant and shocking.

These debates remind us of that well-known line from Isaiah: "Come now and let us reason together, says the Lord" (see 1:18). Reasoning is the last resort which God uses with His people. If there is love, if there is faith, if there is any reverence for God in the people's hearts, there would be no cause for reasoning. The proper attitude for man to have before God, especially for His chosen people, is to bow before Him in humility, listen, and then obey His word. That should be every man's proper attitude; for should the created ever reason or argue or debate with his Creator? How absurd! Yet God, because of His deep love for His people, condescends himself to man's low level and attempts to reason with him. Perhaps through reasoning, somehow some light may break through so that man may repent and be restored. So, in one sense, this is a very sad book, in that it presents God as having to resort to reasoning with His people of that day and exposes them as being so *un*reasonable that they did not even listen to His voice.

FIRST ROUND: I HAVE LOVED YOU

In this book of Malachi there are seven rounds of debate recorded. The first one begins with 1:2: "I have loved you, saith Jehovah; but ye say, Wherein hast thou loved us?" Love is the central issue. The relationship between God and man, between God and His people, is one of love. Love is actually the focus of the entire series of debates, all the remaining rounds turning upon this one issue. God is love; indeed, He always loves. Here He says: "I have loved you." It means that God loved them in the past, loves them now, and will continue to love them to the very end. God's love is unchanging and everlasting. He loves, yet not because the object of His love is lovely or lovable; He loves simply because He *is* love. His love is never affected by circumstances because it comes out of what He himself is.

The Lord said, "I have loved you." What a statement! Can anyone not feel the heart of God when He says that? And yet the people back then said in response: "Wherein hast Thou loved us? Actually, you do not love us anymore. In fact, we do not know if You have ever loved us." Who were these people here? These were *not* the people of the world who do not know God. These were *not even* the great majority of God's chosen people of that day who had decided to remain in the land of captivity because they were interested in their own affairs and not interested in God's affairs. No, instead, these people were the very remnant who had returned to the Promised Land from captivity. When they stood up to return, they had been stirred in their hearts by the Spirit of God. They had returned because at that moment they loved God above all things else. They had returned because they wanted to see His house built. They at that moment had not even cared whether they had a house of their own or not. They only cared for God's house. They had been willing to forsake everything for Him. In other words, they were people who loved God intensely, who loved Him practically. They had forsaken all for the sake of love because their hearts had been stirred by the love of God. They at that time had been reminded how He had loved Jacob—the supplanter, the twister, the deceiver. Yet God had loved him so much that He had been willing to expend much time dealing with him, having been patient with him, having disciplined him until he had transformed Jacob into Israel, a prince of God—no longer a wrestler with man nor a heel-holder of man but now a wrestler with God himself. And out of this Jacob/Israel had come twelve sons: the twelve tribes; and out of those twelve tribes had come the nation of Israel; and oh, how God had loved that nation and had brought them out of Egypt into the Promised Land of Canaan. The love of God had been inscribed indelibly upon the whole history of this nation of Jacob/Israel. And ultimately, God had brought His remnant people even out of Babylonian captivity—yet not at all because they were good but because God had been merciful and faithful.

And yet, this remnant people now had the audacity to say to God, "Wherein hast thou loved us?" Was that not ridiculous? So God condescended to explain to them: "Look, Jacob and Esau were twin brothers, but I loved Jacob and hated Esau." Why so? It was not because Jacob had been better than Esau. As a matter of fact, in Adam all men are equal. But somehow, Jacob had had an interest in spiritual things. He had longed for the birthright, which is a spiritual matter; he had also longed for the blessing of the firstborn—equally a spiritual matter. But Esau had loved the world; he had loved what was immediate and he had therefore been willing to sell his birthright. But because Jacob had responded to God's love, God had loved him to the very end, which had included the discipline of love. Indeed, God had disciplined him in love. He had had to go through very bad times. Even when present before Pharaoh, he had acknowledged this: "My life was different from my forefathers. It was not that easy. In fact, it was very hard, very difficult" (see Genesis 47:9). But God had disciplined him in love in order to mature him, to bring him into sonship and into that birthright he had longed after. But with Esau, it had been different. Outwardly, Esau had probably been better than Jacob. He had been a carefree person, seemingly having forgotten very quickly the wrongs done him by his brother. He had been outspoken, straightforward, not a hypocrite; but he had had no desire for God nor the things of God. Indeed, he had loved the world and, because of that, he had been hated by God. God had punished him and so he had rebelled. The nation of Edom had therefore been the result of Esau. Edom had tried to rebel against God's judgment but God said no matter what Edom did, that people would ultimately be destroyed. On the other hand, God had shown and continued to show how much He had loved Jacob/Israel.

Let us realize that once we respond to the love of God, He will never let us go but will love us to the very end. Though we may depart from Him, though we may go astray, though we may even act like the remnant people back then who had become so hardened, yet love will still pursue us until He brings us back to himself. That is the love of God.

Sometimes, when we are within the embrace of such love, we become insensitive to it. Probably there needs to be a time when love is taken away. Then we begin to appreciate it once more. I came from a family of love. My parents loved us seven children very much.

When I was at home (and I was at home until the Lord called me out in service to Him), I was surrounded by love; but at that time, I did not realize how much my parents loved me. Sometimes I murmured: I thought that my parents loved this one or that one better than me because my birth happened to fall in the middle of the seven. Usually, the mother will love the oldest son and the father will love the youngest daughter, but I happened to be the middle child. After I had finished college and the Lord had called me out, I was away from home, living alone in the upper chamber of a gospel book room. It was at that time that suddenly one day the love of my parents came upon me and I realized how much they truly loved me. I could recall when I was sick and my parents would nurse me at home; they never sent us sick children to the hospital. When I was in college, sometimes I would study late in my bed and fall asleep, and at midnight my mother would come and cover me. Suddenly on that day their love so came upon me that I was overwhelmed by it. So I wrote a letter to tell them how much I appreciated their love.

When we are surrounded by love, we forget that we are loved. God loved the nation of Israel so much; in fact, her whole history is a story of God's love towards her people; and yet these remnant people could now say to God, "Wherein hast thou loved us?" They had forgotten all the goodness of God. Probably, all they remembered was His discipline. They blamed Him for all their distresses. Perhaps they were blaming God that His promise to them had not yet come. Why, for instance, were they still under Persian rule? Why also was their life continuing to be so difficult? Where were the blessings God had promised them? They did not realize, as we learned previously from Haggai and Zechariah, that they were still under discipline, and that that discipline was one of love. They did not understand.

First love is what God is really after. Does He have a controversy with any of us today? Are we not a people loved by Him? Have we not responded to His love? Are we still daily constrained by the love of Christ? (see II Corinthians 5:14a) Or whenever the love of God is mentioned, is it as though it is ancient history to us, even a forgotten history? Where is our first love? Do we love Him above all things? Are we still willing to give up anything and everything for Him? Do we still live for Him and not for ourselves? Where, indeed, is our first love? Is our heart hardened to such a degree that we begin to wonder whether God loves us or not? Do we begin to say, "Wherein has He loved us? He has never loved us."

The relationship between God and Israel has always been one of love like that between a husband and a wife. God has been like a husband to her. He has loved her so very much, but His love has not been reciprocated by Israel. In like manner, Christ loved the church so much that He gave himself up for her, but does the church reciprocate that love back to Christ?

Such was the first round of debate, but it did not seem to have had any positive effect upon this remnant people of Israel.

SECOND ROUND: HONOR ME

God as it were next said as to His wife Israel: "Even though you may forget that I am a husband to you, at least you should recognize and acknowledge that I am a father to you. What you are today here in Jerusalem and Judah was all brought about by Me who am a father to you. Now as a father, should I not be honored? A son honors his father and a servant his master. If I in fact am your Father, where is My honor? Let us not talk about love right now, let us reason about a father's honor. Do you respect Me? Do you honor Me as your Father, as One who has nourished you, cherished you, who brought you up, and supplied you with everything? Do you honor Me? All right, if you do not honor Me as a father, let us go a step lower. Am I not your Master? Have I not redeemed you out of Egypt, rescued you out of Babylonian captivity? At least I am your Master and therefore you are My servant. Where, then, is your fear? If you do not honor Me as a father, at least you should fear Me as a master. Where, though, is your fear? Where is it?—especially you priests." The Jewish priests, of course, had been set apart for the purpose of honoring God, sanctifying Him in the presence of the Israelites. In the past they had stood for the holiness of God. They had taught the people the law of God—that He is holy, that He needs to be honored and to be feared. But here these priests had become so degenerate that they neither honored nor feared God any more. As a matter of fact, they had taken the lead in despising God's name. Think of that!

God's name is holy. Among the Ten Commandments the third one reads: "Thou shalt not idly utter the name of the Lord" (see Exodus 20:7a). In other words, one must not despise God's name but must honor His name and, never utter it idly. When people today take an oath or do something, they often use the name of God loosely as though it were nothing. They in effect are despising the name of God as though He were a nobody, that He is nothing. Even the priests back then had despised God's name and yet they had the temerity to declare to God: "Wherein have we despised You? We have not despised You." Yet in reality God had meant nothing to them. Because to them He had become a nobody, how, then, could they be accused of despising a nobody? They in their arrogance had looked down upon God, and to such a degree that He was simply nothing to them. So they neither honored nor feared Him.

Let us pause here and inquire how we ourselves today relate to this matter. If we do not love God, at least we should honor and respect Him. And if we do not respect Him, we at least should fear Him, for He is God. "Hallowed be Thy name"—that is the prayer the Lord Jesus had taught His church to pray. "Sanctified be Thy name" is another rendering of this prayer. We are a people called by God's name. In other words, His name is vested in us. The issue of whether that name is being honored or is being dishonored seems to be upon us. Do we therefore bring honor to God with our lives or do we bring reproach to Him? Consider the children of Israel in relation to this matter: how seriously God's name was brought into reproach because of what they were.

Let us ask ourselves further, Do we bring glory to God's name or do we bring shame to it? Where are we spiritually in this matter? For let us realize that whenever the heart is hardened, the mind becomes darkened. In Ephesians we read: "Being estranged from the life of God, their mind is darkened" (4:18). The understanding in the mind is darkened whenever the heart has become hardened. We will recall that in the first round of debate, it was a matter of heart—Do we love God? Here in this second round, however, it is a matter of mind—Do we understand? Do we know? The remnant of God's people in Jerusalem had become so blinded that they ended up despising God's name and no longer even recognized it. Do we not often say love is blind? What does that saying actually mean? It means that love is most eager to cover or ignore a multitude of faults and sins. That is blindness. But there is another side to this issue: love also brings in light—where there is love, there is light. God is not only love, He is also light. But where love is missing, the light is extinguished. And hence, that is the reason the mind becomes darkened. It is a very sad and serious situation.

THIRD ROUND: OFFER A PURE SACRIFICE

In 1:7 of Malachi we read what God next declared to His wayward people: "Ye offer polluted bread upon mine altar; and ye say, Wherein have we polluted thee? In that ye say, The table of Jehovah is contemptible." Here God is saying to His remnant people: "You offer polluted bread on My altar." And their response was again one of denial: "Wherein have we polluted thee?" Why could God bring this accusation to them? Because He had read their darkened minds most accurately in that they had been thinking to themselves that in their view the table of the Lord was most contemptible. According to the law of God as given through Moses, the priests were to offer sacrifices to God on the altar and that all such sacrifices had to be without any blemish whatsoever. All these offerings had to be pure because all of them were a type of Christ, the Lamb of God, who is holy and without blemish. That was the law; but during this period of the returned remnant both people and priests had degenerated into offering to God the blind, the lame and the sick. Even when these people made a vow, they changed the sacrifice when they performed that vow by keeping the best for themselves and offered the worst to God (see 1:13b-14a). Why did they do this? If *this* was the way they wished to offer up sacrifices to God, why do it at all? God reasoned with them by saying: "If you were to give such offering to the Governor, would he be pleased or accept your person? Yet who am I that you treat Me like this? For I am not a mere governor; I am a great King—even *your* King. Yet you dishonor My name by polluting My altar and heaping contempt on My table. Oh, that someone would shut tight the doors of the temple so that no further useless fire would be lit on My altar! I do not any longer want you people to offer up to Me because I will neither accept your offerings nor your persons. I am tired of it all" (see 1:7-10).

What had happened? Yes indeed, the returned remnant and the priests had continued offering sacrifices, but to them it had become over time a mere religious act. It was now nothing but a formality—a custom—what their fathers had done, so this, they thought, was what they must reluctantly do. There was no longer any heart in their sacrificial worship of God. In fact, by now the people were simply going through the motions, with the priests having become professionals. They all had been maintaining the form of godliness but without the power thereof being manifested. For both people and priests it had all become nothing more than formality—religious formality. Most likely they had continued to engage in this practice merely as a means of bribing their consciences; but as a matter of indisputable fact, they thought nothing of this practice because, as was noted earlier, they thought to themselves that the altar of the Lord was contemptible anyway. What a weariness, they thought to themselves, that they had to maintain these rituals (see 1:12-13a).

God's reaction to their hypocrisy was to make clear to this rebellious remnant people that He very well knew how to vindicate His name on the earth. Said Jehovah of hosts: "From the rising of the sun to the setting down of the same My name shall be great among the nations; and in every place incense shall be offered unto My name, and a pure oblation: for My name shall be great among the nations" (see 1:11).

This very word of the Lord Almighty has truly come about in His establishing of the church. Even though Israel had failed to honor, respect and love God but had despised Him, nevertheless, God has vindicated His name. Out of every tribe, tongue, people and nation, He has raised up a people for himself, and they are to bring to Him the pure incense of spiritual sacrifices. Are we not to be living stones being built together into a spiritual house and a holy priesthood to offer up spiritual sacrifices acceptable to God through Jesus Christ? Indeed, this is what the church is meant to be (see I Peter 2:5).

What is a pure oblation or sacrifice to be offered by us today? In reality, is not spiritual sacrifice none other than offering back to God the Christ whom He has given to us and whom we have apprehended? That is what a pure spiritual sacrifice is, because only Christ can satisfy God; only He can be God's food. When we try to present ourselves—the produce of our own hands and presented out of our own fleshly energy— even the best of *that* produce, in God's eyes, is nothing but the sick, the blind and the lame. In offering up such sacrifices we verily pollute the table of the Lord.

In worshiping God we today are to worship Him in spirit and truth and not in our flesh. In prayer we are to pray in the spirit and not in our flesh. In service, we are to serve in the power of the Spirit and not in the energy of our flesh. Only such as that is pure incense and pure sacrifice. Are we guilty of polluting the table of the Lord? If so, we are not a holy priesthood as the house of Levi of old had been. For God concluded this third round of debate by declaring to His remnant people: "I made a covenant with Levi, a covenant of life and peace, that out of his mouth there would come forth the law of God. I am therefore disciplining you priests until you cease violating My covenant with Levi and until I obtain for Myself a holy priesthood" (see 2:4-7). God will do the same to us today until He obtains for himself a holy spiritual priesthood in us.

FOURTH ROUND: LIVE A PURE LIFE

"Ye have wearied Jehovah with your words, and ye say, Wherein have we wearied him? In that ye say, Every one that doeth evil is good in the sight of Jehovah, and he delighteth in them; or, Where is the God of judgment?" (2:17).

Ungodliness produces unrighteousness. When people are not right with God, they cannot be right with man. Here we find the returned remnant's relationship with God was wrong. They did not love, honor or fear God. On the contrary, this people had even despised His name and had offered polluted sacrifices to God and had considered it all as nothing to be concerned about. And if they were doing all that to *God*, what could one expect them to do in relation to their fellow man? It turned out that they had begun to oppress their fellow man, to commit forgery and fraud, and to even be unfaithful in their marriage relationships (see 2:14-16; 3:5).

We will recall that when Nehemiah came back to Jerusalem and Judah after a lengthy absence, he found that the remnant people of Israel had begun to marry the daughters of the nations again, just as their forefathers had done. They were divorcing their wives and marrying strange women. And here in Malachi we find that these things were continuing to occur, yet these people were nonetheless going to the altar and weeping and moaning as though they were the most pious people in the world (see 2:10-16). They used their prayer as a cover for their sin—the sin of hypocrisy. They had become a hypocritical people, living a double life.

Not only that, these remnant Jews had even voiced the untrue notion that, "everyone who does evil is good in God's sight, and that He even takes delight in those who do evil. Where, then, is the God of judgment?" In other words, they thought God was not there; and even if He were, He did not care; and hence, they, too, could do anything they liked, free from any fear that God would judge. They further thought, "After all, we are the chosen people of God, so nothing will happen to us." We will recall, however, that John the Baptist strongly disagreed with such thinking; for he said to the Jews of a later day: "Do not say you are children of Abraham. God can raise up children of Abraham from these stones if you do not repent" (see Matthew 3:8-9).

One could therefore assert that the spirits of both Phariseeism and Sadduceeism were already present among this Jewish remnant. The spirit of Phariseeism can be described as maintaining an outward religious form to such a strict degree that those who were members of this religious party considered themselves the most pious people in the world; and yet, in secret, they privately gobbled up even the widow's last mite! Their strict practice required that they carefully wash the outside of all vessels; nevertheless, in their insides these Pharisees were full of all manner of filthiness and hypocrisy. Such was the one thing which the Lord Jesus hated the most. In His entire life, He had meted out a curse only twice. Late in His earthly life He cursed the hypocritical Pharisees by pronouncing upon them, “Woe to you hypocrites!” And on another occasion late in His life He cursed a fig tree for bearing only leaves—when at that season of the year there should have been fruit on its branches; in other words, this was a picture of falsehood and unreality which had come to characterize the children of Israel.

Then there was the spirit of Sadduceeism. The Sadducees did not believe in angels; they did not believe in spirits; they did not believe in resurrection. They, in brief, were marked by gross unbelief. And this same spirit had already crept in among God’s returned remnant people. Where is the God of judgment? they had said to God; He is nowhere. And even if God is present, they had further said, He has no concern for justice anyway; and therefore He will never judge. They also thought, We are a chosen people, for do we not have Abraham as our father? Not so, wrote Paul the apostle of Christ; for not all Israel is Israel, but only those of faith (see Romans 9:6ff.).

Just here we need to look at ourselves and ask in all candor if we today are like those remnant people of God in Jerusalem. God has declared to them: “You have wearied Me with your many words.” Do we, too, wear God down with our words of argument? We, too, may have tested God’s patience. Spiritually speaking, where exactly are we in our Christian walk? What is our relationship with our fellow man? What is our relationship with our brothers and sisters? Are we being faithful to our spouse? Do we live a double life or do we live a pure life before God and man? The apostle Paul once asserted: “I have lived before God and man with a conscience without offense” (see Acts 24:16; 23:1). Where, indeed, are we? What have our actions been like? Do they match our words? Or are we likewise guilty of hypocrisy?

FIFTH ROUND: RETURN TO ME

“Since the days of your fathers have ye departed from my statutes, and have not kept them. Return unto me, and I will return unto you, saith Jehovah of hosts. But ye say, Wherein shall we return?” (3:7).

Recall that these remnant Jews had said: "Where is the God of judgment? He simply has no interest in administering judgment upon the wicked and the unbelieving." They did not know or understand that the explanation for why His judgment had not appeared was the long-suffering and patience of God. One day, His judgment *will* come. For God now declared through His prophet Malachi: "Behold, I send my messenger, and he shall prepare the way before me; and the Lord whom ye seek will suddenly come to his temple, and the Angel of the covenant, whom ye delight in: behold, he cometh, saith Jehovah of hosts. But who shall endure the day of his coming? and who shall stand when he appeareth? For he will be like a refiner's fire, and like fullers' lye. And he shall sit as a refiner and purifier of silver" (3:1-3a).

The God of judgment *will* eventually judge. The judgment does not yet come because of His long-suffering; but when He does finally judge, He will be like a refiner's fire. He will sit like a refiner and refine the gold and silver to remove the dross so that the pure gold and silver may come forth. This passage from Malachi thus signifies that in judgment there is mercy. According to what all of us truly are, we should all be consumed; for we would be saying correctly that there is nothing but dross in us; but thank God that in judgment there is mercy. God who has put His life—even Christ—in us will refine us and bring forth from us God's life unmixed with any of our impurity. But for this to happen God requires this of His people: "Return to Me. If you will only return to Me, I will return to you." But the Jewish remnant back then had responded with: "Wherein shall we return? We have never gone astray. We are righteous" (see again 3:7).

This people's attitude reminds us, does it not, of the parable of the prodigal son. One could easily conclude that there was more hope for the prodigal son than for the elder brother. The prodigal son repented and returned to his father, but the elder son thought he had never needed to repent of anything. And the result was that he found himself outside the father's house.

Let us ask ourselves again: Where are we in our Christian walk? Have we left our first love? Do we honor God as our Father? Do we fear Him as our Master? Or do we despise His name? pollute His table? Indeed, are we hypocrites? Have we committed the sin of unbelief? If so, let us repent and return to God and He will certainly return to us.

SIXTH ROUND: RENDER YOUR HEAVE-OFFERING

"Will a man rob God? But ye rob me. And ye say, Wherein do we rob thee? In tithes and heave-offerings" (3:8).

God declared to His people: "You rob me." And they replied: "Wherein have we robbed you?" God answered: "In tithes and heave-offerings." We know that a tithe is one-tenth. It was the law which God had given to the children of Israel and which called for them to give to God one-tenth of all their substance. The reason for this was to remind them that what they had was not theirs, it was given to them by God. They were simply stewards, not owners. Tithes are therefore to remind God's people that they are only managers of God's gifts to them. But here we learn that the returned remnant had withheld their tithes. They did not bring them to the treasure house of God; and, because of this, the Levitical priests—whose very existence depended on the people's tithes— had to resort to tilling their fields for their livelihood; and thus the temple service had to be neglected.

What, though, were heave-offerings? These were the love-offerings. When anyone was moved by the love of God and wished to devote something to Him—that is to say, to offer it as a gift to God—that was a heave-offering. Moreover, the heave-offering ought to have been of the best quality, not any leftover. But God had accused His people of robbing Him. Therefore, He said for the people to bring their tithes and heave-offerings into His treasure house and test Him and see if He would not open the windows of heaven and pour down His blessings upon them until there would be no space sufficient enough to store them (see 3:10).

I read somewhere (I have forgotten who said it) that we American citizens are very careful to render to Caesar what is Caesar's because if we do not, the Internal Revenue Service—the tax-collecting agency of the Government—will be after us; but that we are not similarly careful to render to God what is God's. Let us clearly understand that it is not necessarily true that we rob God of *money*—yes, we may do this; nevertheless, we can also rob God of our time; or we can rob Him of our life; rob Him of the gifts He has given us; we can even rob God of the grace He has given us. In fact, we can rob Him in any number of ways. Who, therefore, can say that he has never robbed God—that he has always rendered to Him what is rightfully His? Our very life belongs to God. Have we rendered our life to Him as our heave-offering? All the gifts which God has bestowed upon us we are simply stewards of; so whether they be spiritual gifts or material gifts, we are not owners but only managers in determining how they are dispensed. Are we faithful in serving God? Or have we reached the point that we have indeed robbed God but are not at all conscious of it? How sad that God has to contend with His people in saying, "You have robbed Me."

SEVENTH ROUND: A PECULIAR TREASURE

"Your words have been stout against me, saith Jehovah; but ye say, What have we been speaking against thee? Ye say, It is vain to serve God; and what profit is it that we keep his charge, and that we walk mournfully before Jehovah of hosts?" (3:13-14).

Here the returned remnant had degenerated from their first love to such a degree that they fell into rebellion. Their words had been harsh against God: "What is the use of serving God? What profit do we have in serving Him?" Such words constituted open rebellion against God Almighty. And yet they were so insensitive to what had inwardly happened to themselves that they did not realize it.

Now even though this people in Jerusalem and Judah had in general sunk into open rebellion against God, He could nonetheless take pleasure in the fact that He still had a number of people—a minority remnant out of the returned remnant as a whole—who had remained faithful, who had honored and feared His name, who talked positively with each other about their Lord God, and thus encouraged one another in the fear of the Lord. Said God concerning this small but faithful minority: "I have observed and listened to them as they conversed with each other about Me. And so that I can remember each one of them, I am recording their names in My book; for I consider them My treasured possession. In the day when I act in terrible judgment upon the whole earth I shall spare them as a father in compassion would spare his son" (see 3:16-18).

We can be certain that though men may fail, God never fails in ultimately achieving His purpose in man. He will still have a people who fear Him, honor Him and love Him. And though it may be a remnant out of a remnant, even so, they shall be a peculiar treasure to God. He will be honored and loved through them. Oh, that we may be numbered among such a people; and then, when Christ shall return, He will be to those who have revered and honored God's name like the Sun of righteousness with healing in His wings (see 4:2).

REPENT AND RETURN TO FIRST LOVE

Following these seven rounds of debate recorded in Malachi, God concluded with a final word: "Remember the law of Moses ... I will send Elijah" (see 4:4-5). What can we infer from this? We know that Moses represents the Law, and Elijah, the prophets. What do God's Law and His prophets teach? We will recall from Matthew 22 that a lawyer came to the Lord Jesus one day to test Him with a question: "What is the greatest commandment?" And the Lord replied: "You shall love the Lord your God with your whole heart, mind, soul, and strength and love your neighbor as yourself. This is the greatest commandment, and is the sum of all the law and the prophets." In other words, after all that was said and done in these many debates, God's concluding admonition to His people was this: "Remember My law; consider the words of My prophets; and repent and return to love. *That* is what I want."

And hence, the very last message in the Old Testament is one of repentance; but so, too, we shall see that the very first message in the New Testament is likewise one of repentance. And interestingly, upon coming to the concluding book of the New Testament and therefore to the entire Judeo-Christian Bible, we shall find that the very last message sent by the Risen Lord to the seven local churches in the province of Asia—and symbolizing, as they do, the entire history of the church of God—is, once again, one of repentance: repent and return to first love, because God is love.

Let us pray:

Dear heavenly Father, do speak to us. Make us sensitive to Thee that we may repent and return and be recovered to the first love which Thou art seeking after. May Thy heart be satisfied. In the name of our Lord Jesus. Amen.

OTHER TITLES AVAILABLE
From Christian Fellowship Publishers

By Watchman Nee

The Basic Lesson Series

Volume 1 - A Living Sacrifice
Volume 2 - The Good Confession
Volume 3 - Assembling Together
Volume 4 - Not I, But Christ
Volume 5 - Do All to the Glory of God
Volume 6 - Love One Another

Aids to "Revelation"
Back to the Cross
A Balanced Christian Life
The Better Covenant
The Body of Christ: A Reality
The Character of God's Workman
Christ the Sum of All Spiritual Things
The Church and the Work – 3 Vols
"Come, Lord Jesus"
The Communion of the Holy Spirit
The Finest of the Wheat - Volume 1
The Finest of the Wheat - Volume 2
From Faith to Faith
From Glory to Glory
Full of Grace and Truth - Volume 1
Full of Grace and Truth - Volume 2
Gleanings in the Fields of Boaz
The Glory of His Life
God's Plan and the Overcomers
God's Work
Gospel Dialogue
Grace for Grace
Heart to Heart Talks
Interpreting Matthew
Journeying towards the Spiritual
The King and the Kingdom of Heaven
The Latent Power of the Soul
Let Us Pray
The Life That Wins
The Lord My Portion
The Messenger of the Cross
The Ministry of God's Word
The Mystery of Creation
Powerful According to God
Practical Issues of This Life
The Prayer Ministry of the Church
The Release of the Spirit
Revive Thy Work
The Salvation of the Soul
The Secret of Christian Living
Serve in Spirit
The Spirit of Judgment
The Spirit of the Gospel
The Spirit of Wisdom and Revelation
Spiritual Authority
Spiritual Exercise
Spiritual Discernment
Spiritual Knowledge
The Spiritual Man
Spiritual Reality or Obsession
Take Heed
The Testimony of God
Whom Shall I Send?
The Word of the Cross
Worship God
Ye Search the Scriptures

By Stephen Kaung

Discipled to Christ
The Songs of Degrees - Meditations on Fifteen Psalms
The Splendor of His Ways - Seeing the Lord's End in Job
God Has Spoken – Vol. I: Seeing Christ in the Old Testament, Part One
God Has Spoken – Vol. I: Seeing Christ in the Old Testament, Part Two
God Has Spoken – Vol. II: Seeing Christ in the New Testament